I0470970

The Wise Investor

Mark McIlroy

ISBN 978-1492335436

Other books by the author

Introduction to the Stockmarket

The Art and Craft of Computer Programming

SQL Essentials

These books are available in print from Amazon.com

Contents

Summer

4 Principles of Investment

Autumn

5 Specifics

Winter

23

6 Putting it into practice

23

Spring

1 Introduction

1.1 The Characters

John was in a particularly relaxed mood.

One of the benefits of old age was that he could spend a few hours in the park on a sunny day, watching the wind in the trees and the people walking by, without having to hurry from one thing to the next.

It was a beautiful day. Cool, refreshing air blew through the park and the sun shone brightly.

Everywhere he looked, there were trees, birds flitting about and beds of brightly coloured flowers.

And people.

People everywhere, walking along paths, across the grass, sometimes in groups and sometimes alone.

John breathed in slowly, taking the cool, sweet air into his lungs, and watched. Everyone he saw, without exception, had one thing in common.

They were in a hurry.

Such busy, busy lives John thought. It saddened him to see them. Not one person look relaxed, not one soul strolled in the morning sun. So many things missed, he thought, and all because no-one had time to think, time to relax... time to learn.

As he watched, one particular person caught his attention.

In the distance, a lone figure walked towards him. It was a woman in her late thirties, attractive in her own way, but walking with the air of someone with problems.

She, too, was hurrying.

John watched the woman, and wondered what her worries were.

She had an average sort of figure, neither tall nor short, a little slimmer than some but definitely not skinny.

She looked like a fairly sensible person, not stupid, but not blessed with a sparkling intellect either.

Strange, John thought, as he watched his grand-daughter approach, how different children are from each other. There were always some qualities that carried down through a family, and yet each child was their own person.

Kate saw her grandfather as soon as she entered the park.

He was sitting, as usual, on his favourite bench by the small lake. She envied him in many ways.

He had time, time to relax and do the things he wanted to do.

He never seemed to have worries or money problems, and although she didn't know how much money he actually had, she suspected it was a great deal.

Well, she thought, he always does what he wants to, travels when he feels like it, and lives in a beautiful old home.

John's home was modest in size, but filled with beautiful things.

Well, Kate thought, it may not be a classic definition of wealthy, but it was good enough her.

As she came closer, Kate could see the soft wrinkles on her grandfather's face, the slim figure, and the relaxed, happy air he always had around him. Kate often wondered about his life, how he had learned the lessons that had lead him to where he was today.

Clearly he was successful, and successful in a way that Kate desperately wanted to be, but she had faint memories, as a young child, overhearing her parents talk of bitter lessons and hard times her grandfather had suffered.

"Hello, grandad," Kate said with affection. "You're looking wonderful, as always."

"Keep talking like that, Katie", he replied with a smile, "I never get tired of hearing it."

Kate hugged her grandfather, sat down, breathed out and relaxed.

A little.

There was still a worried air about her, a slight tension in her face.

"Such a beautiful day", he said, "look at the wind gently blow through the trees, the ducklings on the lake, the children playing over there. I never get tired of this place. Never."

"Yes," said Kate without conviction, "it is lovely." John sat, patiently, and waited for Kate to speak. She was immersed in her own private thoughts, struggling with some problem or another.

After a while, her face changed, and the worried look turned into a look of sadness. She relaxed, but a quiet depression hung around her. John decided that he would have to prompt a little.

"So, Kate," he said with a playful smile, "What is it? Money or men?" Kate had to smile. She had to admit, that without the worries about relationships, money and health, well, there wasn't much left to worry about.

"Money," she said with a faint smile.

"Oh," said John. It was a common enough complaint, and one that he had heard from Kate many times before.

A pity, he thought, because she had so much going for her. In the past, it had frustrated him to see her mis-manage her money, to do all the wrong things with it until she was left where she started; waiting for her next paycheque.

Such a shame, when a little attention could have changed the picture so much.

He had tried to give her advice, of course, but unsolicited advice simply strained their relationship, and in the end he had decided to remain silent.

"So what's the problem, honey?" Kate's grandfather said with grin. Kate smiled. He often called her "Honey", in a playful, slightly flirtatious sort of way. Even though they were blood relatives, Kate enjoyed it, and she knew he was only teasing her.

"Watch your manners," Kate said, shaking her finger at him with mock irritation, "you're talking to a married woman."

John chuckled with laughter. It was good to see his granddaughter smile again. He looked across at her, raised an eyebrow and waited expectantly.

Kate's smile faded, and the quiet depression returned to her face.

"Things aren't going well, John," Kate said in a serious voice. "I just heard today that my pay rise has been delayed again. I was really counting on it."

John was uncertain how to react.

Kate always lived from one pay packet to the next, and while she had some money put away for a rainy day, she always seemed to be playing catch-up, borrowing money from one of her accounts to keep another one afloat. It still saddened him that she had not learnt to manage her money a little better. Still, she was clearly worried and he felt a strong sympathy for her.

"Are things that bad, Kate?" he said, serious once again. "You're earning a decent salary, and Jim's working too. I thought that things were all right."

"We're coping," replied Kate. "We always manage to pay the bills, and there's always some left over for a night out or some new clothes."

"What's wrong then," said Kate's confused grandfather. He could see that she was not happy, and yet there didn't seem to be any crisis or major problem.

Kate stared into space, silent, thinking about her life and her future.

She didn't speak for a long time. John wondered if he should break the silence, but she was deep in thought, so he sat back, looked out over the park and relaxed.

She would speak when she was ready, he decided. John knew his granddaughter well, and although these moods were rare, she needed time to reflect.

"You know, John," Kate said softly. "Sometimes it get tired of it all."

"We all do, baby," John said gently. "We all need a rest, some time to ourselves. Relax here with me a while and you'll feel better."

"No," said Kate slowly, "that's not quite what I meant. Sure, Jim and I are doing all right, but I still worry about the future.

What if something went wrong? What if I had an accident, or Jim's company closed down?

We just couldn't afford to lose a single pay packet. Then there's retirement," Kate said softly. She turned to her grandfather, a pleading look in her eyes, and said, "I don't want to die a poor old woman, John."

John hugged his granddaughter. Kate was very sad, and her sadness touched his heart.

"You know I love my work," Kate continued, "but sometimes I wish things were different. Nursing has always been a big part of my life, but there's never been time to work on my painting. I want to stay, John, you know that, but sometimes I still feel trapped. I don't have a choice, I have to work, but I wish there was time for the things I really wanted to do."

Kate smiled, a bitter, grim smile, and went on. "Who am I fooling?" she said, "even if I did have the time, I could never do it properly. Those professional oil paints cost a fortune."

John held Kate, comforting her.

Kate's worries may have seemed minor to some, but in other ways, they were the deepest worries of all… the difference between a fulfilled life and a bitter existence that simply passes from one day to the next.

There was little that he could say.

Kate was right about one thing, though.

At the moment, she didn't have any real choice. John wanted to help his granddaughter.

He had offered advice in the past, and leant the hard way

10

that advice was not the way forward. Kate was a funny woman, John thought.

She was a brilliant organiser at work, but her own financial life was a shambles. Kate had a good heart, though, and John loved his granddaughter very much.

Another long silence passed. Kate relaxed in John's arms, and looked out over the park. For the first time that day, she saw the things around her. It was a beautiful park, and a lovely day.

John had chosen his favourite spot well.

Huge green trees bent gently in the wind, the air was crisp and the sky blue. Kate watched the ducklings on the lake. They swam around curiously, exploring the reeds, darting between rocks and fossicking on the lake bottom with their bills.

Every now and then, their mother would swim a little way, and the baby ducks would chase after her as fast as they could. Life would be so simple, Kate thought with envy. Even John, she thought, had a peaceful serenity about him. He did not have the worries that she had, he could go where he chose, and if he wanted to sit in the sun and do nothing, then he could.

"Katie," John said slowly.

"Yes, grandad?" Kate replied.

"I am sad for you," her grandfather said. I have lived a difficult life myself, and everything I learnt, I learnt the hard way.

As a young man, I was full of dreams and hopes, but I was foolish.

"I made many mistakes, and I don't want you to suffer the things that I did. I don't want you to struggle your whole life, never having the money you want, or the time you need."

Kate was taken aback by John's words. Although her grandfather had always been friendly and open, always happy to talk about anything, he had remained a private person. Kate knew nothing of his life before she was born.

He was a mystery to her.

Warm, friendly and serene, and yet sometimes she saw a shadow pass across his face. An occasional, innocent comment, and his face would slightly darken, a distant memory that still haunted him. A moment later, it would be gone.

"John," Kate said, "I am not greedy. I do not care about having ten houses, a car for each day of the week and private jet. But grandad," Kate said, "I just wish my life was easier. I wish I didn't have to worry about the future, that I knew I would always have money when I needed it. I wish I could work because I wanted to, I wish I had the time to do the things I enjoy, the time and money to learn to paint the way I have always wanted to."

Kate lowered her head slightly, a faint image of shame crossed her face, but she continued.

"I wish, grandad, that I had time to spend with my husband, my children and my family. I wish that I had time for myself, and I wish that Jim and I could travel when we felt like it, spend time with each other, just relaxing and enjoying ourselves."

John laughed softly.

There was nothing strange about Kate's wish list, but this was more serious than day dreaming.
A great weight was resting on his granddaugther's heart, and John was not foolish enough to think that there were any easy ways that she could change her life.

"Katie," John said gently, "I wish, too, that your life was easier. I wish that you were free from worries, that you were not trapped in any job, that people treated you with respect.

I wish that you had time, time to enjoy life, time to spend on your interests, time to relax and do nothing." John continued slowly, "I am a practical man. I have learnt, the hard way, that to have freedom and time, you must have money.

You do not need to be rich," he added slowly, "but you must be in control. You must have enough so that you don't need every pay packet, so that you are not struggling from one week to the next. You must have enough money to have choices, to be able to change jobs when you want, or even stop work for a little while if you wish it. Katie," he said, "if you learn about money, you can have this. If you are willing to learn a little, things can change for the better.

Katie bowed her head a little, then raised it and looked into her grandfather's eyes. "I know, John," she said, "and I want you to teach me."

1.2 Achieving financial independence

As John began speaking, his initial hesitation dissolved and his confidence grew. Unsure where to begin at first, the picture became clearer and clearer to him the more he spoke.

"Your wealth, Kate, is your store of assets. These may be properties, shares in companies and cash deposits. Your assets give you security and freedom. If you are ever sick or injured, or unable to work for any reason, you will not suffer from lack of money. When you have a reserve of quality assets, Kate, you will not be vulnerable in the way that you are now. You will have more choices in your life, and you need not fear the future as you do now. This security and peace of mind is invaluable Kate. Even if nothing ever goes wrong, the worries and fears that you feel at the moment reduce the quality of your life. This places a strain onto every day of your life. If you like, I will talk for a while about increasing your wealth, and building a secure financial future."

Kate was listening intently.

"Money comes to us from three sources Kate. First, we may be given it. This includes inheritances, government benefits and lottery wins.

These items are usually beyond our control, although you must make the most of the money that you receive. We will look at this a little later.

The second source of money is our job. I will suggest various ways to improve the income from your job, however the real area to work on is the third source of income.

This income comes from your assets. Investment is the use of your money to make more money. If you invest your money in assets that produce an income, such as properties and bank deposits, then you will receive an income from these investments. At present, this is probably insignificant in comparison to the money that you earn from work. However, wise investment is the key to your financial future, and I will talk about this more than any other topic."

Kate sat in silence, listening carefully to everything her grandfather said.

"John," she said, "we have touched on these topics in the past. I guess that I never really listed before though. I know that you've made suggestions in the past, but I guess that I didn't want any intrusion into my life."

John remained silent.

Kate was right, he thought, his previous advice had been intrusive, and he was sorry for not respecting his granddaughter by trusting in her own judgement.

"However," she continued, "whatever I am doing at the moment simply isn't working. It's that simple. And if you can suggest anything that might help, I would be grateful."

John continued.

"Well," he said, "I will talk about money for a while and let's see how things go.

There are three steps you must take to improve your finances and increase your wealth in the future.

First, you must manage your money wisely. Become more organised in your finances, and keep a close watch on your expenses, your assets and your debts.

I will talk at length about how to do this successfully.

The second step involves saving. Saving part of your income is a necessary step in achieving financial independence.

This does not have to be a difficulty task, and I will talk about ways to make it easier.

However, no matter what your approach, you must save a portion of your income.

This will be used to increase your wealth each year, and set you on the path to greater freedom and security.

The third step involves wise investment. The money you save must be invested wisely.

If you simply keep your money in cash, deposited with a

bank, then you will never achieve independence. Wise investment does not involve large risks, luck or large amounts of skill.

It does, however, require knowledge of the principles of wise and successful investment.

Although they are simple, few people understand these principles fully.

This is the third step, Kate, and the one where many people fail.

Listen to the things I tell you, and I will teach you how to invest your money wisely and safely, and how to increase your wealth for the future."

1.3 Kate's doubts

Kate thought for a long time about the things John had said. Although she desperately wanted the freedom, security and time to herself that John described, she still couldn't see how it could happen for her.

"John," she said in a quiet and depressed voice, "you know I have very little money. I doubt whether I could save anything at all, since there always seems to be another unexpected bill when I least expect it. I am not a wealthy woman, I can't buy properties or shares. Even if I managed to save a little, it would never be enough to invest properly, or make a difference to my income."

John had been expecting some doubts and fears from Kate, and he decided to address each point as she raised it.

"Kate, I know that you have little wealth at the moment. However, you don't need to be wealthy to invest your money successfully. In fact, you actually have some advantages over wealthy people when it comes to investment."

Kate raised her eyebrows in surprise

"I know that your money situation is sometimes tight, Kate, and this has taught you to balance your money carefully, and pay attention to your finances.

This is an invaluable skill that will serve you well in the future. Wealthy people sometimes become lazy about details, as they don't need to be careful with money in the way that poorer people do.

They can loose their financial disciple, and this can lead to making poor investments and paying prices for assets which are too high.

Although you lack experience, Kate, you have learnt some financial discipline and attention to detail that will become very useful.

You are also busy, as I know well, but you still have some time that you can devote to learning and investigating investments.

Some wealthy people can afford to spend their time on leisure activities, and may prefer to spend as little time as possible considering investments.

If you save money in the ways I will show you, then you will be making investments within a few months.

Within a year, you could even invest in property or shares, and increase your wealth through investing."

John had raised some interesting points that Kate had not considered, but she still did not see how it could work for her.

However, Kate had faith in her grandfather. He was successful himself, and although she knew little about the early part of his life, she knew that he had never inherited any money and that he had made it all himself.

"You speak about wise investment, grandfather," Kate said as she thought out loud, "but I hardly know any more about investment than my young children do. I don't have any qualifications or experience, and I just wouldn't know where to start. It's all incredibly complicated."

"The world of money and finance is very complicated," John began, "However, the principles that govern it are very simple indeed.

I can teach you everything you need to know to invest successfully.

The more you know, the better you will be able to manage your investments, but the essentials are very simple. Don't imagine, though, that because they are simple that everyone but you understands them. On the contrary, very few people seem to follow the most basic principles of wise investment.

I am constantly amazed at the mistakes people make but not following a few common-sense guidelines. If you follow the guidelines I give you, you will be far more successful than the average person at investing your money."

Kate pondered John's words.

Some of her initial scepticism was beginning to fade.

John knew her background and situation, and if he was convinced that she could build her wealth by following some simple guidelines, she was interested to hear what they were. There were still things that bothered her though.

"You know, John," she said, "things are difficult financially, but I just don't have the time to work longer hours. I am happy with my life as it is. I really enjoy it when Jim and I have a night out, and I don't want to loose that. More money would really help, but I am afraid that I will have to change my whole lifestyle, and it just wouldn't be worth it."

John was not surprised at Kate's comments, and he sympathised with her fears.

"I understand what you mean, Kate, but you won't need to change your lifestyle to achieve financial success. It really comes down to planning ahead and organising yourself better.

In this way, you can save money without missing out on your personal pleasures."

Kate was relieved that John was not suggesting that she take on extra work, and if anything he was strongly recommending against it.

Her grandfather had answered many of her initial worries, but the larger and more serious ones still remained. Although she hated to admit it to herself, Kate realised that she was afraid.

She was afraid of taking a risk, and afraid of change. She felt intimidated by the world of investment, from banks to the stock market. Kate briefly considered asking John to forget the whole thing, but she had come this far and she was determined to press ahead.

John watched his granddaughter's face, and guessed the thoughts that were passing through her mind.

"You know, Kate," he said in his quiet, relaxed manner, "we are all afraid of change. Even change for the better. Life is a constant source of change and uncertainty, and the most frightening thing we ever do is get out of bed each morning and face the uncertainty of another day.

Always remember, though, that you are taking a large risk by not acting. Although every investment has its risks, you are exposing yourself to the greatest risk of all.

You are financially vulnerable, and if you had a major accident or illness then you would be in serious trouble. The greatest risk of all is the risk that is caused by a lack of resources, and by not making wise investments you are actually increasing your risks, not reducing them."

Kate had always considered money in the bank as the safest investment, but John's comments were starting to place a different complexion on this.

"I have one final point on the issue of change and risks, Kate. Many people see success in investment as a matter of luck.
The stock market is the best example of this attitude, and many inexperienced investors view the stock market like a gambling casino, where luck plays a greater part than skill in success.

Let me tell you, Kate, that there is no luck involved in successful investment. If you follow the principles of wise investment, then you will have a steadily increasing assets, even through your assets may rise and fall in value in the short term.

Kate considered this carefully.

"I understand, too, that you may feel intimated by the world of investment.

There are two important steps you should take which will prevent you from feeling intimidated.

First, you must always remember that you are dealing with other people. Bank managers, real estate agents and stockbrokers are all human beings.

They all make decisions on partly emotional grounds, and they all have worries and fears. Many people that you deal with may have even less knowledge of investments that you have yourself.

The second cure for insecurity is knowledge. The more

you know, the more confident you will feel and the better you will be able to communicate with people in the financial field.

A little knowledge will go a long way, and once you learn the basic terms and jargon, you will feel far more confident and be able to ask for the things you really want, instead of leaving it all up to others."

John's words were making Kate feel much better, and many of the fears and doubts she had possessed had faded away. There was still one major factor, though, and she could not shake this feeling.

It was the one thing, above all else, that convinced her that she was wasting her time. For several minutes she sat in silence, thinking. Finally she spoke.

"John," she said softly, "I am too old for all this. I don't have the energy or the time to learn all these new things. If I had started when I was younger, things could have been different, but it's too late now."

John sat in silence for several minutes, collecting his thoughts.

He had been expecting this, and although his first instinct was to tell Kate to stop being a fool, he realised that he must give a serious reply to her comments.

It was an important point that she had raised, and one that deserved attention.

"Kate, it would be easy for me to be flippant and just say 'it's never too late', but let's look at the issues properly.

First, no matter what your financial position, it can always be improved. Even on the day before you die, there are still things that can be done to organise and improve your financial position.

It is true, that the later in life you start this, the less chance that you will become a rich woman.

However, this is not the goal in any event. You can become financially independent at any stage, with a little work and planning.

You do not need to be rich to have freedom and

independence, but you do need more money than you have at the moment.

Do not forget, either, that you have several major advantages over a young person when it comes to investment.

Even though you have never paid much attention to investment, you have still lived through booms and recessions, and heard about the major news stories in the financial world though your life. Do not underestimate the value of this knowledge.

A young person may have energy and enthusiasm, but they have no experience of life. They cannot put things into perspective, they cannot compare the current environment with past environments and use this knowledge to make decisions.

The older you are, Kate, the longer the period of history you have lived through, the more you have experience of the ups and downs in the financial world.

Our successes may be sweet, but it is our failures that we learn from. The older you are, the more financial experiences and mistakes you have to draw on and learn from.

No matter what your age or income, your financial position can always be improved. Make the most of what you have, and the present and the future will be brighter.

1.4 Common mistakes

Kate had been thinking for some time about John's words. Although he had not explained the details, it seemed a little too good to be true. If things were as simple as they sounded, she couldn't understand why everyone was not successful in the way John described.

Kate's grandfather sat on the park bench, the cool wind on his face and the warm sun on his skin, and waited for his granddaughter to speak. If he was to teach her about money and investment, she must believe that it was worthwhile, and it would work for her. There would always be doubts, of course, but she must believe deep down that it would work in the end. If she didn't, then they would be wasting their time.

"John," she said at length, "if it's so simple. Why doesn't everyone do it?"

"There are several common mistakes people make, Kate. The first, and the most fatal of all, is that most people spend everything that they earn. They may have some money put aside for a rainy day, and they may save up for a new car or boat, but overall they end up spending all money they earn.

To achieve financial success, you must save money and invest it. Even if it is a small amount at first, you must increase your wealth each year.

Each year, you must have a little more money and wealth than the year before. If you save and invest wisely, you will gain wealth and freedom. If you spend all the money that you earn, however, then you will still be financially dependent in fifty year's time. You will be dependent on your salary from work, a government pension, or some other income. Whatever the source, you will not have freedom, security and independence."

Kate had to admit that she was one of these people herself, and although she owned more possessions than she

23

had ten years before, she could not really say that she had built up a store of assets and wealth that gave her an income and security.

"The next common mistake is a lack of planning and organisation. Some people are highly organised in their personal lives, and other are ramshackle and stumble from one moment to the next.

Neither person is better, and a healthy balance of both qualities can make a balanced and happy person. However, when it comes to money, it is essential to be organised. You must plan ahead and budget your money. This will not make you wealthy, but it is an essential ingredient and the first major step on the path. Without being organised, you cannot achieve financial success."

Kate was becoming a little depressed. It seemed that she had made every mistake in the book.

"Having made these mistakes," John continued with a wry smile, "we come to the most insidious and destructive mistake of all. This mistake leads to financial failure, and also bitterness and an unhappy life."

Kate was intrigued.

"Many people blame others for their problems, and rely on others to solve their problems for them. These two attitudes will cause you to fail with money. Not matter what problems other people have caused you, you are the only one who can solve your problems.

You may not be the cause of all your problems, but you must be the solution.

People may blame or rely on a parent, a husband or wife, an accountant or a bank manager.

To succeed, Kate, you must take responsibility for your own finances.

You are responsible for your own financial position, not anyone else. You must take the initiative, take positive actions and learn about money.

Only by learning and taking action will you achieve financial success. Giving over responsibility to others, for our success or our failure, is an easy trap to fall into, but it is unfair and it leads to bitterness and financial failure."

2.1 *Wise financial management*

John stared across the park, silent.

Minutes passed, and Kate become nervous. She briefly wondered if John had fallen into some sort of trance, or forgotten altogether that she was there with him. She waited for him to say something, unsure of whether to speak or stay quiet.

"Err, John," Kate said nervously, "How should we start?" John's face turned slightly red. "I'm not quite sure, sweetie," he said. "Where does one begin with these things?"

He looked a little nervous, Kate thought. She realised that he was unused to sharing his insights, so she prompted gently to reassure him. "Let us begin at the beginning," she said playfully, quoting a passage from Alice in Wonderland.

John raised his eyes and looked beyond the park to the city skyline. Prominent among the buildings was a half-finished skyscraper, a famous project that had been plagued with problems and was never completed. As he stared at the building, an inspiration struck him and he began to speak.

"We will start with wise financial management," he said confidently. "Everything else flows from this. If you don't manage your money wisely, everything else is doomed to failure."

"Isn't that everything, though?" said Kate, confused.

"Not at all," replied John. It is simply the beginning. First, you must manage your money sensibly. Then, you must save part of your income. These savings must be invested wisely. Only then, only once you have done all this, will your financial position begin to improve. When you have done this, your finances will be better with each passing year. Before you know it, you will have independence and choices you never dreamed of."

26

"Oh," said Kate. It was a weak response in the circumstances, but she couldn't think of anything better to say. Kate decided it would be better to keep quiet and listen carefully to what her grandfather had to say.

"Go on, John," she said with encouragement.

"First, let's talk about your income."

"Don't depress me," said Kate with a laugh.

"When we spoke last week," John continued, "you told me your pay rise had been delayed. You were depressed, and a little worried too. Think back to the last pay rise you had, dear. How did it feel?"

"Wonderful," said Kate. "It wasn't much, but it was extra money that I hadn't had before. It was a really good feeling."

"Now tell me," said John, "how did you feel three months later?"

"Well, just normal," said Kate, a little unsure where this was leading.

"So you weren't any richer," her grandfather continued, "you felt the same. Sure, things were a little easier, but it didn't solve your problems. In fact, your worries about the future were probably exactly the same.

Your long term problems hadn't changed in the slightest. You felt a little richer in the short term, but even that faded within a few months.

You were back where you started, making ends meet each week and each month. If the last pay rise made no lasting difference, what do you hope to gain from the next one?"

Kate was embarrassed. She had to admit that everything her grandfather said was true. Uncannily true. Still, it made her feel foolish. She worked hard for her money, and she did what she could to make it last. Kate wished her grandfather would change the subject.

"Don't worry, Katie" John said gently. "I know things are difficult these days. You've done better than most. I know you work hard, and I know you deserve every cent you earn.

I hope I can help you make the most of it."

Kate brightened a little, her confidence restored. "I do my best," she said, "but I'm not an expert on money or investment. No-one ever taught me how. That's why I'm asking you for help." Kate looked at him slyly, then continued, "I don't want to wait another forty years to work it out."

John realised she was getting back at him, and it was fair enough, too. He hadn't meant to criticise. His face slightly reddened, John decided it was better to pass by the comment and keep talking.

"More income is not the answer," He said confidently. "Yes, it does help, and increasing your income is important, but it will all be wasted if you don't manage your money wisely. Sensible money management is the key to it all. You must manage your money wisely if you want to increase your wealth and become more independent.

"Increase my wealth!" Kate exclaimed. "What wealth?"

John smiled. "You'd be surprised, my dear, but that comes later. For now, I want to talk about managing your money."

"The first rule of money management," John said, "is to have control over your money. You must record where it comes from, and where it goes to. I know this sounds obvious, but few people actually do it.

You must record all your expenses, so you know what your money is being spent on. There is an old saying in business management, which says: 'You can't manage what you can't measure'. Let me tell you, Katie, that never was a truer word spoken.

Before you can manage your money and increase your wealth, you must get control. You must write down the figures, and know exactly how much is spent on each of your expenses. Once you have this, you can begin to improve the whole picture. Most people spend money each day, and a month later have little idea where it all went."

John was right, Kate thought, that it did sound obvious.

Still, she had to admit that she didn't actually record all her expenses. She had a vague idea where it all went, but there were days when money seemed to disappear through her fingers like water. It sounded like a lot of work, though, and she wasn't sure she really wanted to do it. "Does that mean that I have to write down every cent I spend?" said Kate, hoping her grandfather would say 'No'.

"Initially, yes," said John. "I know it is a nuisance, but spending a little time now will give you more free time in the future. Once you start, it becomes easy, and it certainly shows up where your money is going."

"Do you do it?" Kate asked. She knew he would say 'No', as he had plenty of money, and he didn't need to be careful.

"Yes, I do," said John. "I withdraw a fixed amount each week for daily expenses, and I write down each thing that I spend it on. No-one is invincible, Katie, and the moment you stop looking after your money, it will stop looking after you."

Kate was surprised. "What do you do with the lists?" she asked.

"Nothing," said John. "At the end of each month, I read through them, then I throw them away. The act of writing it down each night makes me aware of where it has gone, so I never forget what I am doing. I never take it for granted." John looked across at his granddaughter. He knew he shouldn't tease her, but he just couldn't resist. "Money doesn't grow on trees, you know," he said with a perfect imitation of seriousness.

"Bastard!" said Kate, slapping her grandfather on the arm. "I came to you to learn about money, not gardening!".

John laughed so hard his stomach began to hurt. Many people would have been offended by the way Kate had spoken, but John knew her well. She loved to play with him, feigning anger and disgust at his teasing comments. He enjoyed the laughter, and it certainly eased the strain on her face. John wondered if the best thing he could do would be

29

to take her a good comedy, but then the problems would still be there in the morning, and this way things may change for the better.

"Now that you have recorded where your money goes," he said, "look at ways to reduce your expenses. Most people spend their time hoping to earn more money. They wait expectantly for pay rises, try working harder and even take on extra jobs. In general, however, we have far more control of our expenses. Money comes in, and money goes out. You can be in a better financial position by increasing your income, reducing your expenses, or doing both."

Kate grimaced. She didn't like where this was heading. "I don't want to go without, John," she said. "As I young girl, I never had money for the things I wanted. These days, things are better, and I don't think I could ever go back to worrying over every cent."

"Not at all, dear," replied John. "I am simply suggesting a little forethought. Check through your list of all the money that you spent in the last month. I can guarantee, there will be costs in there that you can reduce, without missing out on anything. A little thought and planning ahead will do the trick. Take food. We often buy food when it is convenient, not necessarily at the most inexpensive shops. Planning ahead can save quite a bit. There are numerous examples. Perhaps you have been meaning to change to a cheaper parking area, but haven't got around to it yet. It all adds up, Kate."

"I suppose," said Kate, unconvinced. "But trivial things like this won't make me wealthy." She had been hoping that John would show her some secret investment that would solve all her problems. It wasn't looking very promising.

"True," John replied, "but as I said, every bit helps. Each dollar you save in weekly expenses is an extra dollar every week of the year. After a while, it will snowball into a substantial sum. Anyway, we are really only setting the scene, the real progress comes later." John continued, building each point he made on the last.

"We have now looked at two aspects of money management; recording money in and out, and reducing expenses. You should also look at increasing your income in the longer term."

"Why the long term?" interjected Kate, "what's wrong with right now?"

John laughed a little. "Fine if you can do it, Katie," he said, "but increased income is usually a long term proposition. In the short term, it is important to focus on reducing expenses, but there are limits to reducing your expenses and keeping a high quality of life. In the longer term, you will need to increase your income. Later we will talk about strategies for achieving this."

John paused, resting for a moment. It was harder work than he had imagined. "Records, income and expenses. A good start. You must, of course, have a budget."

Kate face brightened. "I have a budget!" she said excitedly. On reflection, John was not surprised. She ran her finances so close to the bone, a budget of some sort was inevitable, he thought dryly. Still, he suspected it was more of the catch-up variety than the plan-ahead variety. "That's great, Kate dear," he said. "Now, make sure you budget for everything. Make sure you put away a fixed amount each week for bills, make sure you save up for Christmas, and don't use credit or personal loans."

Kate face lost some of its brightness. "Of course, John," she said, avoiding his eyes.

John looked across the park. The sun was lower in the sky and long shadows stretched out from the trees. It was quieter now, the children had gone home and the wildlife in the park had settled down. Ducks swam slowly on the lake, feathers glowing in the rich golden sun. The birds, too, were quieter, preparing for the night.

Kate's grandfather loved the park. It was the largest in the city, and the most beautiful place within a great distance. John hoped his words would be of some help to Kate.

"Katie," said John slowly.

"Yes?" she replied.

"I have talked a little about managing your cash flow, your income and your expenses." He paused, collecting his thoughts.

"Go on," said Kate gently. She wanted him to see that she appreciated his efforts.

"Overall, though, this all comes to nothing for most people. We all earn a fortune though our lifetimes, and yet few people could last more than a month or two without a paycheque. It is the same for people with high incomes and low incomes, the young and the old."

"I know," said Kate.

"There is only one reason for this, Kate. Most people spend everything they earn. Pay rises don't help their situation, because their lifestyle adjusts to spend a little extra. They buy slightly better clothes, or go out to dinner a little more often. Nothing changes, because they still spend all that they earn. If anything, they are even more vulnerable, because their whole lifestyle is built around a high income, and if it disappears then they are in serious trouble. Kate, there is only one answer to this, only one way out of the cycle of rising income and rising expenses."

"Go on, grandfather," Kate said tenderly. She could see the sense in his words, and she could see that memories were haunting him.

"Kate," he said, "you must save part of your income. You must save on a regular basis, you must save a fixed amount each week. It is the only way to build a strong financial future, to give you choices and freedom in your life. If you save at least one tenth of your income, and invest it wisely, your future will be assured."

Kate looked at her grandfather, unsure what to say. "John," she said, "I have a little put away, but I couldn't possibly save a large amount each week. I simply couldn't afford it."

"Kate," John continued, "remember the pay rises?

Remember how great they were for a few months, but then your lifestyle adjusted, and everything seemed back to normal? Well, starting to save is the same.

For the first few months, it seems a real pain. The extra money missing each week makes a real difference. After a while, however, things return to normal. It gives you the incentive to complete some money-saving ideas that you had been planning, but hadn't bothered putting into practice.

You may find that your routine changes slightly, and you spend a little less time on pastimes that are expensive, and a little more on ones that are cheap. Overall, however, in a few months time, everything will seem normal again." John paused, took a deep breath, and continued.

"Think about your expenses, Kate, and take action to reduce them. Don't waste money, when you can achieve the same thing in a cheaper way. As the old saying goes, 'necessity is the mother of invention', and we only solve problems when we are forced to.

Don't let yourself be ripped off. If you buy something, and it's faulty, make sure you get a full refund. Even small amounts of money make a difference, and if you don't have the courage to stand up for small things, then it will be almost impossible when really important issues come along.

One of the hallmarks of successful people, Katie, is that they never let themselves be ripped off, even for trifling amounts. They always demand what is rightfully theirs, and they refuse to be a victim in any situation. If you can develop this attitude, Katie, it will be your constant companion and friend throughout your whole life.

Re-organise your expenses, and you may even find that you can save money without having to miss any of your personal enjoyment at all."

John paused again, and rested. It was difficult to collect his thoughts, to organise the jumble of ideas and wisdom into some sort of order. It was frustrating, too. He wanted to pour all his knowledge into Kate's mind like a jug of water into a bowl, and yet he knew there was no quick and easy

33

way. It would take a long time and a great deal of patience.

"This is the only way, Kate," he said. "If you save what is left over each week, you will save nothing at all. We all spend everything we earn. The secret is to take one tenth out of each pay packet, put it away, and then spend everything that is left."

Kate sat in silence, reflecting on what her grandfather had said. She didn't want to tell him, but she couldn't imagine how she could possibly find the extra money for saving.

Still, there was sense in what he said. Every bit of extra money seemed to be absorbed into the mass of expenses, and perhaps it worked in reverse as well.

Perhaps, if she began to save, the expenses would re-adjust themselves, and she would not go broke after all. Perhaps, if she looked at ways to save money, she could save and still enjoy herself whenever she wanted to.

"Two final points I should make, my dear," said her grandfather. He was beginning to tire. "This money you save is your wealth, your security and your freedom for the future. It is not money saved for expenses. You must also budget and save for expenses, but that does not count as your savings.

Second, you must invest these savings wisely. Do not worry, for I will teach you how to do this. Investment is simply placing your money into forms that may increase in value. If you do this carefully, it will begin to snowball into more and more money.

The money you invest will earn more money, and this in turn will earn more money again. Over time, your investments may begin to produce so much income, that you may not be totally dependent on income from your work.

This is when the freedom begins to come into play. Perhaps, one day, if you learn these lessons well, your investments will be so strong and profitable, that you will not even have to work at all, unless you chose to for

34

enjoyment."

Kate was excited. Finally, the things John said were really beginning to interest her. She could see the sense in what he had said, and she could see it was a necessary part of the process, but the idea of money coming in the door without any personal effort sounded like heaven.

She determined that she would start to save, even if it was difficult at first. She wanted to manage her money better, so that she would have cash left over to save and invest, and so she could escape from the rut she had lived in for so long.

John was tired. It had been a long afternoon, the sun was below the horizon and the daylight was beginning to fade. "Another day, Katie," he said slowly. "More talk another day."

"Thank you, " said Kate. "I am not worried any more. I am full of energy, I can't wait to do the things you have told me. Things are going to change, John.

I am going to change them." Kate beamed at her grandfather. He suddenly looked old, she thought, very, very old. "Let me take you home, grandfather," she said softly. "Its time to go home."

2.2 Budgeting, provisions, saving and investing

It was a sunny day, as it always was at this time of year. Kate sat with John on his favourite bench in the park. It was a week since they had last spoken, and John looked relaxed and happy. Kate had been a little worried after their last talk, for it had clearly been a drain on her grandfather. Still, it was Sunday again and he looked fitter than ever.

"I swear," said Kate with a smile, "you don't look a day over fifty, John. If I was a single woman, I'd be after you myself."

John laughed. "Flattery, flattery, my dear. I love it!" Kate was feeling good. Over the week, she had thought about the things her grandfather had said. Although it was just a start, and things had not really changed yet,

Kate's whole attitude had shifted. She had known John for many years, and she loved him dearly, but she had never stopped to think about how he lived his life.

After listening to him the previous week, though, it dawned on her that he was rather a unique person. He rarely complained, and when he did he always took some action about the problem.

His life was his own, he controlled it himself, and when something was not right, he did his best to change it. The problem was not always solved, but at least he had acted. In short, thought Kate, he was never powerless, never a victim. For the first time, Kate began to feel that she, too, could control her future. She was optimistic and positive, ready for action, and eager to listen. Kate thought more about her grandfather's attitude, and decided it deserved a great deal more attention.

"So tell me, John, what is the lesson for today?" said Kate playfully. She was a trifle worried that he had forgotten about teaching her, and would not wish to continue the discussions. Her fears were soon put to rest.

36

"The lesson for today comes from the book of Exodus," said John in a deep, solemn voice, reminiscent of Charlton Heston's portrayal of Moses.

"Bastard!" said Kate, slapping him on the arm in her traditional way. "First a gardening lesson, and now religion!"

John's face burst into laughter, unable to maintain it's mock sincerity. "On the contrary, my dear, the topic is highly relevant. The Jews' exodus from Egypt was a trying time, and resources had to be allocated and managed very carefully." Kate's face betrayed confusion, and John quickly decided that a more traditional approach would be more effective.

"Kate," he said confidently, "today we will begin with budgeting. Have you ever had the feeling of receiving a large bill, and not knowing if you will have enough spare cash to pay it?"

"Of course not, John," said Kate with mock irritation. They both laughed.

"Well, you won't ever have that feeling again. You may not be any richer next week, but you will know that every bill you receive can be paid on the spot. Believe me, Kate, it's a very satisfying feeling."

"What's this all about?" said Kate, not quite following him.

"Its about budgeting," John replied. "Let me continue, and you'll soon see. First, remember that most bills and expenses are predictable. Yes, there are accidents, and cars break down at random, but on the whole we know what is coming. Insurance, electricity, the telephone and servicing the car all come around at regular intervals.

It is well worth the effort of putting aside a fixed amount each week to cover all these items. When you add up the total amount that these things cost each year, you'll probably have a heart attack."

Kate laughed. Often the bills seemed reasonable, but when she imagined adding them all into one lump sum, he would probably be right.

"Remember, though, that you would be spending this money anyway. All you are doing is being more organised about the whole thing. You will need a moderate amount from each pay packet, instead of a small amount from one pay packet and a massive amount from the next.

In business, this money is called 'provisions', because you are providing for expenses that you know will be coming up.

"OK," said Kate with conviction, "the first rule of budgeting is to put aside a fixed amount for bills; to make provisions. This way, I have the peace of mind of knowing that I will be able to pay each bill when it arrives, and my cash flow will be smoother, not up one week and down the next."

"Excellent," John said with pride. "One more point on provisions, Katie. You can go overboard with provisions, allocating money for all sorts of things, such as the chance of expensive car repairs, possible health problems. Life is full of possibilities, both good and bad. On the whole, I suggest you put aside provisions for the predictable, regular bills. All other possibilities are best covered by increasing your overall wealth."

"Fine," said Kate. This talk was going well and she felt she was keeping up all the way. "Now the second rule, John."

"The second step in budgeting," said John, "is a little more difficult." He hesitated a moment, unsure of how to continue. "Let me ask you, Kate, what you do at Christmas time."

"Well," she said cautiously, "I save up a little if I can, and I buy the rest on credit. Credit cards are so convenient, John."

"True," her grandfather said, "and they do have their place. I have one myself.

However, we all know that Christmas is coming up, and we usually know who we will be buying presents for. Kate,

I know it takes some discipline, but you should save up for all your purchases.

There are some very large items, like a car or a house, where it is not practical to save up, and a loan is normally required. However, apart from these, you should save up for everything else."

Kate looked glum. If she kept putting aside money for so many things, she reasoned, there would soon be nothing left over for herself.

"Don't look so depressed, Kate," her grandfather said. "Remember that you are spending this money already. The budget is simply to allow you to be better organised with your finances. This approach will leave you with more money for yourself, not less.

Saving has several advantages. First, it eliminates the interest that you pay on credit.

Right away, you have more money for yourself. Second, it makes it brutally clear just how much money you are spending on all these different items. If you choose to spend your money on large purchases and gifts, that is all very well, but at least you will see clearly why your week-to-week cash seems a bit tight.

The chances are, you will decide that you don't really want all of these things after all. Since you are allocating money before you purchase, and not afterwards, you can change your mind and spend the money on something else."

John paused for a rest, and looked at his granddaughter. She was not as bright as she had been, and he briefly wondered if it had been wise to paint the picture so honestly.

"I know you're right, John," Kate said with a weak smile. "I guess I'm just a kid at heart, and I want everything right away. Gifts, too, just seem to be free when I don't have to hand over cash." Kate took a deep breath, and looked up at her grandfather. "OK, John," she said with renewed determination, "the second rule of budgeting is to save up for all your purchases."

"I know it sounds like a nuisance, Kate, but it will leave you better off at the end of the day. You will have greater control of your money, and you will have more to spend. It will be you, for the first time, who decides exactly where it will go, instead of it just disappearing through your fingers like water."

John leaned back on the chair and rested. They had been talking for a while, and it had become quite warm in the sunshine. As he sat there, a cloud passed over the sun, and a slight breath of cool air blew past him. It was a wonderful day, a little warm perhaps, but relaxing all the same.

John watched the families picnicking, the children running around and playing games. Their small faces were glowing and alive with energy.

Their parents rested on the grass in the shade, relaxing after a long week. John watched the innocent joy on the children's faces, and then looked at the parent's faces. They were resting, and yet there was no real peace for them.

There was the tinge of tiredness, the slight stress and the faint air of jaded cynicism. Perhaps it was his imagination, he wondered, but then he looked at the children again, and was saddened by what would become of them on their difficult journey through life.

Kate watched her grandfather. He was deep in thought, watching the children at play. A curious man, she thought, loving and wise, but full of mystery. He was still, in many ways, a private person, and Kate wondered what thoughts travelled through his head.

She looked at his face, and had to admit that it held character, and was more than a little attractive. She could see some of her husband's face in John's, and perhaps this had attracted her to Jim when they had first met. And yet, this was a very different man from the one she had married. John suddenly turned to her, almost as if coming out of a trance.

"Let us continue," he said briskly. "Your income will be broken into four parts.

First, money put aside for regular bills and expenses, such as insurance and electricity.

Second, money you put aside to save for purchases.

Third, money saved and invested. This is your wealth, a wealth that will increase when you invest it wisely. It will give you security, and one day, when it has grown, it will give you an income without labour of your own.

Finally, what remains, you may spend on your daily expenses and entertainment. I will caution you, however, to keep a little aside for the unexpected expenses which pop up from time to time. If you manage your expenses wisely, the money you can spend on yourself will be the same as you have now, or perhaps even more."

Kate thought about John's words. The approach he was suggesting was a hell of a lot more organised than anything she had done before, and yet she could see that it made a great deal of sense.

Kate decided that it was worth trying, but she still hoped that john would soon tell her how to have more money, not just use the amount she already had more effectively. Suddenly, a curious thought struck Kate, a question that she felt would be very revealing. "John," she said innocently, "do you organise your finances in this way?"

John smiled, a smile of amusement, a secret sort of smile. "My finances," he whispered softly, "are complex enough to keep several people in full-time employment."

Kate was shocked. Her head spun with a whole range of possibilities and she was dying to ask more. She looked at John.

He said nothing, just stared into space, relaxed, with a slight amused smile on his face. Kate sensed that she was wiser not to push, and she would have to wait for another day. She sat while he rested, and waited for him to being his next topic.

2.3 Controlling expenses

Rested and refreshed, John prepared to tackle the next topic on the agenda.

"I hope that I have been able to illustrate," he said, "the benefits of being organised and budgeting your money. In fact, if you don't become more organised, the other things I tell you will do more harm than good."

John had made his point, and Kate listened in anticipation for his next words.

"Having gained control of your money," he said, "the next step it to have more of it."

Kate liked the sound of this. At last he was getting down to the real business of getting more cash through the door. "Improving your cash flow," he said, "involves reducing your expenses and increasing your income. First, I will talk about reducing expenses, as this is the first area you should tackle. You have more control over your expenses, and any improvements you make usually take effect right away.

First, as we have already discussed, it is essential to record your expenses and work out where all your money is going. A month's worth of figures would be a good start, and the longer you record things the better. Take each expense, no matter how big or small. As the old saying goes, 'if you look after the cents, the dollars will look after themselves'. This is very true, my dear.

Every expense, no matter how small, should be examined. Think about ways to reduce or eliminate each item. Many things can be bought more cheaply by shopping around and planning ahead. Have a close look at all your insurances. Make sure they are not too small or too large, and don't pay for anything that you don't really need.

Have a close look at your recurring expenses, things that come up on a regular basis. Servicing the car is a perfect example.

For each regular activity, make sure you perform it as

infrequently as possible. Now, don't neglect anything, or much bigger problems will arise in the future. Cars, for example, should be serviced regularly and promptly.

However, don't do anything more often than it needs to be done. In the long run, this can make a big difference to your overall expenses.

My next suggestion," he said, "relates to gifts. It is a wonderful thing to give gifts to loved ones, and one that I indulge in myself. However, don't overstretch yourself. Decide how much you can afford to put away each week for gifts, and keep to your limits on Christmas and other occasions.

Sometimes, we receive expensive presents, and feel obliged to buy an equally expensive one in return. If a present is given, however, and an equal present is expected in return, then it is not a true gift; it is a business transaction.

It can be difficult, I know, to show restraint in purchasing gifts, but you have your own future to think about as well. One final point on gifts. A gift is an expression of love for a person. The more personal involvement you have in a gift, the more meaningful it is.

Become involved in your gifts. Select something carefully that the recipient really wants. Wrap it yourself, or have it specially wrapped. Write a personal, descriptive card.

If you have a hobby, consider using your hobby to make gifts for your loved ones. A gift with this involvement can have more meaning and have less monetary cost than an 'off the rack' present."

John turned to his granddaughter, smiled, and continued speaking. "Now," he said, "for the big one… Interest."

"Interest?" Kate said curiously.

"Interest. Interest, for many people, is a significant expense. It is often hidden, though, within repayments for various loans, credit and overdrafts.

Re-arranging your finances can reduce the interest you pay, saving you significant amounts of money. Remember, my dear, that interest is completely wasted money. It is not paying for the item itself, the interest is simply paying someone for the privilege of borrowing money.

There are many ways to reduce the money you waste on interest, and I will go through these shortly. The number one way, however, it to simply save up for purchases, instead of buying them on credit. It is quite common, my dear, for people to pay double the price for items, once interest charges are taken into account.

This is money that you can't afford to throw away. I have heard people complain that they can't afford to pay cash for an item, and they need some form of credit.

Well, my dear, if someone can't afford to pay for a purchase, how the hell can they afford to pay twice the price for it?"

A fair point, thought Kate.

"The topic of borrowing and credit is so important," John continued, "that I wish to devote the whole next hour to it. First, however, we must get our priorities right. See that icecream van over there?" said John, pointing to a van under a nearby tree.

"Yes," replied Kate.

"Let's eat!" he said with a childish grin as he leapt from the chair.

2.4 Borrowing and credit

John and Kate were refreshed, relaxing on the park bench and eating icecream. Kate felt a little embarrassed. She felt like a little girl being naughty, sitting on a park bench eating icecream with her grandfather.

"I'm too old to be playing around like this, John," Kate said with a sheepish look on her face. "Can you imagine what my kids would say if they could see me now?"

"Rubbish," said John, smiling. "The moment you're too old to eat icecream with me, you may as well pack it in. Michael and Sarah are good kids, I'm sure they wouldn't tease you for more than, say, a couple of months at most."

"Bastard!" said Kate again, almost spilling her icecream into her lap. "You'll get me into trouble yet!"

"I sincerely hope so, my dear," John said with a twinkle in his eye. "Now, where were we."

"Credit, I think," replied Kate. She wasn't looking forward to this topic, as she was an offender herself. Still, If she could reduce all the various repayments, it really would be a major step forward. "Go on, John," she said between mouthfuls.

"Now, the first point I want to make," said John as he finished his icecream, "is that all forms of credit are simply different ways of borrowing money. Personal loans, credit cards, overdrafts, financing through stores, all these different arrangements are simply different ways to borrow money.

In life, there's no such thing as a free lunch. If you want to borrow something from a stranger, then you have to pay for the privilege.

If you want to borrow someone's flat for a year, then you pay rent. Rent is simply a charge for borrowing someone else's building for a while.

If you wish to borrow a car from a car rental company, then you will pay for each day that you have it. Money is no different.

If you wish to borrow money from someone, then you must pay for the privilege. The fee you pay is called interest. For each day you have the money, you are charged a fee.

Now, imagine you go into a shop and buy some furniture. Instead of paying cash, the salesman offers you repayments over twelve months. What is actually occurring here? Essentially, there are two transactions going on.

Firstly, you are borrowing money, and repaying it over twelve months.

Secondly, you are using the borrowed money to purchase the item. Because the whole thing is done at one time, you simply sign a stack of papers and take the item home.

However, Kate, it is essential to understand what is happening. You must separate the financing arrangements from the purchase of the item, to properly understand what you are doing.

Now, let us take credit cards. The same situation applies, you are borrowing money from the credit card company and using it to purchase goods. I know, Kate, that when you buy something on credit it almost seems free. It is a hard feeling to shake, I have experienced it myself. You must think about it, however, and realise that everything bought on credit must be paid for out of your own cash, plus any interest as well. Items bought on credit aren't free, they actually cost more that the same item bought with your hard-earned cash."

John paused for breath. Kate was listening intently, hanging on every word that he said. Although there was nothing new about what he said, there was something about the approach that was different.

John's descriptions showed the whole issue in a different light, and Kate felt she had a deeper understanding of the things she had been doing.

"I have, I believe," said John, "shown the disadvantages

of borrowing and credit. You only have a certain amount of money to spend, Kate, and there's no use in giving it away to people for borrowing things if you can avoid it. Having said that, do you have any forms of credit yourself?"

"John," said Kate with a sudden rush of honesty, "I have every form of credit that you have just mentioned."

"Oh," said John. He had expected her to be up to her eyeballs in debt, but this was worse than he had expected. "Well, Um, my dear," said John, unsure how to react, "let's look at strategies for improving your situation."

He paused to collect his thoughts. Perhaps, he thought, this was a good thing. Kate was spending so much on interest, she would have learnt to live from a modest amount each week. If the interest payments could be reduced or eliminated, she would have massive amounts of cash left over to save and invest.

"First, my dear, think about any money you have in the bank. Although you should have a little cash for emergencies, it is pointless to have cash earning a low rate of interest, when you are paying a high rate of interest on credit.

Effectively, you are borrowing money from the bank, paying a high rate of interest, and depositing it right back in the same bank at a much lower rate of interest!

Is it any wonder that the rich get richer and the poor get poorer?

Now, my dear, keep a little cash for emergencies, but use everything else you have to pay off your credit and loans. Paying off these items is the most profitable investment you will ever make."

Kate felt like a fool. There was no way she was going to admit it to her grandfather, but she had money in one bank account, and an overdraft on another. The bank charged her double the interest on her overdraft compared to the interest she earned on her deposits.

It seemed obvious, but she had never got around to transferring money from one account to another. Every month, she paid large amounts of interest to the bank, simply because she hadn't bothered to make a trip to her local branch.

"That's a good idea, John," said Kate. She was trying to sound business-like, although her face was quite red. "Still, that won't be enough to pay all my debts. Besides, it always made me feel good having the cash squirreled away in that other account."

"In a way, Kate, that is an illusion. A person with 5,000 in cash and 3,000 on a credit card has exactly the same wealth as a person with 2,000 in the bank and no debts. However, you are right in one respect. Once a lump sum of money is dissipated, it is difficult to have the discipline to save and rebuild it. If you cannot save a fixed amount from each pay packet, though, you will not achieve that things you have been asking me about anyway."

John sat in silence for a few moments, contemplating the information that Kate had just given him. It was worse than he had thought, and Kate could not even repay her short-term credit with her cash assets.

It was, he thought to himself with grim humour, what one could call a 'challenging situation'.

"Time for the next strategy, my dear," he said brightly. "Rearranging your finances can be a hassle, but once you get things under control it will be a whole new ball game. Next, you should investigate refinancing and consolidation loans."

"Consolidation loans?" said Kate. She had no idea what he meant.

"A consolidation loan is simply a loan you take out to pay off several smaller loans," said John. There are several reasons you should do this.

Firstly, many forms of credit have high rates of interest. By taking out a single personal loan, you can pay off several other loans and have a lower rate of interest.

Secondly, you will have a fixed repayment period. With credit cards, the balance usually goes up and down as you spend and make payments.

It is hard to set yourself a schedule to actually repay the whole amount. In fact, you would probably never pay it off completely.

The balance would simply go up and down like a barometer of your financial health.

With a loan, however, the repayments are fixed and you know exactly when the entire amount will be paid off. The final advantage is simplicity. You have one fixed payment a month to budget for, rather that running around from pillar to post paying different people different amounts each month."

John paused, looked at Kate, and said, "Once you have done this, Katie, for God's sake destroy your credit cards and cancel your overdraft so you don't ever get into this situation again."

Kate sat back on the chair and thought over everything John had said. It was a major change to her whole financial situation, in fact a major change to the way she did things in general.

She had asked John for advice, and she had certainly received what she asked for. She looked across at her grandfather.

"OK, John," she said. I will use my cash to pay off my loans, and what is left of the loans I will refinance with a single personal loan. I will pay off the personal loan over the shortest period that I comfortably can."

"Good girl," said John giving her a hug. "Did you get more than you bargained for when you asked me for advice?"

"Yes," said Kate dryly.

She had been hoping for some secret investment technique that would solve all her problems, and yet, she saw that John's method would work, and she did appreciate his efforts to help her.

"A few final comments on debt, and then perhaps we should take a quiet walk," said John gently. He could see that Kate was overwhelmed, that changes that they had discussed would mean some big changes for her.

"Credit cards," said John, "are one of the most useful modern inventions."

Kate looked at her grandfather with surprise.

"Not as a form of borrowing," John said hurriedly, not wishing to dilute his earlier points, "but they are convenient. I suggest you keep a single credit card, with a low credit limit. Every time you receive a statement, pay the whole amount religiously.

This way, you can have the convenience of a card without using it as a form of expensive, long-term borrowing. You might also consider having one other card, with a large credit limit, locked away in a cupboard for dire emergencies like medical operations. However, my dear, it requires discipline not to use it, and you are the only one who can know whether this will work for you or not.

If in doubt, don't have it. Overdrafts are of questionable use. If your account rarely goes negative, then they can be useful to stop the occasional cheque from bouncing. However, if you are one of the people who runs their account close to the overdraft limit, then they are a complete waste of time.

You do not have the protection factor, as cheques will bounce anyway because you are close to your limit. All you have is an expensive long-term loan that has not even bought you a specific item.

Overall, I suggest that you cancel your personal overdrafts. Incidentally, overdrafts are quite useful in business, but that is another story."

John paused and rested. The discussion on personal debt had gone longer than he had expected, and yet it was a critical issue for Kate to understand. Soon, he hoped, Kate would understand how to borrow for investment, how to borrow for items that increased in value, not items that declined in value. She would, he hoped, eliminate borrowing for purchases and consuming, and use loans as part of her investment portfolio. Still, he had a long way to go before Kate was ready for this.

"Finally, Kate," John said, "there are times when we all need to borrow. Some items, such as a house, are so large that it is rarely practical to save up and purchase them in cash. One day, you will have enough money to buy everything you need in cash, but that day is a long way away. When you borrow, chose the shortest term that you can manage. Remember, every day that you have someone else's money, they will charge you for it.

The sooner you pay it back, the less interest you will have to pay.

Remember, too, that interest rates make a big difference, especially on long term loans, so shop around for the lowest rate you can get.

It might help," John continued, "to understand what lenders look for when assessing a potential loan.

There is an old saying in banking and credit circles, that the 'three C's' are the three essential factors in assessing credit risk. They are 'Cash flow', 'Collateral' and 'Character'.

If you can improve your appearance in these three areas, bankers and lenders will be more likely to give you loans, and they will offer you lower rates of interest.
First, the most important issue is 'Cash flow'. Try to maximise your income and reduce your expenses to show the lender a healthy cash flow. Taking out a consolidation loan to pay off credit may help with this, as the monthly repayments can be less than the original loans that it replaces.

List all your sources of income, including anything you may earn from hobbies or extra work. Second, 'Collateral' is very important. This is the assets you have, which give the lender the security of having an asset that can be sold if you cannot meet the loan payments.

Include everything you have of value, such as furniture and jewellery, as well as the obvious items such as cash, a car and a house. Last on the list, but equally important, is

'Character'.

Lenders love stability, and they hate change.

Remember, the lender is looking at your application, and trying to guess whether you will still be making payments in another five or ten year's time. Frequently changing jobs and frequently changing homes causes them to worry, and when they worry, they might reject your application or charge you higher interest to cover the extra risk.

If you have successfully repaid loans in the past, mention this as it gives the lender confidence.

Remember, the bank manger or lender does not know you from a bar of soap, and they are guessing the chances that you will repay the loan fully, based on very little information. Your aim is to present yourself as close to the ideal loan applicant as possible. The ideal applicant has a secure income with modest expenses, they have assets in reserve, and they have a stable, responsible, conservative attitude.

The more you can make yourself look like this image, the more chance you have of being accepted and the lower your interest rate will be.

John stopped talking, leaned back on the bench, and relaxed. They had covered a great deal of ground today, and he was becoming tired.

It was late afternoon, the sun was softer and the air had cooled a little. The park seemed more peaceful, and the hustle and bustle of the city seemed further away than it had been under the mid-day sun.

John breathed slowly.

The serious talk tired him, and he almost regretted the attempt to help Kate. He was very weary now, and talking was difficult. "Kate," he said slowly, "I am tired. I am a tired, tired old man."

Kate looked at him. His face was drawn, and the light in his eyes seemed a little dimmer than before. "You are the strongest man I know, John," she said with a gentle smile, "you are not tired, you're beautiful."

A slight smile crossed John's face, a moment of thanks and pleasure, but the tiredness remained. He turned to his granddaughter, breathed slowly, and spoke. "I am ninety two years old, Kate," He said in a whisper. She could barely hear his words. "I am past my time, I am at peace, but my energy leaves me so quickly. So very, very quickly."

Kate took her grandfather's arm, and lifted him to his feet. "Come and walk with me a while, my dear," she said softly.

2.5 Increasing income

Kate and John were sitting, once again, on John's favourite bench in the park. They had walked along paths, under the shade of huge trees and past the still water. Sometimes the paths twisted and turned so much that John felt he was lost in a peaceful, enchanted forest. It was a wonderful feeling.

"How do you feel now, grandfather?" said Kate inquiringly.

"As the old black woman said to Martin Luther King after a long rally," he said with a happy smile, "'my feets are tired, but my soul is rested!'."

Kate laughed. He was a tough old bird, but she did worry at times. She was relieved to see her grandfather smiling and full of energy once again.

"Now, Kate my dear," he said with gusto. "We have more ground to cover yet today. A subject that is dear to your heart; increasing your income."

"Wonderful!" Kate said happily. "Where do I start?"

"Relax, my dear," John said. "As I said before, improving our income is a long term journey for most of us. Like the race where the slow tortoise beat the flighty hare, the one who takes steady consistent steps wins the race in the end. First, and most important, you must look after your skills and career like an old friend.

Life takes us through many unexpected turns, and your skills are the most valuable asset you have.

Money is also important for security, but the greatest security of all is in having a broad range of well cared-for skills. Unlike money," John continued, "skills cannot be lost or stolen, they cannot be taken by tax or inflation, and wherever we go, they are always with us.

Skills are an eternal source of income, a fountain of money that never runs dry."

John's voice dropped slightly, and his tone became

cautionary. "However, skills are like any friend, if you take them for granted, you will eventually loose them.

Keep your skills maintained and up-to-date, as you would maintain a valuable piece of machinery. I have several suggestions for you.

First, keep up-to-date with changes in your field. The modern world moves quickly, and skills will become out-of-date if you are not prepared to put some effort into training and keeping in touch.

Second, consider formal qualifications. It is possible to put vast amounts of effort into formal study, and receive little gain in return. On the whole, however, formal qualifications are valuable assets.

You will learn a great deal, and qualifications are one of the few things an employer can reply on when assessing an applicant for a position.

Next, be prepared to branch out into other fields, and learn new skills. A person with a wide range of skills is more valuable than the sum of the skills put together.

She can apply all her talents to any task at hand, and has a stronger chance of finding employment that an unskilled person has.

The more you learn, Kate, and the broader your skills, the more valuable you will be to an employer. Don't forget, either, that I have spoken of skills, not a paid career.

Kate, there are many documents that will pass under your eyes during your lifetime, but few will be as important as your resume.

Those few pages represent the greatest security that you possess, and probably the greatest income-producing asset that you have."

In the circumstances, John though dryly, it was a fairly safe assumption.

"Keep you resume up-to-date, and include all experience, skills and qualifications. Even unpaid work that you have done, and serious hobbies and interests can be relevant.

Keep an open mind, and do not restrict it to the full-time jobs that you have had. If you think back carefully on the many things you have done through your life, there are sure to be many relevant items that don't immediately come to mind.

Along with your resume, collect references from people you have worked for. A good reference is worth its weight in gold, it can open doors for you for the rest of your life. Ask for references, collect them, and guard them well. They are an asset that money cannot replace.

John paused for breath. Kate was listening intently, absorbing everything he said.

"I have spoken about your career, your skills and your work," he said, "and how important they are. I have spoken about caring for your skills, expanding them, and keeping in touch with skills you have not used for a while.

This is the most important advice I can give you about your income and security. When you have built up a reserve of strong assets that produce good income, you will not be dependent on your career, but even then it will be an asset that should always be nurtured."

Kate sat in silence, contemplating the things John had said. He, too, sat in silence, giving her time to mull over his words.

As Kate thought, John looked at the trees, gently bending in the breeze. From a distance, the leaves looked tiny and soft, almost like pale green cotton blowing gently in the breeze.

He watched the trees sway back and forth with the puffs of wind. It was calming, almost hypnotic. John's heartbeat slowed, he took a deep breath, and he absorbed the calmness into his body and his mind.

A long silence had passed when Kate spoke. "You know, John, I have always been proud of my work. Nursing has always been special to me. In many ways, I felt it satisfied so many of my needs. It is hard work, but I have the best of many worlds as well. It involves working with people, which I enjoy greatly, and it also involves technical skills and scientific knowledge." Kate looked at her grandfather. "It's not an easy job, John."

"I know that well, Kate dear." John had always admired his granddaughter's work. She took it very seriously, and, he was sure, did an excellent job.

"I have always kept up to date on my training, although I did it because I liked it, not just for the money."

"Wonderful, my dear," said John. "I, more that anyone, believe there is so much more to life than money. However, if you have done something for enjoyment, there's nothing to stop you using it to your advantage in other areas as well. You should make the most of everything you have achieved."

"You know, John," Kate said slowly, "I have always felt good about my career. I always felt that this was one area that I succeeded well in."

"And you have, Kate."

"Even so, I have never really sat down, and listed my skills and achievements on a single piece of paper. A resume, I suppose. The last time I did that, I was still wearing braces," Kate said with a smile. She was thinking, mentally listing all the work she had done, the different courses and the study.

Little things, many of them, but the more she remembered, the better she started to feel.

Suddenly, she sat bolt upright and beamed at her grandfather. "John," she said, "you're absolutely right. I have been feeling trapped, as if I had no choices. I've just made a mental list of everything I have done in my working life, and it looks damn good.

Even if I stay in my job, I don't feel bad now. When I think of that list, I realise that I do have choices. I realise that there are other things I could do, other jobs I could work at. In fact," she said, getting more excited, "I was even a little embarrassed about my pay. It's not wonderful, but in some ways I even thought I was being over-paid. Now, I've just decided that the bastards aren't paying me enough!"

"Don't get too excited, now Kate," said John. She did have an emotional streak, and John had visions of her charging into her boss's office the next day and demanding a doubling of her pay. Still, her attitude had changed for the positive in a rather dramatic way.

"It's good to see you being more assertive and confident about the whole thing. Now, there are three steps to increased income.

First, increase what you are worth. This is done by improving your skills, experience and qualifications.

Second, get a clear and objective idea in your mind about what you are worth. Don't underestimate yourself, as most people under estimate what they are worth, but don't become filled with pride and vanity and overplay your hand either.

You must be realistic.

Third, insist on being paid what you are worth. A little give and take is required here, and it is rarely worth leaving a job if the only reason is a minor increase in salary. However, if you are paid much less than you could get elsewhere, then it's time to leave. If your assessment of your worth is accurate, then there will be someone who is willing to pay you the full amount.

Of course, job satisfaction and enjoyment is critical, but no person is indispensable, and no job is perfect.

Don't put up with something that is far below what you could be doing. One final point on jobs, Kate. As well as the pay, you should take into account the training and experience you are receiving.

If you are receiving valuable training or experience, then it may be worthwhile staying in a job that is not highly paid, as the skills you are receiving will be invaluable in the future.

Above all else, Kate, be prepared to take action. The key to financial success, and other success for that matter, is willingness to take action.

Don't put up with a situation if you can do something to improve it. Most people fail with money because they simply live with what they have.

They complain from time to time, but in the end they just adjust to their circumstances, and don't do anything to change them. Whatever you do, and whatever your reasons, be prepared to change. Have the courage to make things different, to make things better.

Kate was impressed. Sometimes, she thought, John displayed a real talent for speaking. She wondered where his life would have lead if he had been more open, not as secretive with his thoughts and his inner feelings. He was one of the rare people who could capture the imagination with his words, who could paint a picture with his voice that startled the mind.

Kate felt a sense of power, a sense of hope and strength that was unfamiliar to her.

She had, in many ways, imagined herself as a cog in a massive machine, powerless to change her situation. This feeling was fading quickly. "Tell me John," she said, "have you any more advice on increasing my income?"

"Only this," he replied, "that you should look at every source of income that is available to you. Specifically, any hobbies or interests you have. If you are serious about any hobby, there are usually ways to earn a small amount of money from it. It may seem small compared to your job, but remember that every dollar counts. If you ignore the part of your pay that is spent on essentials, like rent or a mortgage, then the amount left over, your 'disposable income', is often quite small.

Even a small amount of extra income can increase your disposable income quite significantly. It may be those extra few dollars that tip the scales in your favour, so things get a little better and a little easier each week, instead of staying the same. You may even think about overtime, but I caution you with this.

Many people work very long hours, but continue with

the lifestyle of spending everything that they earn. For these people, their quality of life may become terrible. They miss out on many things, and a few years down the track they have nothing to show for it. If you want to work extra hours, I strongly suggest that you save the extra money, so that your sacrifices will pay dividends for you in the future."

It was time for another rest. John had been talking for a long time, and they had both become tired again. He wondered whether he was going too quickly, whether he should give her more time to think over the things he was saying.

"How do you feel, Kate?" he asked.

"My head is swimming," she said quietly, "swimming with new ideas. I never imagined that you would say all these things. I simply thought you would give me a few tips, and that would be the end of it."

John felt a bit put out. Perhaps he had done the wrong thing, perhaps he was going too deep, saying things that were better left unsaid. She was right; all she had been expecting was a few hot tips.

"Don't worry, John," she said looking up at him. "I am very grateful that you have taken the time to tell me these things. It's all very new, I must admit, and I have never sat down and thought about my finances in such a deep way. I can see clearly now, that if you had just made a few comments, instead of starting at the start, you would have been wasting our time."

This made her grandfather feel better, and he decided that it was the right approach after all. It had taken him a lifetime, a very long lifetime, to learn the things he was teaching Kate, and he could not expect her to absorb the ideas over-night."

"Let's rest a little, dear," he said. "Let us sit in the cool evening together. Let us say nothing, just enjoy being here."

They sat together in silence.

2.6 Financial affairs

Although they had been sitting in silence for quite a while, in a strange way John and Kate felt even closer to each other than when they had been talking.

In the quiet of the evening, without words to distract them, they sat together. The air was cool, but each of them felt a warmth inside, and they were glad that the other person was with them.

"It has been a long afternoon, Kate," John said at length. "Perhaps we should stop soon."

"Yes," Kate replied, "but you told me there was more still for today. I would like to hear it all, John. I am learning very much."

"Very well," her grandfather said. "Next week, we will begin the journey to investment. For now, there is only one more topic concerning your personal money management we need to discuss."

"And what is that," said Kate, listening intently once again.

"Handling your financial affairs," John replied. "There are several more things you should do to handle your financial affairs effectively and responsibly."

Kate was a little annoyed at her grandfather. She considered herself to be very responsible and did not appreciate the implication that she was not.

John noticed the look on her face, and guessed correctly what his granddaughter was thinking. "Forgive me, Kate, if I seem to be talking to you as a child. These are important issues, they are issues for adults and issues to take seriously." He smiled at her mischievously, and continued. "When I have finished speaking, if you have already done everything I suggest, the icecreams next week will be on me."

"Bastard!" replied Kate with an affectionate slap on the arm. "You can pay anyway for daring to suggest it!"

John laughed. Typical of a woman to twist his words and trap him in a no-win situation, he thought to himself, but wisely he kept his mouth shut. How he wished he had learnt to stay silent much earlier in his life.

"Kate, my dear," he said becoming serious, "firstly we should talk about wills. We all like to avoid the topic, but as sure as the sun rises, we will all die one day. It's simply a matter of when. If you have people who you love, and I know that you do, then it is essential to have a valid will.

Anyone with children should have a will.

Anyone with significant assets should have a will. If you die without one, your money will be distributed to your next of kin, but there can be delays and extra costs.

Then, of course, your money may not be distributed in the way you would prefer." John was tempted to make a joke about Kate having a boyfriend on the side, but thought better of it and waited for Kate to speak.

"Very true, John," Kate said without humour. "I have a will myself." Somehow, she did not feel the same satisfaction she had felt about other issues, and she was glad to move on. John was perfectly relaxed and business-like about it, but to her it was still a rather morbid subject.

"Besides a will," John said, "there is the issue of insurance. Every situation is different, but I will tell you my impressions from the things I have seen during my lifetime.

First, every person who has dependants should have life insurance. A married couple, where both partners work and there are no children, have little need for life insurance.

In the tragic event that one partner died at a young age, the other would still have their own income. As soon as a person is responsible for a child, however, regardless of the relationship or situation, they should have life insurance.

Children are completely dependent on their parents for many years, and no responsible parent can afford to be without life insurance. Incidentally, this includes both the mother and father, as a child is dependent on the efforts and income of both.

One should also consider any other dependants, such as elderly parents in a poor financial position. The simple rule, Kate, is that if anyone is financially dependent on you, then you should have life insurance."

John paused, gave Kate a few moments to consider this, then continued. "Next, consider 'disability income insurance'.

This type of insurance goes by various names. It purpose is to continue paying you a salary if you cannot work due to illness or injury.

As we have clearly seen," John said dryly, "you would be in serious trouble if you were unable to work for several months or even years. This type of insurance will pay you your normal salary, for as long as you are unable to work.

Even in the extreme case that you were lying in a hospital bed for two years, the policy would pay you your salary each month as usual.

Kate, I strongly suggest that every person in full-time employment should have one of these policies. Yes, there are various types of insurance to cover you at work, and in other situations, but these are all full of loopholes and exceptions.

This is the best protection you can have against sickness and accidents. Even if you are never injured or sick, the extra peace of mind is well worth the money."

Kate thought about the things John had described, and had to admit that they sounded very practical. Even though there was a cost involved, Kate determined to take out appropriate policies on herself, and encourage Jim to do the same.

"A few words of warning," John said, his tone becoming cautionary.

"First, don't take out too much insurance, don't buy more cover than you need. It all costs money, and I have seen poor people struggling under the burden of large premiums for policies that they didn't even need.

Look at your insurances carefully, and make sure you

have the right amount, not too much and not too little. Shop around and get value for your money. Later, I will talk about the different kinds of policies, and how much cover you really need."

"Next item on the agenda," John said briskly, "is insurance of assets." Every major item, such as a house or car, should be insured.

The basic rule, is that if you can't afford to loose it, then insure it.

However, don't take out specific insurance for small items, or items you could afford to replace. The insurance company calculates the odds of the item being destroyed or lost, and charges premiums accordingly.

However, because they are in business to make a money, they charge extra on top of the risk premium to provide a profit. If you don't insure small items, then you are effectively becoming your own insurance company for these items, because you are carrying the risk yourself.

The only difference, is that you get to keep the profit margin yourself, instead of giving it to the owners of an insurance company."

This was quite long speech, and John was a little breathless. He rested, while Kate thought over the things he had said. At length, she spoke.

"I do have various insurance policies," she said, "but to be honest with you John, they are a bit disorganised.

In fact, if you include my superannuation through work, and the policies we had to take out with the mortgage, I'm not exactly sure what I'm covered for and what I'm not. Over the years, you know, it all gets into a bit of a mess. Tonight," she said confidently, "I'm going to sit down, make a list of every single insurance policy I have, and see how the whole lot fits together."

"An excellent idea," her grandfather replied. "Who knows, you may even find you've been paying for something you don't really need, and you can save some money right away.

On the other hand, you may find that you aren't covered for some serious risk, and the sooner you correct the situation the better."

The sun had sunk below the horizon, and the soft dusk light lit the park. Another hour, and it would be dark. Time, John thought, to finish their discussions. Time, soon, to go home.

"There is one last thing I must tell you, Kate," he said. "The key to managing your money wisely is to be organised. Keep receipts and records for everything you do.

Make sure you understand clearly where your money comes from, and exactly where it goes. Have a clear record of all your insurances, what they cover, and how much they cost.

If you can be organised, Kate, you have made the first major step along the road to financial independence.

Being organised will not make you rich, but being disorganised will surely make you poor. Everything else I will teach you, about investment, building wealth and independence, hinges on managing your money wisely and in an organised fashion."

John turned to his granddaughter. The light was very dim, now, and he could barely see her. "Kate," he said softly, "it's time to go home."

Kate breathed deeply. He had said so much over the day, that yesterday seemed a million miles away, a whole lifetime away. She turned to her grandfather and hugged him. "Thankyou, John," she said. She looked at his face, barely a shadow in the dim light, and smiled.

"Let me take you home, grandfather," she said gently.

3 *Our economic system*

3.1 *Basic concepts*

Several weeks had passed since John and Kate had last discussed finance. Each Sunday, they met in the Park as usual, walked, rested and talked about many things.

John insisted that Kate needed time to think over the advice he had given her, and he needed time himself to restore his energy.

'You must keep these things in perspective, you know' he had said to her. 'Never too much thought, and never too little'.

Although she had been anxious to learn more, John had refused to say anything more on the subject.

Over a few weeks, Kate became more relaxed about the topic, and thought back over the things John had said to her. She had implemented several of his suggestions, and a few more of her own that were in the spirit of the whole exercise.

Kate felt more optimistic and positive about her finances and her future than she had felt for a long time.

Although she was not any richer, she was certainly less worried, and that made the whole thing worthwhile already. She was in control of her situation, instead of floundering around like a rudderless ship in a storm.

Kate's only worry was that John would never finish the things he had begun to teach her. Although she had taken a large step forward, there where still many holes in the picture.

Her grandfather had talked about the need to save, and to

invest her savings wisely. She still had no idea of how to achieve this, and although everyone she met was full of enthusiastic suggestions, John was the only one she trusted to steer her through the traps that she would inevitably face.

Kate had given up prompting him, to avoid the risk of deterring him altogether, and hoped he would resume the discussions on his own. She tried to avoid thinking about it, but secretly she was scared that he would never say another thing, and she would be left with unfulfilled hope.

One afternoon, as they sat on John's favourite bench, Kate's grandfather fell deep into thought and said nothing for a long time. Kate knew these moods of his, and relaxed in the warm afternoon sun. He would speak, she knew, when he was ready.

"Kate," her grandfather said slowly.

"Yes?" she replied hopefully, praying that he was ready to discuss the things she desperately wanted to learn.

"Kate," he said again, "I have been watching you these past few weeks. You have become more confident, and the depressed air you had around you has lifted. There is still tiredness, but you seem more happy and positive than you have been for a long time." John looked across at his granddaughter, waiting for her to confirm his observations.

"Yes," she said excitedly, "I feel much more positive now that I have made these changes. Still, it is only a start."

"Very true, my dear, very true," her grandfather replied. Again, he lapsed into silence for several minutes. Kate's excitement began to fade, and she decided that he was not going to say anything after all.

"As you say, my dear," John said suddenly, "it is only the beginning. I can see that you have taken control of your money, and it makes me happy to see this.

Even now, the future is looking brighter. However, if you are going to have the freedom and independence we have spoken about, there is far more you must learn."

Kate's excitement returned, and she realised that he was going to talk after all. She beamed at her grandfather.

John looked down at his granddaughter. She was smiling like a little child, her face a picture of naivety and innocence.

'Sweet, innocent little child' he thought. 'How little you really understand. If only you knew, if only you understood how your life is used as a pawn in the games of the rich and powerful.

If only you saw how cleverly your own values are used to make you slave willingly for others. If only you understood the system, then you could be freed from it.'

John looked at his granddaughter, smiling openly at him, waiting for him to speak. 'If only she truly understood.' But she didn't. Still, perhaps he could teach her enough to make her own life easier. Perhaps her ignorance was a blessing. Perhaps he could teach her enough to have freedom, to have independence and choices, to have, one day, wealth of her own.

He had failed to help others, and in fact had barely survived the attempt at all, but perhaps this one last effort would be worthwhile.

"Kate," he said to his granddaughter, "we have covered personal money management. You have listened carefully, and I can see that you have followed my advice. The other major factor in financial success is the ability to invest your money wisely."

"Tell me, grandfather," said Kate, unable to contain her excitement.

"Slow down, honey," John said with a smile. When all was said and done, her spirit and natural enthusiasm bought him a great deal of happiness and relief. "Just take it easy."

"Bastard!" said Kate, slapping him on that arm for fun. "You know I can't wait to hear it!"

"Take it easy," John replied. "You know I can't resist fiery women."

They burst into laughter and hugged, the tension broken. It was a beautiful friendship, and one that they both relied heavily on.

"Now, Kate," John said after they had relaxed, "there are things I must teach you before we speak about investment. Investment is using your money to make more money. If you are going to do this successfully, it is critical that you understand how our society and economic system operates. Only then can you understand how the different investments work, and apply them successfully."

Kate was flabbergasted. John had implied that it would be easy, that the principles were simple and that a little hard work would be all she needed to become a successful investor. The way this was progressing, it sounded like she needed an economics degree just to get started.

John saw the look on his granddaughter's face, and guessed correctly what she was thinking. "Relax, my dear," he said with a smile. "There are only a few simple principles you need to understand. These principals have operated in very society since Babylonian times, and although political systems sometimes get in the way, the principals are so universal that they are part of life itself. Let me tell you a story. Listen to my words carefully, and everything will become clear.

One day, a very, very long time ago, there lived a small group of people. There were fifteen or twenty families, enough for a small community, but not too many that they did not know each other well. These people travelled through the forest, collecting food and hunting as they went. They travelled long distances, and lead a simple and fulfilling life. They had virtually no possessions, as everything they owned they had to carry with them. When work needed to be done, everyone helped out. There was, of course, still fights and arguments, jealousy and greed, but on the whole it was a simple and effective lifestyle.

One day, on their travels, the people stumbled across a valley. The hunting had been poor of late, and the people had not seen rich forests for several months.

They were weak and hungry. It was a large valley, and one that was different to any other valley they had seen.

There were plants and flowers, trees and animals, and yet it was different from other valleys they had encountered.

There were many flat, open areas at the bottom of the valley, and few large trees. There was a plentiful supply of water from a river though the valley's heart, and yet there was no dense rainforest. Just an occasional tree, an occasional animal, and grain.

Lots and lots of grain.

Everywhere they looked, it seemed there was wild wheat and barley, corn and rice. Rice grew in the wet, dark areas around twists in the river, and wheat grew on the sunny ridges and plains within the valley.

The people were hungry after the last few months and they ate ravenously. There was plenty of food for all. As well as the grain, there were fruit trees.

However, these fruit trees were tall and straight, not the twisted mass of vegetation the people were used to from the rainforest. Overall, the weather was good, the food plentiful and the water fresh.

Normally, the people would have stayed a while, used the food that was available and then moved on. In this valley, however, there seemed a limitless supply of food. More importantly, the surrounding land was barren and dry, and the food there was scarce. The people had travelled far, across much dry land when they had arrived at the valley.

There was no telling whether the next valley would be like this one, or whether there would be another long, slow journey to the next source of food. So, after much talking, the people made an important decision.

It was a decision that would fundamentally change the course of their future. For the first time in living memory, they decided to stay in one place.

There was no need, they felt, to move on.

In the past, the food and game in an area had been used up quickly, and it had been necessary to search for new hunting grounds. Here, however, the valley seemed rich enough to support their needs almost indefinitely.

Time moved by. Although the weather in the valley was good, some winters were colder than others. Since they were in no hurry to move, the people put more and more effort into building shelters against the cold nights.

What began as makeshift huts, gradually developed into solid, warm houses. On their travelling days, the people had done all the work together. It was an effective way to work, as no job was particularly long or hard on its own.

Now that they were in one place, however, some people took more care building their shelters than others did. Over time, each person worked on a shelter for their own family, and the homes and families developed their own shelter and areas of land.

More time passed, and slowly a change developed within the valley. Although the food had seemed limitless at first, the people became aware that the grain was running out. As the food became scarcer, two significant changes happened to the people.

As they became hungry, the people began to fight over food. The hungrier they became, the more they fought.

After a while, each family began to protect its own housing, and the land around it, as their own property, and attacked anyone who ventured onto it. For the first time, people began to see areas of land as their own personal property.

Previously, the people had simply wandered around the forests and the plains, but now, they stayed in the one place and treated it as their own. Still, however, the food became scarcer and scarcer.

It was then that the second significant event occurred.

The people had always known that new plants developed from the seeds of a mature plant. In order that they would have more food to eat, the families collected the seeds from the heads of the grain and kernels from the fruit.

They planted the seeds and kernels in the ground around their homes. After a few years, large areas around the homes were covered in healthy crops and fruit trees.

All this time, however, the number of animals in the valley had also been decreasing. The people had been hunting them at a faster rate than they reproduced. The people had been in the valley so long, however, that the animals had become quite tame.

In order that they would have meat, with the salt and protein their families needed, the people began to collect the animals into groups, and fence them into small gullies. No longer would the infant animals wander into another family's area, or into dense forest where they could not be captured. As time passed, the animals feed on the grass, bred, and grew into large herds.

It was at this time that the next major change took place. The lean times had passed, and each family had developed crops, herds of animals and strong shelters.

The desperation of the past faded, and the people began to mix once again. On each farm, the families developed simple tools to help them in their work. Primitive ploughs and sickles were used to sow and harvest the crops. At one farm lived a particular young man. He was interested, as many of the young men were, in making things with his hands. He had no interest in working in the field, and although he had to help support the family's crops, he was always glad to have a break and work on one of his devices.

The young man's ploughs, in particular, were looked on with admiration by the other families. They were strong and they moved through the soil with ease. One day, one of the people from a neighbouring family was talking to the man.

He suggested, that if the man was willing to exchange one of his ploughs for some sacks of grain, the man would not have to work in the fields, as his contribution to the family's food stores would already be made.

In return, the other farmer would have the use of a good plough, which would make his daily work easier.

The plough-maker readily agreed. Everything went as expected, and both men were happy with the trade.

Other farmers soon made the same offer, and before long

the man was spending all his time making ploughs, which he traded for grain. Time passed, and it became apparent that other people, too, had special skills of their own, and particular products they liked to make. More trading began, and soon there was an active and healthy trade between the families. This trade benefited everyone involved, although it soon became apparent that some people were wiser in trade than others, and some seemed to accumulate more grain over time than their neighbours.

As the trading of goods expanded, it soon became obvious that there were other needs, as well. Some people had need of items for short periods of time, such as a borrowed plough while the their main plough was under repair.

Many items were lent and borrowed. In return for borrowing an item, the borrower would give the lender some sacks of grain. The item would be returned, however the lender would retain the grain as compensation for not having use of the item. Soon, there was a thriving exchange of items on loan, and a corresponding flow of grain in exchange for the loan of the items.

Trade in ploughs, grain, cut wood and many other products had been going on in the valley for some time, along with lending of tools and machinery in return for fees.

The families found that they were all better off, as the people who were best at each job were the ones who were doing it for all. One year, however, a tragic accident occurred. Three young men from one family were fishing in the river, when a landslide crashed down the side of the valley and killed all three. All the people the valley mourned the tragic event. When the mourning was over, the family of the boys was in serious trouble.

It was harvest time, and the youngest generation was not quite old enough to complete the harvest by themselves. Without the full harvest, the family would be critically short of grain. Some families offered help, but it was their harvest time as well and they could ill afford to spend the extra time to help the grieving family.

As luck would have it, however, this was the same family whose son had first begun to trade his ploughs for grain. There was no grain to trade, as harvest time was not complete, but the young man had an idea. He offered his best ploughs to the other families.

In return, they would work in his family's fields and help complete the harvest. Everything went as hoped, and all were satisfied with the exchange. Soon, other families realised that they, too, had a shortage of labour and an excess of goods, or perhaps the reverse.

In no time at all, people all over the valley were working on each other's farms in return for fees. Thus, while families had long since exchanged their goods, they began to exchange their labour as well.

Through these processes, the four pillars of commerce were formed; the creation of assets, such as housing and machinery; the ownership of assets, such as land and skills; the trading of assets, such as grain and tools; and the lending of assets in return for fees. On these four pillars, the society developed into a thriving, productive community, rich in food, shelter and possessions."

John paused, resting, while Kate pondered the story he had just told her.

"It's a very simple story, John," she said, and yet it does make things clearer. Still, I can't quite see how it relates to me. I mean, the modern world is far more complicated, and I am just a nurse, I don't buy and sell goods for a profit."

"On the contrary, my dear," John said with a smug smile, "I am pleased to say that everything you have just said is completely wrong."

Kate was a little taken aback.

"The society that I just described included all the fundamental elements of our modern economic system. There are several concepts I have not yet covered, and the modern world has many complications, but the basic issues remain the same.

In fact, when we look at investment in more detail, you will be amazed at how little has changed.

Economic systems revolve around creating products, buying and selling products or services and lending items or skills for a fee. Even your job revolves around these principles.

You sell your time to the hospital, which pays you money in return. As well as selling your time, you are effectively lending your skills to them for a period, and charging them for it. Everyone is in business, Kate, even you."

Kate was perturbed. She had never quite thought of her work in this way. It was clear, though, that the viewpoint John was proposing brought everything to do with money into a common perspective.

"While we are discussing this system," he continued, "I would like to talk about this concept of an 'asset'. An asset is anything you possess which is valuable to other people.

It may be a tangible item, such as a car or a house.

It may be the title to some land, which effectively gives you control over the land, or 'ownership' within certain limits.

It may even be an intangible asset, such as your skills and your labour.

There are two types of assets.

First, anything you possess which is capable of earning income is an asset. This is the most valuable type of asset to own.

As long as it produces an income, other people will have a use for it and it will always be valuable. These assets include your skills, and also include investments such as a rental property.

The second type of asset includes possessions that are desirable to others. These include paintings, your own home, and some investments such as gold.

Anything that can generate income, or be easily sold, is an asset. Kate, you should care for your assets like your own children. All through your life, it is these assets that will give you security and freedom

. Maintain them well. Keep properties in good order, keep your skills up-to-date, and never let any possession fall into disrepair.

Your wealth is your collection of assets. You may feel that you are poor, but consider all your assets.

Compare yourself with another person who has no skills, and is reliant on an investment property for income. Their property would have to be worth ten to twenty times your salary for them to earn a comparable income to yourself.

Kate did a quick mental calculation, working out exactly how much twenty times her salary was. It did not take long. She quickly realised that if she owned a property worth more than twenty times her salary, she would indeed feel like a wealthy woman.

"This, Kate, is how much your skills and labour is worth. However, if you do not want to work your whole lifetime, if you want to have time to yourself and cash to spend, then you must build up a store of other assets.

You must build a reserve of assets that can earn income all by themselves, without any effort and labour of your own."

John leaned back on the park bench, exhausted. He had been talking for quite some time, and although he and Kate often talked for hours, that was different to an uninterrupted speech.

He was hot and tired.

It was a warm time of year, mid summer, and the sun was high in the sky. Evening, though, was always cool, and John loved the climate that they lived in. Warm, sunny days and cool evenings. Autumn was he favourite season, though. The days were cool and crisp, the sky blue, the sun warming on the skin. The trees were at their best in autumn, golden leaves on the young trees and rich red colours on the older ones. In autumn, the earth was warm and the air was cool.

This was still summer, though, and tiny green shoots bravely faced the burning sun as they grew into branches and leaves.

How sad, he mused, that the people of the city knew so little of the park. John loved the bright lights himself, and had spent many evenings as a young man in dim bars and bright nightclubs, but it was only in the park that he had found himself, and learnt the exquisite joy of being alive. If the city held the rhythm of human life, the ebb and flow of people, then trees, flower and lakes held their soul and their spirit. It was only here that John had found peace.

Kate was deep in thought, contemplating the things her grandfather had said. It was not a set of facts that she had learnt, or even concepts, it was a fundamentally different way of viewing the world. She had never seen the world in this way before. Suddenly, many confusing things became clear, and Kate saw the simple wisdom and truth of John's words. She turned to her grandfather, a peaceful, relaxed expression on her face, and softly spoke. "Tell me more, John. I want to know more."

3.2 Corporate enterprises

"Very well, my dear," John said.

"One sunny afternoon, several of the valley's families were gathered together, picnicking by the river. The children played in the water, swimming, diving and generally having fun. While the children played, the old people of the families sat in the shade and talked.

It seemed an ordinary afternoon, a day much like any other, but this day was special. This day, the people would take another fundamental step forward in life of their community.

Grain had been grown in the valley for many years.

The families had long since learnt to make flour from grinding wheat, and bread from the flour. Indeed, bread had become one of the staple diets of the valley people.

However, grinding the grain was a time-consuming process. Some families had built small water wheels by the river to drive the grinding stones, but these were small devices and had limited capacity.

The families who were picnicking lived near the top of the valley, where the river ran through a narrow gully, and the farm land was less fertile than on the plains below. As the old men sat talking, one of them pointed to the children at play and laughed.

The children had built a small dam, blocking off a small off-shoot of the river. As the water built up behind the dam, higher and higher, the pressure grew greater and greater. Finally, when the dam walls could hold it no more, the dam burst, sending a torrent of water over the excited children.

So powerful was the flood, that several children were swept a small distance downstream, and their older brothers and sisters had to rescue their frightened siblings.

The man who had spotted the children's adventure sat deep in thought. All afternoon, he had been discussing the difficulty of obtaining flour for the family. Like others, his family had built a small water wheel, but it was a difficult job and the grind-stone was small. Suddenly, the man spoke. He suggested, to the considerable surprise of the other families, that there was a way to solve all their problems.

The was, he said, a way to provide all the flour the families needed, along with a new source of income for trading. After encouragement from the others present, he outlined his plan.

The idea was to dam off the entire river, high up in the valley near their homes.

Beside the river, a large grinding mill would be built, as large as a small house. This mill would have enough capacity to grind the wheat of all the families at the picnic.

In addition, other families could be charged a fee for grinding their wheat, and a new source of income would be had for all. The man's words were greeted with howls of laughter.

Never before had a project this large been attempted in the valley. It was a job requiring dozens of people, and clearly the man's family did not have enough grain or possessions to pay this many people for their labour.

Then, when the laughing had died down, the man outlined the critical ingredient of his plan. All the families, he said, would contribute. They would all contribute their own labour, along with grain and goods which could be traded for the necessary wood to build the mill.

In turn, each family would receive an equal share of the grain and goods that the other valley people were charged for use of the mill. When the mill was built and operational, another man would be hired to look after it.

This man would be responsible for organising the use of the mill and ensuring that it was properly maintained. In return, he would receive a share of the grain and goods the mill earned, equal in size to the other family's shares. When the man stopped speaking, he was greeted with silence.

The laughter had long since stopped. After much

discussion, and many more meetings, the project went ahead as the man had described it. Everything went well, and the families who had built the mill received a generous income from the fees the other families paid to use their new project.

Time passed, and the mill ran smoothly. A man was employed to manage the mill, and in turn he employed others from time to time to make repairs. The grain used to pay these people came from the overall store that the mill received, before it was distributed to the families.

As more time passed, other large projects were undertaken in the valley. Soon there were many large constructions in the valley, all owned by groups of people. Each project employed people, paid them wages, owned buildings and generally behaved much like a whole new person of its own.

One day, one of the original families found itself in a difficult situation. Through a series of developments in the life of the family, it found itself with a large number of children, not quite old enough to work in the fields, but old enough to have ravenous appetites.

The family still owned its share of the original grinding mill, and this mill provided an income of grain each year to the family. However, this grain was not enough to feed them. So, after talking with other families, a major decision was made. The family traded its share of the mill to another family, in return for a large amount of grain.

This grain would be sufficient to last them several years, until the children were old enough to work in the fields. The other family was happy to pay a large amount of grain, as they knew they would receive a steady flow from the mill for many years to come.

After a while, other families in the valley tried the same idea, and soon there was an active trade in shares of projects throughout the valley. Thus began the next great step in the economic life of the valley: group ownership of projects, projects which acted like an entity in their own right.

John paused to let Kate ponder the story he had just told her. "This story is one of the most important that I will tell you. It is essential that you understand this idea of a 'corporate body' or 'company'.

In the modern world, most of the trade, employment and money is managed by companies, not individuals.

First, consider the project I just described. Building a large grinding mill had never been attempted by the people of the valley. It was simply too large a project to be undertaken by a single person. Like a bridge over a river, there is no point in building half of it. Either they went the whole way, and dammed off the entire river, or there was no use doing it at all.

Many projects have a minimum practical size, and are simply too large for any one individual to pay for.

In these situations, people form groups, pool their resources, and attempt the project as a team.

In the early days of history, this was done on an informal basis. Over the last few hundred years, however, the law has developed to the point where a 'company' can now act in much the same way as an individual.

Each company has a name, and can own buildings, equipment and any other assets. Companies can enter into contracts, and have binding agreements with individuals and other companies.

A company can borrow money and lend money, it can employ people and make decisions. You can sue a company, and a company can sue you. In fact, there are few differences between the things a human being and a company can do. One could even say that each company has a personality, character and culture of its own, although their conscience and memory can be rather limited.

There are only two significant differences between a company and an individual.

First, a company lives forever, it never has to die. The owners of the company will change over time, but the company itself can continue forever.

The second difference, is that a person has their own skills and labour with which to earn income, whereas a company does not. In the case of an individual, she may earn income from her own personal exertion, or from her assets and investments. A company, however, is totally reliant on the use of its assets, and the employment of staff, to produce an income and a profit.

This distinction between individuals and companies has little practical significance however. As well as large projects, companies can be formed whenever a group of people wish to get together to carry on any kind of business enterprise.

The owners of the company all own a share of the company's assets, and they are all entitled to a share of the profits that the company makes. Owners can even sell their share of the company to someone else. In fact, buying and selling shares of companies has become so common that there are 'share exchanges' all over the world where people can buy and sell shares in companies."

Kate pondered this. "Does this mean, John, that in any form of business dealing, I could be dealing with a company or a person, and it would make no practical difference? Does this mean, for example, that if I owned every single share of a company, then it would be just the same as owning the assets and employing the people myself?"

"Yes," her grandfather replied. "Once you realise that a company is like a living, breathing, thinking person, then many economic issues become much clearer."

Kate followed the things her grandfather said, but she wasn't quite sure why they were important. Still, by this stage she was willing to take some things on faith, and wait until the whole picture began to fit together.

3.3 Government

John continued with the story.

"Many years had passed in the valley, and the population had grown until there were people living on every part of the land. Whole new families were formed as each generation grew up and established farms and trades of their own.

As the population of the valley increased, new problems arose for the people. In the past, a young couple would move from their parent's home and establish a farm of their own.

However, land was becoming scarce, and disputes over boundaries were becoming more and more common.

Other problems were arising, too. The river, for example, was the life-blood of the valley. Every farm depended on the river to irrigate its crops and provide water for the family. In the early days of the valley this had not been a problem.

The river had always flowed with clear, crystal water.

Now, however, there were so many people living on the river that it was becoming polluted. From time to time, someone would dump rubbish into the river, and incur the angry complaints from his neighbours downstream.

These days, with so many people putting small amounts of rubbish into the river, there was no single person who could be blamed for the decline in the quality of the water. It was a problem that the community as a whole needed to address together.

The families were accustomed to meeting, once or twice a year, to discuss among themselves any problems that arose in the valley. At these meetings, disputes were discussed, and generally the majority would support one point of view and the other party would be forced to give in.

Trade was so prevalent in the valley that no one person could possibly support themselves in isolation from the others. The threat of being cut off from the trading system was enough to force the most ardent complainer to settle his grievance.

It was a simple disciplinary system, but one that was effective and did not require violence. It was at one of these meetings that a new proposal was put forward.

In was clear to everyone that land in the valley was rapidly filling up. To counter this problem, a suggestion was made that the valley should be completely divided among the people living there. Every part of the valley would be allocated to the person who was currently using it.

Any land that was not in use would be retained by the group and allocated to young families who wished to establish farms of their own. Each person would be given a written document, a 'title', showing the land which was theirs.

They would be free to do what they wished with the land, including trading part of it to another person in return for grain or anything else of value. Much discussion took place, and it was eventually agreed by the majority that the idea was a good one.

Several families disagreed, however the threat of being cut off from the trade in the valley was enough to force them to submit to the majority consensus.

The system was set up as the man had described, and each person was given a written description of the land they owned. Buying and selling of titles to land became a common occurrence in the valley, as people required more or less space to suit their needs.

More time passed, and the population continued to increase. The system of land division was working well, however the number of disputes was increasing along with the population.

The families were meeting more and more frequently to discuss issues and solve disputes. It became clear to everyone that something had to be done, that the current system of managing the land was simply too much to be handled by an occasional meeting.

Things were becoming desperate when a completely new suggestion was put forward. This change was to have profound and far-reaching effects on the lives of the people in the valley.

The population had grown to the extent where it was not practical for everyone to meet to solve every single problem. Therefore, the suggestion was made that one person be given the task of managing the land titles and the disputes.

This person was to be paid a salary, which every family in the valley would contribute to. This person would have the power to make a decision on disputes, and the majority would support their decision at the next full meeting of the community.

With little other choice, the community reluctantly accepted the idea.

More time passed, and the population expanded rapidly. One person was no longer sufficient to mange the land titles and solve disputes, and eventually a whole team of people were employed by the community to handle the affairs of the valley.

This, however, caused a problem. There were now many people working on community issues, and it had become almost impossible to collect the entire population together in one place.

At this point, another major step was taken.

The people who were employed by the community were broken into two groups. The first group was given the authority to make decisions. This small group of people was chosen by the community, and given the power to handle the affairs of the valley as they saw fit. Each year, the people would meet again, and choose the best-equipped people to take on the role of running the valley for the next year.

The second group were simply employees of the community, and subject to the direction of the ruling group.

As was suggested, this system was set up and it worked well.

Over the years, the group that was employed to manage the valley's affairs hired more and more people.

In order to pay these people wages, it collected grain and goods from all the people in the valley. As long as the amount was small, the people were willing to make the sacrifice, as they could see the benefits that were provided.

Schools for the children and hospitals for the sick were built. Canals were built to supply water to everyone living in the valley.

Since it was now impossible for the entire population to meet and vote on rules and laws, the ruling group was given the task of creating all laws for the valley. This was done on the understanding that the ruling group would not be re-elected for a following year if the general community was not satisfied with their decisions.

To enforce these rules and laws, the ruling group was allowed to hire a small number of strong men. These men would detain any person who broke the valley's rules, and force them to work on community projects for a period of time as a punishment.

Thus, the community defined standards and physically forced everyone in the valley to adhere to them.

On the whole, the system was fair, and few honest people had any serious complaint with the arrangements.

Problems arose from time-to-time, but in general the system allowed the valley people to live free and happy lives.

In a similar way to the projects in the valley, the new ruling group acted as a single entity. It hired employees, it collected grain from the valley people, and it made decisions on new laws. Indeed, although the individuals changed over time, the group as a whole continued to operate as a single person.

It bought and sold goods, it owned assets, and its decisions were still binding long after the individual people

86

working within it had been replaced by others.

The group borrowed money and lent money, it entered into contracts, it sued people and people sued it. Over time this entity became the single richest group in the valley, and employed a significant proportion of the entire population. Thus was born a fundamental element of a large society; government.

3.4 The banking system

Many years had passed since the people had settled in the valley, and an active, thriving community had developed.

There were numerous farms, trades and businesses operating in the valley. In the early days, trade between the families had been done directly. Perhaps some grain was swapped for a plough, or a sickle for some building timber. As time went by, however, the limitations of this approach became apparent.

A farmer, for example, may have some excess grain in his store. There may be nothing that he needed at the time, and yet the grain would have to be disposed of before it rotted and became useless. To solve this problem, it had become customary to swap items for gold.

Gold was always in demand for jewellery, so the local goldsmith could always be relied on to swap the gold for any other item that the person happened to need. This approach had several advantages, and made life much easier for the valley people. Gold was small, it did not rot or break down, and it could be kept indefinitely.

Rather than swapping a plough for some grain, the farmer could swap the plough for some gold, and then swap the gold for some grain when he actually needed it.

The system was much more flexible, and everyone benefited from the easier method of trading their goods. This system continued to operate for many years, and there was a steady flow of gold around the valley as items were traded, 'bought' and 'sold'.

There was one serious disadvantage with using gold, however. It was easy to steal. In the early days theft had not been a major problem, as sacks of grain were not easily spirited away, and if they were, then it soon became obvious who had stolen the goods.

Now that gold was in common use, however, theft became a serious problem. A farmer could swap everything he owned for gold, and carry his entire wealth in his pocket. Since one piece of gold was much like another, if it was stolen it was impossible to determine who had taken it.

The goldsmith had worked with large amounts of gold for years, and to counter this problem he arranged for the blacksmith to build a large, heavy vault. The vault was strong and secure, and the goldsmith had the only key.

From time to time, people in the valley would come to the goldsmith, and ask for the use of his vault. Since there was plenty of space in the vault, the goldsmith was happy to let other people store their gold there, and he charged them a small fee for the privilege.

This system continued for some time, and the number of thefts in the valley was drastically reduced. This was fortunate, as the rising number of thefts had lead to resentment and bitterness in the valley, and there had been a serious risk of outright battles between families and a breakdown in the operation of the community.

After a while, most of the gold in the valley was stored in the goldsmith's vault, and people only removed it when they needed to trade it for some other item. By this time, several other goldsmiths had begun to operate in the valley. They, too, offered space in their vaults to their customers, for which they charged a fee.

So much gold was stored in the vaults now, that these fees had become a large proportion of the goldsmith's income. What had begun as a small side-line had turned into a serious money-making operation.

It was at this time that the original goldsmith had a brilliant idea. Since the earliest days of the valley, goods had been lent and borrowed in return for a fee. As gold came into common circulation, people did not bother to borrow goods anymore, and simply borrowed gold instead.

This was simpler and more flexible, as they could use the gold in any way they wished. Of course, a fee was still required for borrowing the gold, and this was usually paid to the lender in the form of gold as well.

The borrower, then, had to repay the original gold, plus extra gold as a fee for having the use of the gold for a period of time. The goldsmith's idea was simple.

He would take some of the gold from his vault, and lend it out to people who needed to borrow. This way, he would get two sources of income; the fees from his customers who deposited gold in his vault, and the fees from the people he lent the gold to. There was one serious flaw in this system however.

Should his customers all come in on the same day, and demand their gold, he would not be able to give it back, as it was lent out to other people. At first, the goldsmith was nervous. He lent a very small amount of gold, hoping that his customers would not notice that some gold was missing from the vault.

Time went by, and as one might expect, there was a constant flow of customers depositing their gold and removing their gold. The total amount in the vault, however, remained fairly steady. The goldsmith became braver and braver with each passing day, and eventually he was lending out 90 percent of the gold in the vault.

There was, he realised, some risk with this, but as long as the gold kept coming in at about the same rate that it was going out, the system remained stable. When customers withdrew their gold, there were always some new customers the next day to replace it.

The goldsmith's customers realised that the goldsmith was a frequent lender of gold, but it did not really dawn on them that is was their gold that was being lent, and far from being safe in the goldsmith's vault, their gold was actually jingling around in someone else's pocket.

This system continued for many years without incident. As long as the lending and repayment, depositing and withdrawing continued at a steady pace, the whole system worked well. Needless to say, the goldsmith was making a large profit from these operations, and spent most of his afternoons relaxing under a tree drinking beer.

He had long since given up making jewellery, and left that task to his young apprentices. It was during one of these lazy afternoons that the goldsmith had his second brilliant idea.

The profits that he had made had not gone unnoticed, and many other goldsmiths were beginning to follow the same practices as the first goldsmith. As competition increased, the customers were spread more thinly. The fees the customers were charged were reduced in order to attract as many customers as possible.

On this sunny, warm afternoon, as he relaxed under a tree, the original goldsmith contemplated his idea. Instead of charging his customers to deposit gold in his vault, he decided he would actually pay them to do it. He would, of course, pay them less than he received when he lent out the gold, and the difference would be his profit.

When he announced to his customers that he would pay them, they thought he was crazy. For years, they had required protection for their gold, and they had been happy to pay a small fee for this protection.

Now, one of the goldsmiths was actually offering to pay them instead of charging them! People were amazed, and decided that he would quickly loose all his money if he continued in this way. However, they were not going to miss out on the opportunity, and the goldsmith was greeted with a flood of new customers.

He paid them to deposit their gold in his vault, and then he lent it out to other people for a larger fee. Far from loosing his money, he quickly became the richest man in the valley.

As he lay back in his chair, drinking his favourite beer, the man reflected on the operation he had created. It was, he realised, fundamentally unstable, as he only had enough gold in the vault to pay about one-tenth of his customers back their money. The rest of the gold had been given out for loans.

As long as the people didn't realise the significance of

this, however, business continued as normal.

The ultimate irony, the man thought with a satisfied smile, was that customers often deposited gold in his vault, and then later he would lend them back their own gold, and charge a higher fee.

In effect, they were simply giving him money for free. The man lay back in his chair and smiled. It was a pleasant lifestyle."

John stopped speaking and looked at Kate. She was, he realised, shellshocked. Hardly surprising, as he was certain that she had never thought through the true nature of the banking system. He sat in silence, watched the birds flying through the trees, and waited for Kate to compose her thoughts.

"John," Kate said timidly, "this is an interesting story. But banks don't work like this these days, do they?"

"I'm afraid they still work in exactly the same way, Kate," John replied. "A bank simply channels money from one place to another. When you deposit money with them, they promptly lend it out to someone else at a higher rate of interest.

When you borrow money from a bank, you are not borrowing money 'from the bank', you are really borrowing money from the bank's customers. The bank is simply the half-way house that manages the whole transaction.

Don't get me wrong, Kate, banks performs may useful functions. They combine a mix of depositors with the mix of borrowers, so you can deposit money for any period of time and lend money for any period of time.

They provide a place to store your money when you are not using it. The banking system is the backbone of our financial system, and provides the main opportunity for the public to borrow and lend money."

John paused again, watching Kate's face. She was still a little stunned.

"But what about the depositors, surely everyone could withdraw their money if they wanted to?"

"I'm afraid not, Kate. In fact, if ten to 20 percent of a bank's customers decided to withdraw their money, the bank would have to close its doors and cease operation.

It simply does not have enough money kept aside to pay back more than this many people. All the rest of their deposits have been lent out on loans, often long-term loans that will not be repaid for many years. The finance industry are the ultimate gamblers, Kate.

Insurance, banking, is all about playing the odds. The institutions that we believe are the safest and most secure, are the ones that simply survive on confidence and statistics. In many ways, it is the best example of the 'self-fulfilling prophecy'; as long as the public believes an institution is secure, then it will be, but if the public looses confidence and begins withdrawing their money, then the whole operation is on shaky ground."

Kate looked exceedingly glum.

"I am telling you these things, Kate, so you will understand how the financial system operates. Once you understand it, you can use it to your benefit. You will not be throwing your hard-earned money away because you do not understand how the system works.

To be a successful investor, you must understand the basic concepts that our financial system is built on. Keep everything in perspective, though.

Take banks as an example. Although banks and other financial institutions do sometimes fail during major crisis, these failures are very rare. In fact, over the past hundred years, you will find that a very small number of financial institutions have actually ceased to operate and lost money for their depositors.

However, it does happen, so I will caution you with the golden rule of investment. I have not mentioned this rule to you yet, but now seems an appropriate time. This rule, Kate, is the most important principle of investment. It is the most critical rule in money management, the single most valuable thing I can teach you.

Its importance is beyond measure. It will protect you, and protect your money. Anyone who follows this rule will never loose all their money, regardless of their approach to investment."

Kate looked at her grandfather, curiosity growing on her face.

"Kate," John said, "the golden rule is this: *never put all your money in one place.*" John paused, letting his words echo through Kate's mind. These were the most important words he would speak to her, and he desperately hoped she would see their importance and follow them.

"I realise, Kate, that this seems pathetically obvious. However, very few people that I know follow this principle properly. The only true security is in spreading your money around. Choose different types of investment, the more different from each other the better.

We will cover the important investments later, so have no fear, I will show you what to do.

There are many different risks in the financial world. The best way to protect your money is to put it into several different investments. Always, of course, choose high quality investments in every field. However, make sure you invest in different fields, not just several purchases in the one field.

Even with the safest investment there are tiny risks. Loaning your money to the government, in the form of government bonds, is the safest possible investment. If the government of the country fails to repay its debts, then the whole society will break down and the only true wealth would be food, medicine, and accurate weapons.

Even with this, though, there is the one-in-a-million risk of a mistake.

Your cheque may lost in the mail, a computer error may occur, or deliberate fraud by an employee may happen. It may be a one in a million risk, but this is no consolation if you happen to be the one person in the million who suffers from it.

The only way to truly protect your money, Kate, is to spread it into many high-quality, diverse investments.'

3.5 Business operation

John was tired. He had been talking all afternoon, and although Kate was obviously intrigued by what he said, it was all old hat to him.

He had thought long and hard about these things over the years, and in the end, he was tired of it all.

John would be happy to sit in the park forever, to listen to the birds and watch the flowers. All he wanted was to hear beautiful music, to see the beautiful things in the world, to be relaxed, peaceful and happy. There were so many complications, so many difficulties and problems in the modern world.

It almost made him angry, that the greed and desire of people had created such a complex edifice to live in.

They could do what they wanted, but when it made his life difficult then he wasn't impressed. Then, of course, there was Kate.

It first, he had been glad to help her, and he hoped his efforts would make a real difference to her life. As the weeks went by, though, John realised what a huge task he had taken on.

There were some topics that interested him, but on the whole he had said it all before, and there were more interesting ways to spend his time now.

Still, it was not in his nature to start a job and not finish it, so he resigned himself to some difficult afternoons ahead.

"John," said Kate after a long silence, "where did you learn all this?"

"My dear," John replied with a weak smile, "there are three steps I took to learn these things.

First, I watched.

I watched the things around me. I noticed that some people were successful, while others were not. I watched the newspapers, the television, and everything around me.

Second, I listened. I listened to what everyone had to

say, even the most flippant and off-hand comment.

Often these comments taught me the most. I listened to the famous and the obscure, the rich and the poor.

From every person I learnt something, even if it was only how the rest of the world thinks.

Finally, and most importantly," he said after a pause, "I made mistakes. Many, many mistakes." John turned to his granddaughter, and said with half a smile, "hell, Kate, I've made so many mistakes, if you lined them up like matchsticks, you could pave a road to China."

Kate laughed and hugged her grandfather. There was, she knew, times when you had to laugh, smile and relax. This was a flaw in John's character, and for all his success, he still had trouble just playing around. She sometimes wondered why he was like this. Perhaps even he, himself, did not know.

The afternoon was growing old, the shadows were lengthening and the air was cooling down. John was in two minds whether to stop for the day, or continue with his last topic. At length, he decided to continue, as next week would begin a whole new area of discussion. "Kate," he said, "there is only one more topic I would like to talk on today."

"Very well, grandfather," Kate said with resignation. It had been a long day for her, too, but she wanted to finish their talks at a sensible place.

John breathed deeply for a few moments, then looked up at Kate. For all his age, she thought, he recovered his strength remarkably quickly.

"Think about the valley again, my dear. In the valley, there were many businesses, trades and farms in operation. One day, one of the blacksmiths looked at his bellows, and realised he had a problem. His whole operation was based around a very hot fire, kept alive by a leather bellows.

However, it was a small bellows, and the fire was not large enough to work the bigger pieces of iron. Much of the work his customers wanted done was lost to other blacksmiths, because his equipment could not handle the job.

Large bellows were expensive, and the blacksmith did not have enough money to buy one. After much thought, he went to the goldsmith and borrowed some gold.

With this gold, he purchased a larger bellows, and expanded the range of work that he did. He had to pay a fee to the goldsmith, of course, but he found that he earned even more from the new work.

Although it cost him money to borrow the gold for the bellows, the income he earned from it was even greater, so overall his financial position was improved.

In a few years, he had completely repaid the loan, and the business was now larger and generated a greater income for his family. While this was happening, the blacksmith's friend, a baker, also had a problem. Even though he worked from dawn to dusk, he could not bake enough bread to satisfy his customer's needs.

Every day, he sold all his bread, and still they wanted more. The baker could have continued like this forever, but like the blacksmith, he saw an opportunity to expand his operation.

He hired a young man as an apprentice.

Although he had to pay the apprentice a wage, he found that he earned a greater amount from the extra bread that was baked, and overall he had a higher profit. As time went by, the baker hired several employees to bake bread.

Although each employee required wages, the amount of income they generated for the bakery was higher that their wages and the extra amount was more profit for the baker. After a while, the bakery was far larger than it had originally been, and the baker became a wealthy man."

John stopped speaking and rested. The sun was below the horizon, now, and there was little daylight left. Soon they would have to go home.

"The two stories, the blacksmith and the baker, illustrate two important principles of business. First, it is often necessary in business and investment to borrow money.

I know I have told you that borrowing is a bad idea, but that was for personal items and purchases. When we spoke about personal money management, a loan was simply a substitute for saving up for a purchase.

In your personal purchases, you should save up wherever possible. However, when it comes to business and investment, the situation is different. If you borrow money to purchase an asset, and the asset produces a greater income that the loan interest, then you have made a profit overall.

Many business and investment transactions are not practical without the use of borrowed money.

In the case of the blacksmith, he borrowed money to buy a larger bellows. Because the income from using the bellows was greater than the loan interest, he was making a larger profit in total.

In fact, the more you borrow, and the larger the asset, the greater your profit will be. Of course there are limitations and problems with this approach, which we will discuss later. Overall, however, I wish to illustrate that borrowing money for business and investment is quite normal and healthy, and can increase your profits."

John paused for a few deep breaths.

"Now, the baker. The baker employed staff, who produced an income for the bakery. As long as the income they produced was greater than their wages, the baker made a larger profit from the business. Of course, he still needed equipment for them to use, so there was a limit to how many people he could employ, but within limits, the more people he employed the greater his profit would be.

Kate, if you are simply investing your own money, and not operating a business, you will not need to deal with employees. However, it is still very useful to understand how this system operates.

The use of employees to make a profit is so fundamental to our economic system, that you could not hope to see the complete picture without it,.

3.6 Cash and other currency

It was a bright, sunny day. The wind blew strongly through
the park, so strongly that Kate's long skirt needed constant
attention. John sat on the bench, absorbing the feeling of
nature into himself.

As he sat on the bench, he was no longer old, he had the
strength of a young man and felt the sweet joy of a child.

Kate watched her grandfather.

She was having considerable trouble with the wind, but
it didn't seem to bother him at all. In fact, he had a wild,
excited look in his eyes. Kate had never seen him like this
before, and she didn't know what to make of it.

He didn't look like an old man any longer, he was alive,
fresh and full of energy. John turned to his granddaughter,
his eyes bright and wild with energy. He was a different
person, almost in a trance. "Can you feel it Katie?" he said
excitedly, "Can you feel the wind? Can you feel the power
flowing though you, the energy of life?"

Kate was scared. She had never seen John like this
before. He had always seemed such a calm person, a little
mysterious perhaps but not weird in any way at all. Now,
she saw the fire in his eyes, the joy on his face, and she was
afraid. She could almost feel the strength of his will, the
power he had within him.

He was no ordinary man. He was very special, and at
that moment, he looked like he could conquer the world
with ease.

Kate was glad he was on her side, for she wouldn't want
to have him as an enemy.

Eventually, the wind died down, and John opened his
eyes once again. He looked at Kate, a serene, peaceful look
in his eyes. There was no tiredness, no ghosts and no pain.
"I love you Kate," he said softly. "You are a beautiful
woman, and a very kind friend." He hugged her for a long
time.

Kate and John had rested in the park for some time, and talked about family and the things they had been doing recently. John was stronger and more relaxed than Kate had seen him for a long time.

"Kate," John said confidently, "I have not forgotten our talks about money. We have made a great deal of progress. When I look back on the way you thought when we started," he said with a mischievous grin, "I realise just how far we have come. Now, my dear, it is time to move along to the next topic. Once again, we will visit our old friends in the valley."

Kate was pleased. She had begun to feel guilty that the talks were a drain on her grandfather. He was an old man, and they had talked long and hard about many issues. She had even noticed a slow deterioration in his energy, and this had worried her even more. Now, however, he looked ready to take on the world.

"Many years had passed since the valley had first been settled. An active trade and commerce had developed. There was buying and selling, lending and borrowing, companies and a government.

The government collected taxes, as all governments do, and companies carried on business between themselves and with individuals. The activities of the goldsmiths had developed into a banking system, and now there were organisations that acted solely as banks, without any other business such as goldsmithing.

By this time, gold was used exclusively for buying and selling. It was far simpler than trading items directly, and gave the people of the valley much more flexibility in their financial affairs.

The banks accepted deposits, which they paid interest on, and lent out money for which they charged a higher rate of interest. This system had operated for many years without incident.

There was one disadvantage with using gold, however. Gold is one of the heaviest metals, and a wealthy man could not hope to carry his entire store of wealth with him because of the immense weight of the gold. Initially, this was not a major problem, as most of the gold was stored in vaults anyway.

As more gold was mined, however, the value of each individual piece of gold became less. After a while, the amount of gold required for even a modest transaction became prohibitively heavy. To avoid this problem, people in the valley developed a new method of buying and selling. Instead of going to the bank and withdrawing their gold to pay for a purchase, the buyer would give the seller a piece of paper.

On this piece of paper, the buyer would write an order to the bank, to give the seller a certain amount of their gold. In this way, the buyer avoided the inconvenience of going to the bank to withdraw their gold. There were other benefits, too. There was more security for both parties. The buyer never touched any gold at all, so there was no chance of his gold being stolen on the way from the bank to complete the purchase.

The seller of the goods benefited as well. He did not have to carry the gold to the bank, and take the risk of being robbed on the way. The piece of paper had both people's names on it, and was signed, so it was no use to anyone if it was stolen. As well as the convenience and security of not carrying the gold, there was one more benefit for the receiver of the paper.

If he happened to keep his gold in the same bank, all he had to do was present the piece of paper at the bank, and they would simply transfer ownership of the gold from the first man to the second.

In this way, no gold ever had to leave the vault. The bank, too, liked this arrangement. There was less work for them, as people did not need to withdraw gold as often. It also meant that more gold stayed in the vault, which gave them more opportunities to lend out the gold at a profit.

These pieces of paper were the first cheques, and the

personal cheques we use today operate in exactly the same way."

"Interesting," Kate said with enthusiasm. "I use cheques all the time, of course, but I never really stopped to think about what they are. Are you telling me that a cheque is simply a written order to my bank, to give some of my money to another person?"

"Yes," replied John. "I told you this as a curiosity, more than anything else. It's interesting to understand how these things work."

"Go on," Kate said with encouragement. "I am learning a great deal from these stories."

"Very well," said John with a pleased smile.

"This system worked well, however there were certain limitations. When many small transactions took place, a great deal of paperwork was generated. This created a large workload for the bank, which it disliked, as it meant they had to employ more staff and this reduced their profit.

The goldsmith who had first started the banking business was an old man by now, but his mind was still as sharp as a tack. One afternoon, he sat under his favourite tree, sipping beer, and thought about this problem.

He employed quite a large number of people to handle the transactions that customers required to complete their business. People were constantly withdrawing and depositing gold, and writing and depositing cheques.

The cheques had helped the situation greatly, as the customer did not have to withdraw gold to pay for an item. However, the person who received the cheque had to either withdraw the gold, or transfer ownership of the gold in the vault to themselves.

The goldsmith had become rich by making the customers happy, and although the customers were often worse off, as long as they believed they were being looked after then the profits kept rolling in.

This afternoon, the goldsmith had another brilliant idea. He thought of a system which would drastically reduce his costs, and also appear to benefit the customers as well. The secret, he reasoned, was to transfer all the work in financial transactions from the bank to the customers.

If the customers were handling their own financial transactions, then he would not have to employ staff to do it for them, and his profits would be even higher. He could even convince the customers that it was a benefit for them, too, as they would have more flexibility in their financial affairs.

So, the next day, the goldsmith put his idea into practice. He went to the local printers and paid them to print a large number of small pieces of paper. On each piece of paper, there was an attractive picture of the valley, and a drawing of the bank building itself.

In small writing at the bottom of the paper, the following words were printed: 'The valley bank will pay one once of gold to the holder of this note'.

Also printed on the note was the goldsmith's signature. The next day, the bank wrote letters to all its customers. The bank, the letter said, had developed a wonderful new system for the benefit of its customers.

This system would make the customer's lives much easier, and as a special favour to the existing customers, there would be no charge for the use of this service. This special discount, of course, only lasted a short period of time.

The system worked like this. In the past, every customer had a piece of paper, on which the bank wrote the number of ounces of gold that the customer had deposited in the vault. When the customer wished to withdraw or deposit some gold, they would bring the piece of paper with them. The bank would adjust the figures on the paper, sign it, and accept or pay out the gold.

The new system, however, would work differently. The bank would accept gold for deposit, and in exchange the customer would be given a piece of paper for each once of gold they deposited. If a customer deposited 50 ounces of gold, they would be given 50 pieces of paper.

They could, of course, come back at any time and exchange the paper for the gold. As the words on the banknote said, the bank promised to exchange each piece of paper for one once of gold.

At first, this seemed like an unnecessary complication to the customers. However, the bank's letter proceeded to explain the benefits that the new system would provide. Rather than paying a debt in gold, a buyer could simply hand over some of the banknotes.

The seller would be happy to accept them, as the paper held a promise from the bank that the holder would be paid the equivalent amount of gold. Buying and selling could now be carried out using paper banknotes instead of actual gold. People could now carry their wealth with them, in the same way as carrying gold, but with much less weight.

Cheques had become popular, but there was the nuisance of not knowing when the recipient of a cheque would actually take the gold that the cheque promised him.

By using banknotes, the debt would be settled immediately and without fuss.

There was another major benefit with using banknotes compared with cheques. A cheque was simply a written order to the bank, a promise that the gold would be paid.

The recipient of a cheque had no way of knowing whether the writer of the cheque actually had the gold to meet the promise they had just made. A banknote, however, was almost as good as physical gold. It was a promise from the bank, not the individual, to pay the holder an once of gold.

By skilful manipulation of public opinion, the goldsmiths had managed to convince people that the banks where the most stable and secure organisations around.

There was another benefit for the bank as well. Gold was deposited with the bank in return for banknotes. The banknotes could be converted back to gold at any time, but the amount of gold was always fixed. Each banknote was worth one ounce of gold. In effect, the customers would be depositing money with the bank, but not earning interest on it.

The goldsmith would lend out this money at a high rate of interest, and increase his profits even more. The system was put into practice, and everything went as the goldsmith had expected.

Soon there were a large number of his banknotes in circulation. The banknotes made buying and selling much easier, and the goldsmith was widely praised for his contribution to the community.

That year, the goldsmith was awarded the civic prize for services to the public. He made a famous speech about sacrifice and service to the community, and humbly accepted the cash prize and trophy that he was awarded.

All this time, the original aim of the exercise was also being fulfilled. The general public was now buying and selling between themselves at a frantic rate, without any intervention whatsoever from the bank.

From time to time, an old person would trade their banknotes for real gold, but as time went by this disappeared completely. All business was done with cash banknotes, and the administrative load on the bank was drastically reduced.

The goldsmith, however, was a wise man, and did not sack a single member of his staff. Bad publicity and low staff morale was a problem that he never created for himself. The banknote idea took off so well, that many new customers joined his bank. This new business was enough to make use of the existing staff, and with lower costs per customer he was able to increase his interest rates on deposits and attract even more customers.

Time moved by, and it was not long before other banks in the valley began to issue their own banknotes as well. This caused some confusion, but it was a minor problem as there were only a few banks in the valley and they were all well known.

It was at this time that the government of the valley began to turn its eye to the arrangement. They saw the potential to improve their own financial position, and so the government issued notes of their own. These notes contained a promise from the government to pay the holder of the note one ounce of gold.

All one had to do to obtain a government currency note, was to hand over one ounce of gold to the government.

In return, the government would give the person a single note. This note could be used to pay debts, and at any time returned to the government and exchanged for gold.

The bankers, understandably, were furious. They were making large profits from the arrangement and did not want to share them with the government.

Many people, however, withdrew some of their gold from the banks, and deposited it with the government in exchange for currency notes. The government, they reasoned, would be even safer than a bank. The government bravely ignored the banker's protests.

They made grand speeches about free and open trade in the valley, and about how a single currency note would make the system even easier.

The government, of course, began paying all its employees using this new currency. Since this comprised a large percentage of the valley's population, the new currency notes quickly dominated the valley's finances and the banks gradually gave up issuing banknotes of their own.

There was, however, another reason why the government took this course of action. It was a less noble reason than the one that it presented to the public. The government now had large amounts of money sitting in its vaults. Although it may have to pay it all back to the noteholders, there would be no interest due.

A currency note worth one ounce of gold would still be worth one ounce of gold in ten year's time. Because of this, the government had a large amount of gold which it didn't have to pay interest on. Effectively, everyone who had exchanged gold for currency notes had given an interest-free loan to the government.

Although they did not have to pay interest on this gold, there was nothing to stop the government earning money from it by lending it out or depositing it in banks.

The governemt proceeded to lend the gold out in return for interest, and to deposit the remaining gold in bank vaults, which also earned interest. Through this process, the government soon had another source of income in addition to collecting taxes.

To this day, if a person has a currency note in their hand, then this represents an interest-free loan from them to the government.

Over time, real gold was used less and less in financial transactions. The government passed laws to make their currency 'legal tender', which meant that a person was legally obliged to accept a currency note in payment of a debt.

A long time passed, and eventually gold was no longer used at all. The government stopped printing the promise to exchange the note for gold, and simply printed: 'legal tender of the valley' in small print on the bottom of the note. Thus developed the modern system of currency."

Kate was impressed. It was an interesting story, and one that put the whole business of cheques and dollars into historical perspective. "Is it necessary that I understand all this, John?" Kate said with a smile.

John looked a little embarrassed. "Not really, Katie, but I got a little carried away. Still, I hope it was an interesting story. Everything that I tell you about the history of our financial systems helps you understand the mysteries of its operation."

"Bastard!" Kate said with a smile, slapping her grandfather on the arm. "You know I'm desperate, and you're telling me bedtime stories!"

John went even redder.

"Don't worry," Kate said quickly, "It was very

interesting. The more you tell me, the more I see the complete picture, how the whole system fits together. You know John, you were right. When you reduce it down to the basic elements, the system is really very simple."

This made John feel better, and has face returned to its natural colour.

"There are a few points about cash that you can glean from these stories. First, cash is simply a convenient way of carrying your wealth around. Wealth is everything of value you own. Your wealth can be in the form of cash or other assets. Cash, however, is the most convenient way of buying and selling. I should emphasise, Kate, that you are still trading, just like the people in the valley. You are simply trading part of your wealth, in the form of cash, for something else. Hopefully," he said with a dry smile, "something of similar value. Now, a small rest. We will sit and soak up the stillness.

One cannot work too hard, Kate, without becoming very ill." As John had said, they sat, quietly, and rested. They rested a long time.

3.7 Markets

"The next step," said John after a long break, "is a discussion on markets.

Markets for selling produce developed quite early in the valley, but I have left a discussion until now to avoid complicating the other issues.

In the earliest days of the valley, trading was done between individuals on a ad-hoc basis. The population was small, and the trading of food and goods was done whenever two people happened to have something that was useful to the other.

Price was negotiated between the two parties until both people were satisfied.

As the population increased, however, a new system was developed for buying and selling food. Once a week, all the valley people would gather together to buy and sell food.

By now there were many farmers, so each buyer had a choice of several people from which to buy their goods. The natural laws of supply and demand operated, so that if pumpkins were in demand, for example, then the farmers would charge a high price for their pumpkins.

Since the demand was high, all the farmers would sell their pumpkins, even though they were charging a high price. Other foods, however, might be out of fashion. Beans, for example, may be tough and stringy at a particular time of year and there may be little demand for them.

The farmers would be willing to sell their beans at a low price, as this was their only hope of selling them at all. When demand is high, the sellers tended to set the price. When demand for an item was low, however, the buyers tended to set the price. Whichever the case, the buyers and sellers bargained until both were prepared to complete the sale.

This, Kate, is the basic operation of a market. Some markets take place at a particular time and place, whereas other markets are distributed across the land.

Any time there is a large number of similar things for sale, the nature of markets comes into play. As well as markets for food and goods, there is the market for buying and selling properties, and even the market for labour. Wages are determined by the supply and demand for labour. If many people wish to hire employees, and there is a shortage of labour, then they will offer higher wages to attract staff.

Back in the valley, the operation of the food markets continued unabated for many years. The price of the goods was determined by the supply and demand for the goods.

However, two other factors also affected the volume and prices of goods that were sold.

If demand for an item was high, the price would be high,

and so more people would try and produce the item. One year, for example, strawberries were particularly popular. The farmers that produced strawberries made handsome profits when they sold their strawberries at the local market.

The following year, strawberries were just as popular. Most of the people had eaten strawberries by now, and although they were expensive, they were delicious and worth the price.

All the farmers noticed this, and the following year several more farmers planted strawberries on their land. Again the strawberries sold well, but the price was slightly lower, as there was a greater supply of strawberries and the farmers had to lower their prices and compete with each other in order to attract customers. The following year, even more farmers planted strawberries. A large number of strawberries were sold, but there were so many produced that year that no farmer sold his entire production.

It was quite expensive to grow the strawberries, as they needed careful attention. The farmers were not able to charge enough to cover the cost of growing the strawberries, and few made a profit that year. The next year, many farmers abandoned the planting of strawberries.

This story, Kate, illustrates how the supply of goods changes over time to reflect the natural demand.

If the desirability of an item is greater than the available supply, prices will be high and more people will start to produce the product.

As production increases, the prices will drop. Eventually, the price will reach a point where the profit on selling them is small, and no more people will produce the product. In short, Kate, there are four things that determine the price of goods in a market.

In the short term, the price is determined by the demand for the goods and the supply of the goods.

In the longer term, the price will adjust itself to reflect the natural desirability of the product, and the difficulty and cost in producing it."

John paused for a breath. He felt he had illustrated the basic operation of markets, how prices were determined by supply and demand.

It was important that Kate understood this, as virtually all investments operated on market principles. She seemed to be following the things he said, so he decided to continue.

"The food market had been operating successfully for several years, when a small group of people decided to set up another market. This was to be a market for buying and selling furniture, and was held once a week.

At first, few people attended, but with encouragement and time it grew to be as large and active as the food market.

One day, an old man arrived at the market with a desk. It was beautifully made, an expensive desk which he had owned for many years.

The desk was made of the finest timber, inlaid with gold leaf and polished to a warm glow. The man was sad to sell the desk, but a large debt was due the following week and it was the only thing of value he possessed.

At least, he reasoned, he would get a high price for the desk and be able to pay off the debt and have money left over for himself. The man set up the desk in a corner of the market, and waited. Lunchtime came, and still he was waiting. Mid-afternoon arrived, and the man reduced the price a little. Many people stopped to admire the desk. They all agreed that it was a beautiful desk, and that the price was fair, but unfortunately none of them needed a desk at the time. Evening came, and the desk had not been sold.

The man returned home with his desk, dejected. The following week, he attended the market again.

His debt was now overdue, but he had no other possessions to repay the debt and the bankers had no choice but to wait for payment.

Again the desk was not sold.

Finally, several weeks later, a new buyer attended the market. He was a wealthy man, and happened to be in need of a new desk. The sale was made at the agreed price, and the man was able to pay off his debt."

John stopped for a breath, and checked that Kate was still listening. She was concentrating deeply on his words.

"This story illustrates an important characteristic of markets," he continued. "Some items are sold in massive quantities. The perfect example of this is fresh food. Other items, however, are bought and sold at less frequent intervals. Rare furniture is an example here.

This quality of markets is called 'liquidity'. A market that is liquid has a high turnover of goods. There will be many similar items that are frequently bought and sold.

The price will be clear to all, as there will be many sellers competing with each other and their prices will be similar. In a market with low liquidity, however, two additional affects come into play.

First, it may take some time to sell an item. If sales happen only occasionally, it may take a while for a buyer to come along. This was the case with the man with the desk. Although it was a good desk, a desk is an item that one buys rarely, and he had to wait until some-one came along who happened to need a desk at the time

In some markets, such as expensive and unique property, it can take six months or even a year to find a buyer. Always remember this Kate. Just because an item has a certain natural value, never assume that you can actually sell it for this price at a moment's notice.

The second factor that comes into play in markets with low liquidity is the price of items. In a liquid market, such as a grocery market where there are twenty-three farmers selling cabbages, the price of a cabbage will be clear to all.

The farmer's prices will vary slightly depending on the quality of their cabbages, but the difference will be small. In markets with low liquidity, however, the price of items is not so clear. The particular item may be unique, so there are no similar items to compare it with.

There may not be any similar items offered for sale at

114

that time. In this case, the price may be affected by how desperate the seller is and how much the buyer wants to buy. In an illiquid market, with few buyers and few sellers, the price will often be determined by what the buyer is willing to pay and what the seller is willing to accept.

In an illiquid market, Kate, prices are hard to predict and will partly depend on the individual buyer and seller. The liquidity of a market depends on several things.

Firstly, a liquid market requires a large number of buyers and a large number of sellers, and frequent transactions. This tends to happen for low priced items that have a high volume of sales, such as food.

In liquid markets, prices tend to find a natural level based on supply and demand. Markets with low liquidity tend to have a small number of buyers and a small number of sellers, and infrequent sales.

They operate for large, expensive or unusual items. Expensive and unique properties are an example of this type of market. Remember, too, that you cannot sell something unless someone wants to buy it.

You may believe an item is worth a particular amount of money, but at the end of the day, if no-one wants to buy it then it is worth zero.

It is critical to realise the difference between an item's worth and natural value, and the price that would be paid for it.

This will become an important issue later when we discuss investment strategies. An item may have a natural value, such as its beauty or its ability to earn an income, but in the cold light of day, the value of an item is what people are prepared to pay for it."

Kate was still listening intently. John decided not to break her concentration, and continued with his final point on the nature of markets.

"There is one last point I wish to make on markets," he said. "This is a subtle point, and one that few people take into proper account. Still, it is very important to understand this. Let me tell you another story and you will see what I mean.

The population of the valley was now so great, that people lived in every corner of the land. Some parts of the valley were more attractive than others, of course, and some places were more popular with the people than others.

Trading in land titles and buildings had gone on for many years, and it was common for a young family to sell their house and move to a bigger property as their need for space increased.

There was always a high demand for properties in desirable parts of the valley, and these homes always fetched a good price. One might expect that people would stay away from the expensive areas, areas they could barely afford, but in fact the reverse happened.

People being people, one of their goals in purchasing a home was to impress their friends and the people around them. If they purchased an expensive house, they reasoned, then people would assume that they were wealthy and wise. In fact, the purchase of an expensive home may have ruined their financial situation completely, but no-one was too fussed about that.

As long as appearances were kept up, the rest was left to fate. When families moved house, they generally bought a new property in the most expensive and desirable place they could afford. However, this created a problem.

Since there was so much demand for homes in the desirable areas, the prices rose higher and higher. Buyers would compete with each other, and offer higher and higher prices, in order to win the sale.

The sellers simply sat back and watched with satisfaction as the buyers tried to outdo each other. Whoever had the highest bid was sold the house.

Time went by, and the prices in these areas reached ridiculous heights. Few people could afford a home in these areas, but they were not prepared to admit this to their friends. And so, another interesting social change took place

. In order to live outside the expensive suburbs and still maintain the facade of being wealthy and fashionable, certain poor areas became trendy and fashionable. People turned their back on the expensive suburbs and the latest fashion was to live in a poor area and renovate a house.

Not just any poor area, of course, but only special ones that had come into favour. The whole reason for this trend was to preserve the pride of the people who were desperate to live in the rich areas but could not afford to.

Some time passed, and an interesting change occurred. Since many people were moving to these particular poor areas, and houses were being updated, the prices started to rise. The areas that were previously in demand had become less fashionable and the prices there began to fall.

The people who had moved to the new areas felt proud and vindicated about their choice, as everyone wanted to live in an area where prices were rising. Since prices where now falling in the old expensive areas, these areas became even less fashionable, as there was nothing more embarrassing to these people than to own a property in an area were the values were going down.

More time passed, and the areas that were poor were now fully renovated and in great demand. The prices had risen dramatically. All the people who lived there believed their wisdom and foresight had led them to an area where values would rise strongly.

However, the next generation was growing up, and they could not afford to live in these areas. Houses in the suburbs that used to be fashionable were now run-down and in need of repair. Prices had fallen drastically. The young people abandoned the new trendy suburbs, and began moving into the older areas.

These areas became the new, trendy places to live, and the cycle turned full circle. Nothing stays in fashion forever, and the longer an area has been in fashion, the more overdue it is to become unfashionable.

Over a long period of time, the cycle repeated itself

many times, and areas moved in and out of fashion. As they moved in and out of fashion, the prices rose and fell."

John stopped talking and leaned back in the chair, resting. It was still a beautiful day, the air was cool and the sun was warm. It was a pleasure talking in this weather. Had it been cloudy and grey, John was not sure he would have the energy or the desire to finish his speech. In this weather, though, he could talk forever and not grow tired.

"That's a very interesting story, John."

"Indeed it is," John agreed with his granddaughter. "If you are going to predict which areas of property will increase in value, then you must be able to identify social trends.

This will become very useful when we look at property investment.

There is an important factor in the nature of markets that we have not yet covered. I have set the scene, and soon you will see what I mean.

One day, one of the men who lived in the valley had some spare money to invest. He watched the prices of property carefully, and after a long time he decided to buy a house as an investment.

He bought a house in one of the new trendy areas, where prices were beginning to rise sharply. Time moved by, and the value of his house increased every month. In a short time, the value had doubled. The man was ecstatic.

He bragged to everyone he knew that he had doubled his money. He explained that he had made a profit equal to the entire amount he had paid for the house. He friends were impressed, and not a little envious.

They wished that they, too, had made so much money.

Then, one day, the man noticed that something was wrong. Harvest time had recently passed, and the harvest had been a poor one. The weather had been very bad that year, and the farmers had only managed to grow a fraction of their usual crops. The farmers were very short of money.

As it happened, the past few years had been good ones,

and many farmers had used their excess money to buy houses as investments.

In fact, many of the houses were in the same suburb as the house that the man had bought. As soon as the harvest was completed, it became clear to the farmers just how bad the situation was. They had put money away for a rainy day such as this, and they had invested it in houses. Now, with no income from the crops, they began to sell their houses.

A trickle at first, a few houses one week and a few the next. As more houses were sold, however, the prices began to fall.

There were more sellers than buyers, and the laws of supply and demand began to take effect. Sellers had to compete for buyers, and to do this they lowered their prices.

All the property owners in the suburb had been watching the prices closely. Their houses had all greatly increased in value, but now the prices were starting to fall. The property owners panicked, as unskilled investors often do.

Almost in unison, they decided to sell their houses and pocket the profits. In the space of a few weeks, a flood of houses was offered for sale. Buyers, too, had noticed the fall in prices, and were beginning to re-assess their choice of suburb.

The buyers had been desperate to buy a house in the area, since prices were increasing rapidly, but now they began to have second thoughts.

If prices were falling, then they did not want to own a property that would decrease in value. All this added up to a large number of sellers, all desperate to sell, and very few buyers, all reluctant to buy.

Prices crashed.

Within the space of a few weeks, the prices had dropped by half. The house the man had bought was now worth the same amount that he had paid for it.

Things became even worse, however.

Although the house may be worth that amount, there were so many sellers and so few buyers that there was no-one to buy the man's house. Several months passed, and eventually someone came along and offered to buy the man's house.

He reluctantly accepted the deal. The buyer had offered a price that was even lower than the amount he had paid for the house, but the man realised it was his only chance of selling it at all.

In total, the man lost a large sum of money on the purchase and sale of the house."

John stopped to rest again. Kate was staring into space. A fleeting worry passed through John's mind, that perhaps her thoughts were elsewhere and she had missed everything he had just said.

"Go on, grandfather," Kate said quietly. "I have learnt more today than I learnt in my entire time at school."

John decided to continue. Kate was obviously in the mood to listen and learn more, and he sensed it was not the time for jokes or playing around.

"There is one critical message from this story, apart from the fact that the man broke every single rule in the book of wise investment.

When the man was bragging about his profits, he made one fatal mistake.

Although his house was worth more, he had not made a cent of real profit. It was not until he sold the house that his profit became real.

The fact that the value of the house had gone up was in many ways irrelevant, as it could drop just as quickly.

All that mattered was the price that he actually obtained for the house when he sold it. Now, don't get me wrong, it is clearly more pleasant to have a property that has gone up in value that one that has reduced. Just like the saying that 'a bird in the hand is worth two in the bush', however, it's not until the item is sold and the profit is in your pocket that it becomes real.

What the man had, Kate, is called an 'unrealised gain'. Certainly, the value of his house had increased, but until he

120

sold it he had not actually received any profit from the property.

Selling the item is called 'realising' the gain or 'crystallising' the gain. After the stockmarket crash of 1987, a famous wealthy investor held a news conference. Speculation was rife about how much money the man had lost in the crash, and most estimates were in the billions of dollars.

One brave journalist plucked up her courage, and asked the man on national television how much money he had actually lost. 'I have,' he replied with a smile, 'not lost a single cent'. There was silence in the room. For a moment, the journalists thought he was joking, or perhaps had gone mad after the whole experience.

A few moments later, however, it dawned on them that the man was absolutely right. He had not lost a cent. Although his shares were worth half what they had been the day before, he had not sold a single share, and so he had not lost any money.

If by some miracle the value of the shares returned to their previous value the next day, then he could sell them all and not loose anything. Never, Kate, confuse an 'unrealised' gain or loss with a real gain or loss. If the value of a marketable asset increases in value, then it is not until you actually sell the item that the gain becomes real."

John had been speaking for quite some time, and yet he was still full of energy. This was his forte, telling stories to illustrate simple points. Although their discussions on budgeting were necessary, John had found them a little boring.

Many of his ideas were new to Kate, and so he had kept her interest, but with the benefit of hindsight they were all simple.

Now that they were talking about wider issues, though, John was beginning to enjoy himself. He was not used to sharing these thoughts with people, as he had long since learnt the wisdom of remaining silent. As the bible said, 'cast not thou pearls before swine, lest they trample them in the mud, then turn and rend you'. How true, John thought.

Often it was the wisest and most heart-felt comment that attracted the most scorn and criticism. Kate, however, had an open mind, and was anxious to learn.

Some of his comments had surprised her, but she had never lost faith in him and had always listened until the story was over. Invariably, he had demonstrated some new and important insight.

"John," Kate said with a weak smile, "you've worn me out. I think I need a rest."

"Heaven forbid, my dear," her grandfather replied with a devilish grin, "you must restore your energy. We still have a long journey ahead of us today." For a change, it was Kate who had called for a break. The rest would do them both good, though, so they sat together on the park bench, silently, and soaked up the afternoon sun.

3.8 Markets and cycles

Kate had rested a long time, and John had also taken advantage of the time to relax and enjoy the cool breeze. At length, Kate spoke. "Very well, John," she said grinning. "Let me have it. What is the next item on the agenda?"

"Well my dear," he said enthusiastically, "we have discussed markets in detail. A few more points, however, will not go astray.

Market forces, and the consequences they produce, are everywhere.

There are obvious markets, like the grocery market and the second-hand furniture market. These operate in one place and at one time.

There are also less obvious markets, such as the market for houses. This is a market, the same as any other, but it does not operate in a single place or at a single time.

However, the property market is subject to the same principles as a vegetable market. I will give you two examples of markets you have probably never thought about, yet they affect your finances every day.

First, the labour market. We have already discussed how your job is simply selling your time and labour to someone, in return for money.

Millions of people sell their time through jobs, and millions of people buy time and labour by hiring employees.

This system has all the ingredients of a market. Say, for example, that there is a low demand for employees. Unemployment will be high, as there are few jobs to go around. Employers will be able to offer lower wages, since there may be several people competing for each job.

Take the opposite situation, where there is a strong demand for new employees but there are few people looking for work. Employers will be forced to offer higher wages to attract employees, as each person will have the choice of several jobs.

In this way, the average level of wages is determined by the supply and demand for labour. If there is a big demand for labour but the supply is low, in other words the number of unemployed people is small, then the wages offered will be high. The opposite, of course, applies when the number of unemployed people is higher than the number of positions.

My second example relates to interest rates. Interest is simply a fee that is charged for borrowing money for a period of time. Like borrowing anything else of value, if you want to borrow money, then you must pay for the privilege.

Now, at any one time, there will be a certain number of people who want to borrow money and a certain number who want to lend money. If there are a large number of borrowers, but a small number of lenders, then the lenders can charge high interest rates. They will get away with this because there are several people wishing to borrow their money, and whoever is most desperate will pay the high rate of interest in return for the money.

In the opposite situation, where there are more lenders than borrowers, the lenders will have to offer lower rates in order to attract customers. Interest rates, then, are simply the cost of borrowing money. Like everything else, interest rates are subject to supply and demand."

Kate was still listening carefully.

"Now Kate, we need to talk about a whole new area. It is related to markets, but this topic is special all on its own. This topic is fundamental to our economic and financial system, and yet it is one that receives little real consideration.

Everyone knows it is there, and yet few people think through the real implications for their investment strategy. I am speaking, Kate, about cycles.

Nature loves cycles.

Take the seasons, autumn follows summer, then comes winter, then spring, then summer again. The endless cycle of the seasons. At my age, the cycle of life becomes painfully clear. Babies are born, grow up, have children then grow old. Eventually they die, their children have babies, and the whole cycle repeats itself.

Everywhere one looks in nature, one sees cycles. Money and finance is subject to the same natural laws as the seasons. Interest rates, unemployment, production, the price of property and the price of shares. These things all go up and down in regular cycles.

All markets are subject to various cycles. Take the stories we looked at with the strawberries, the man who lost money investing in a house, and how interest rates are determined by the demand for borrowing money.

There are only two factors required for a system to have regular cycles. First, there must be competing forces, such as supply and demand. Second, there must be delayed reactions, or inertia in the system.

Let's look back at one of our earlier stories, the story of

the strawberries. The price of strawberries was high, as there was a strong demand and few farmers were growing them. Since prices were high, many more farmers began to plant strawberries in the hope of making good profits.

It took time, however, for the strawberry plants to mature.

Once all the new strawberries became available, the price gradually dropped, as the supply was now greater than the demand.

There were so many strawberries, that people became tired of them and the demand reduced even more. Many farmers stopped growing strawberries, and gradually the prices rose again. Once the prices reached a high peak, the whole cycle started again.

Now, Kate, you may ask why the system did not reach a balance, with an average number of strawberries and an average number of farmers producing them.

There are two reasons for this.

First, there is a delay between the demand changing and the supply changing. It takes some time for the farmers to grow new strawberry plants, or for the old ones to wither and become useless.

The supply of strawberries was always trying to catch up with the demand, which was constantly changing anyway.

The second reason, is that nothing ever repeats itself exactly. Although the strawberry supply, interest rates, and other economic factors go up and down in endless cycles, no cycle is exactly the same as the last. The farmers, for example, were always at the mercy of the weather and the fickle public tastes.

They tried to predict how many strawberries they should grow, but they were never exactly right. These random factors ensured that the demand would never exactly equal the supply, and that cycles in markets would be guaranteed until the end of time.

Kate was nodding sagely. John's words made perfect sense, and it would be hard for anyone to argue against them. There was one factor that worried her though.

"You talk about economic variables, like unemployment, moving in cycles, but doesn't the government control those things these days? I mean, they have economists working all day to predict all these things."

"So they do," John replied drily, "and they are consistently wrong. Ever since the dawn of time, governments and economists have promised steady growth and moderate unemployment, without peaks and troughs.

Time and time again they have failed.

In fact, surveys have been done of economists' opinions, and the years when they were closest to agreeing with each other in their predictions, were usually the years when they were the most wrong!

Governments have never succeeded in achieving steady growth without booms and recessions, and I can see no reason why they ever will.

Until they are willing to accept that cycles are inevitable, that recessions and booms cannot be completely avoided, then they will never understand the economy that they are responsible for managing. Nature will not be denied, and the most strenuous efforts to prevent her cycles are the efforts that make things even worse

. The best a government can aim for is to smooth out the cycles, so the booms are not too massive and the recessions not too deep. The economy is like a living organism, not a predictible machine. The more they interfere and try to drive the economy like a tractor, the more it rebels and the more extreme the booms and recessions are."

John sighed deeply. Kate looked across at her grandfather. He was staring into space, a distant, thoughtful look in his eyes. Kate was not even sure he was aware of her presence. He seemed to be thinking aloud, his thoughts wandering from one topic to the next. She was fascinated by his words, and didn't dare to speak lest she break the spell.

"The reason economists have never understood the economy, is because they think of it as a machine. Some even built little mechanical models, supposed to simulate the flow of money, unemployment and the growth in business. These models were deceptively simple, and seemed logical at the time.

Without exception, though, every economic model and theory had failed to predict the behaviour of the economy. From time to time, a new school of thought will be developed, and this will be heralded as the answer to an economist's every question.

Without doubt, some theories have contained a good deal of sense, and have widened our understanding of the system in which we live.

And yet, each model has failed.

Even today, economists cannot predict how the economy will change, what will go up and what will go down. Their every attempt to create steady, consistent growth has eventually fallen apart. The reason is simple. The economy is not a machine at all, it is like a living organism.

It is composed of many inter-connected systems; the transport system, the education system, the financial system and the social system.

Each is affected by the others, and only a fool would believe that he can change any system without effecting all the others as well. A living organism has many special features, and behaves quite differently to a simple machine.

Living organisms have a general state of well-being; they make be sick or they may be healthy. There may be no single part that is sick, but the organism as a whole may not be functioning at its peak.

In these cases, the organism is not being cared for properly, and not being given an environment in which it can flourish. Living organisms cannot be changed suddenly. They can grow and develop, given the right conditions and encouragement, but any attempt to rapidly change them is met with disaster. Since every system within the organism depends on every other, any drastic change to one system has dramatic effects on the whole organism.

The organism can become unstable, and react in totally unpredictable ways. Some parts begin operating faster, and others slower.

The more drastic the change that was made, the more violently the organism reacts. Any attempt to rapidly change an organic system is met with extreme reactions from unrelated parts of the organism.

The economy of a country, the human body and complex computer programs all have one thing in common. They all display the behaviour of a living, breathing organism.

In their arrogance, politicians and economists believe that they have complete control, believe they can achieve any economic conditions they wish. The greater their arrogance in managing the economy, the greater the penalty that nature rewards them with.

Until they can accept that they are not in control, that the economy is a living, growing organism and not a machine, until they can accept that cycles are healthy and inevitable, they will never understand the system they are responsible for. Until then, they can never fulfil their responsibility of providing a healthy environment where the economy can grow and flourish."

John stopped speaking, and remained silent for some time. Kate said nothing, not wishing to disturb him. Finally, he seemed to come out of a trance, and turned to her with an embarrassed smile on his face.

"I'm sorry, my dear," he said, "I've been rambling on.

I have been talking like a silly old man, instead of keeping to the practical things you asked me for. At least I kept to economics, but I'm sure you don't want to hear all these boring things."

"On the contrary, grandfather," Kate replied in a strong voice, "I very much want to hear it. It may not be directly relevant to my own finances, but it is fascinating all the same.

Everything you tell me about money is opening my mind.

I am beginning to understand what you meant, when you said I needed to understand the 'system'. I am beginning to see my money and life in a completely different way.

Grandfather, I will never be able to think the same way after this.

I understand the world so much more, and I don't feel powerless any longer. Yes, I don't have any money, but at least I don't feel like a naive schoolgirl."

John and Kate rose from the bench and walked slowly through the park, past still ponds and through clusters of green trees.

It was late afternoon now, and most of the people had left for their homes. Only the sounds of the animals met their ears; the sweet song of the sparrows, the splashing of the ducks on the lake and the excited barks of dogs in the distance.

There were still the faint sounds of the city, the hustle and bustle of people as they went about their business, and the quiet hum of distant traffic. Here, though, it seemed a million miles away. It was comforting to know that there were people around, and yet still hear the sweet sounds of the animals.

The air was noticeably cooler, and the sun had become a rosy glow on the horizon. Eventually, the path lead them back to where they had started, as paths often do.

"So, John, one last topic before dinner?" Kate said with a playful smile. "Something useful this time, I hope," she said with a passable imitation of seriousness.

"Bitch!" her grandfather exclaimed. He had never said this to her before, but now that her jibes were becoming more regular, be felt safe in taking a risk and teasing her.

Kate simply laughed.

3.9 Inflation

"Well," said John becoming serious, "there is one more thing we should discuss today. We will return to the valley and see how things have developed.

The valley people had established a thriving community. Their economic system had all the elements of your modern system, and sport and art were also developing within the valley.

The economic exploits of the people were so successful that they easily produced the things they needed, and they did not need to toil in the fields all day long.

They had time to develop the finer things in life.

Currency notes were used for all buying and selling, and the whole system worked extremely well. Over time, however, the people noticed that a strange thing was happening. Gold was still gold, and property still property, but the value of currency notes seemed to be declining. Things that once cost a certain number of dollars, now seemed to cost a little more.

Each year, the value of a single dollar became a little less than the previous year. It was a slow change, however, and the valley people were not unduly concerned. Still, they did not understand why this occurred.

Perhaps, they thought, it was due to the growth in population. Perhaps there were more dollars in circulation, so each one would be worth a little less.

Whatever the reason, people with their wealth in the form of property, gold, or shares of companies seemed to keep it, while the people who had dollars in the bank seemed to loose their wealth.

Of course, many of these people earned interest on their dollars, and this often compensated for the reduction in the dollar's value. Depending on their interest rate, some people had a greater wealth at the end of the year, but others had less wealth, even though they had earned extra dollars in interest.

This was because the value of a dollar was reducing at a faster rate than the dollars they were earning in interest.

Various theories were proposed for the cause of this strange effect, and although actions were taken, and the effect was greater some years than others, it became an integral part of the financial system.

To this very day, inflation is an integral part of most modern economies. It may be eliminated for short periods of time by drastic government action, but it is a fundamental element of the economic system and it always returns sooner or later."

John paused to breathe in the cool air. It felt wonderful as it flowed into his lungs.

"Inflation is a strange beast," he said."Most people, Kate, view inflation as things becoming more expensive. They see a dollar as a constant value, but everything they buy or sell becomes more expensive.

I suggest that you look at inflation from the opposite point of view, in order to better understand it. Imagine that wages, the cost of food, and the cost of property all remain constant.

After all, we all have to buy food from our wages, so the price of food must always be a certain proportion of our income.

Throughout time, regardless of the type of currency in use or its value, the relationship between wages and the cost of food and shelter remains fairly constant.

I will go even further, and say that a person who has wealth in the form of assets, apart from cash, will keep the same wealth over time. Even if the value of the currency changes, their real wealth is the same. Of course, if they use their assets to produce income, then this mayl increase their wealth.

Assets also change in value for many other reasons, and may increase or decrease in true value. So, rather that saying that prices go up in time due to inflation, say that the value of items remains the same.

Now, however, we must look at cash. If we assume that the value of assets remains static, then the value of cash reduces over time due to inflation.

As the years go by, the value of each dollar reduces.

More dollars are required to buy an asset with each passing year, not because the asset has more value, but because each dollar has less. This may be due to government actions that result in an increase in the number of dollars that are in circulation with each passing year. It is essential that you understand this, for two reasons.

First, any investment in the form of cash, such as loans to people or deposits in banks, will be subject to inflation. You must always take inflation into account when calculating whether you are making a profit on these investments.

If inflation is 10 percent and you are depositing your money at 12 percent interest, then you are actually increasing your total wealth by only two percent a year, ignoring taxes.

Even worse, if your deposit earns only 8 percent interest when inflation is 10 percent, your wealth is actually reducing by two percent each year.

There is a second reason to clearly understand inflation. If your wealth is in the form of quality assets, like shares in large companies or property, then inflation should not be a major problem. As we have said, these items keep a constant real value, so their price will increase at the same rate as the value of a dollar reduces.

Overall your wealth has remained constant. If you have chosen your investments well, their real value will increase due to other factors.

Now, when you compare the price that you bought an asset for with the price that you sold it for, you must take inflation into account.

If the price has only increased by the same amount as inflation, then you have not made any real profit at all. Your total wealth at the end of the deal is the same as it was at the start."

Kate contemplated John's words. It was true that she

thought of inflation as the cost of things rising, and that John's approach was the opposite. It was a little strange at first, but the idea of real things staying constant in value, and cash notes reducing, put things in a different perspective.

After all, John had shown her how possessions and assets had real value, but cash was just an artificial invention to make trading easier.

It also made it easier to understand how different investments were affected by inflation. She realised, too, that the old saying about investments being a 'hedge against inflation' was completely the wrong way around.

Wealth in the form of assets was the natural store of wealth, and it was only cash, the artificial creation of banks and governments, that was subject to the ravages of inflation. Kate looked at John and nodded approvingly.

"Continue, grandfather," she said with confident pride. "I am following everything you say."

John smiled to himself. He was pleased that Kate felt more confident, so he moved on to a new topic. There was still time left in the afternoon, and he did not want to waste her confident and receptive mood.

3.10 Foreign exchange

"Now, Katie, we come to a turning point in the valley's history. This event would forever change the lives of the people in the valley.

You will remember when the people first settled there. Many generations had passed since they had arrived, and the people had never seen any reason to leave. When they arrived in the valley, they had been travelling for months through dry and rocky country.

There was little food, and the people were thin and malnourished. There could well have been another valley,

133

just as rich, beyond their valley, and another one beyond that, but the people would not take the chance.

The valley provided everything they needed, and they did not want to risk being trapped in the desert with little food or water. So much time had passed since the people had first settled there that they had completely lost their skills as nomads and bushman, and had forgotten how to live off the land.

So, the people were happy to live in their valley, and occasionally explore the fringes of the desert that surrounded them.

As far as they knew, they were the only people on earth.

One dark night, as the wind howled in the trees and rain beat against the roves, a child was born in the valley.

Years passed, and the child grew into a young man.

He was a strong young man, but restless and unsettled. He explored every part of the valley, from the high hills to the deepest gullies. It was a large valley, but still it was not enough to satisfy him.

He began to explore the desert around the valley, riding long distances on horseback. There was no food in the desert, however, so this limited the distance he could venture from the valley.

As he grew older, he grew bolder and bolder, and his trips away from the valley became longer and longer.

One day, when he had been away from the valley for longer than usual, his parents began to worry. A search party was sent out after the man, but no trace was found of him.

Weeks passed, and the parents' hopes for the safe return of their son gradually faded. More weeks passed, and eventually all hope for his safe return was lost.

A funeral service was held, and everyone in the valley consoled the grieving parents on their loss. He had been a good boy, they said, but just a little too wild and adventurous.

Months passed, then one day a dramatic event occurred.

News spread through the valley like wildfire, that the man had returned, weak, thin and barely alive.

His parents were filled with joy. It took several weeks to nurse him back to health, and it was some time before the man was strong enough to tell his amazing story.

While riding, he had discovered a pool of water in a cave. He drank thirstily, as his water supply was limited and he would need all of it to return safely to the valley.

The next day, however, he had developed violent stomach craps. He became delirious, and was completely unable to control his horse. He simply lay across the horse's back, hoping that the horse would know the way home and return him safely to the valley.

They were, however, many days ride from the valley, and the horse had never travelled though this land before. The horse walked slowly all day, walking directly away from the hot sun. As luck would have it, though, this lead them away from the valley, not towards it.

The man was still suffering from severe headaches and stomach cramps, and was unable to steer the horse in the correct direction.

All the water was exhausted, and there was no hope of returning to the valley. The horse walked on, patiently plodding all day, while the man lay across its back and waited to die.

His only faint hope was that they would find another cave, where the water was not bad, and he could survive a few days longer.

One morning, as the man slipped in and out of consciousness, he saw a vision in the distance. It was cruel, he thought, how the eyes played tricks on the weak and delirious.

As the came closer, however, the vision became clearer and clearer. Finally, when they arrived, the man saw that the image was real.

They had arrived in another valley. A farmer discovered the man, and nursed him back to health.

Although they spoke a different language, and the man could not understand their words, he saw that the valley was similar to his own, and that the people lived similar lives. Once his strength had returned, the man began the long journey home. The farmer generously gave him all the supplies he needed, and by riding into the sun every day he had eventually made his way home.

The valley buzzed with news of the amazing story. Some people doubted the man's words, and accused him of lying or telling the whole story in a delirious fantasy. It was clear, however, that the man could never have survived for several months in the desert alone, and so it was accepted that the story must be true.

After much discussion between the valley people, an expedition was launched to contact the other valley. The strongest horses where loaded with large amounts of food and water, and a small group of people set out in search of the other valley.

Contact was made, and the first real meeting between the people of the two valleys took place. Over the next few years, the language barrier was broken and regular contact was established between the two valleys.

Although they were similar in many ways, there were differences too. Some products were more developed in one valley than the other. Silk, for example, was widely used in the second valley, and the clothing was finer than anything that the people of the first valley possessed.

The machinery in the first valley, however, far surpassed the machinery in the second valley. Thus, over time, brave and enterprising people set up trade between the two valleys.

Wells were dug along the route between the valleys, and over time the journey became a commonplace occurrence. There was only one major problem with the trade between the valleys. Each valley had developed their own currency, and this was used exclusively for buying and selling.

The earliest trade between the valleys was done by the

old method of swapping goods, but all the limitations of this approach soon reared their ugly heads.

The goldsmith who had created the first bank had been watching these developments with interest. He was a very old man now, but one of the most powerful, wealthy and respected men in the valley.

In the early days, he had avoided trade between the valleys because of the risks and expense involved. Now that the route was better known, however, his agents were regularly seen travelling between the valleys with goods to trade.

The problem of the two currencies remained, and was a stumbling block to the expansion of trade between the two valleys. So, the goldsmith decided to offer a new service to the customers of his bank.

He would offer to exchange one currency for the other. His agents would take goods to the second valley, sell them for the second valley's currency, and return with the currency to the first valley. This would be kept in the goldsmith's bank, and anyone planning to travel to the second valley could come into the bank and exchange some notes between the two curencies.

The goldsmith calculated how much of each currency was needed to buy similar items. These figures were then used to determine how many notes of one currency would be swapped for the other currency.

Of course, the goldsmith intended to make a profit, so he charged a fee for the conversion. Over time, prices in each valley changed by different amounts, and so the conversion ratio between notes changed as well. As long as the same value bought the same goods in each valley, people were happy to freely convert their notes from one currency to the other, as they needed.

This, Kate, was the beginnings of foreign exchange, and it is a system that we still live with today."

3.11 The individual within the system

The soft dusk light filtered through the trees of the park. Even though it was midsummer, the air was distinctly chilly.

Kate held her coat tight around her to keep out the cold. She looked at John.

The cold did not seem to affect him, and she could still see the warm glow of fire in his eyes and the relaxed smile on his face. They had been resting a short while, as they always did after each major topic, when John spoke again.

"Next week, my dear," he said like an excited little boy, "we will begin the really interesting subjects.

Investment.

This is when your hard work will finally start to pay off, when you will learn how to manage and reduce your risks, especially the greatest risk of all, the risk of dying poor."

Kate could see that the topic excited him, and she was anxious herself to hear what he had to say. All the talk had been useful, but she was more interested in actually having money so she could do the things she wanted to do.

"Now, however, we must finish the things we have been discussing these past few sessions. I have tried to show you a little about how the world works, how business operates, how the banking system works and how market forces affect almost everything related to money.

I am not trying to make you an economist, but you do need a general understanding of how the financial world works, if you are going to invest your money successfully."

John paused for a moment.

"Investment, as I have said Kate, is using your existing money to make more money.

It involves keeping your wealth in the form of assets that will generate an income and rise in real value. Always remember, though, that you are part of the system that I have described.

You live within the economic system that we have talked about. Your wages are affected by the demand for labour, which in turn is related to the level of employment.

The same factors that affect other businesses affect you. You are selling your skills and time for a profit.

Having said this, though, do not ever feel that you are trapped by the system. You are an individual. Just because the average level of wages stays constant, is no reason why your own wages cannot increase. It will be harder, of course, if no-one else's wages are going up, but it is still possible.

Every situation is different.

It you follow the principles that I have taught you, such as caring for and improving your skills, then you will be successful regardless of the environment around you.

You must always be aware of the environment, as this will affect you, but never believe that you are trapped by it.

Never believe that you have no control or no power.

In the deepest depression, some people make a fortune, and in the greatest boom, others loose all their money. Every situation is different, and at the end of the day, your financial success or failure is determined by your own actions, and nothing else."

John paused for a moment to let Kate absorb the full impact of his words.

"Now, I want to make a few final points about the economic system before we leave the topic. First, there are two distinct parts of your life that relate to earning money.

First, your business.

This is your primary job, your career. It may be a trade, a profession, a small business, or any other activity you work at to earn an income.

We have already discussed strategies for maximising the benefits you gain from this employment. Pamper your career and treat it well, for it is your greatest asset in the changing fortunes of life.

Second, there are your investments.

Virtually everyone has some form of wealth, no matter how modest. If you have nothing, then by following the methods I have suggested you will soon be able to save a small amount.

A wise investor protects their wealth, and uses it to earn more income and to increase its value. To do this, you must keep your wealth in the form of quality assets.

The best assets are ones that earn a steady, reliable income. Even money in the bank fits into this category, however tax and inflation usually make it a very poor investment.

Remember the valley, Kate.

There are only three main investments, three things you can do with your wealth to increase it. First, you can lend it to people, and charge interest.

Even money on deposit in a bank is effectively a loan from yourself to the bank.

The second form, is property. All people need shelter, a place to live and a place to work. Popery is the second major form of investment and store of wealth.

Finally, shares in a company. Most money and business in the modern world is managed through companies, and part ownership of companies is the third major investment and store of wealth.

Think about the things that I have told you Kate.

Think about them well.

This is the system that you live in, this is the system that takes your money from you, or gives you more money, depending on how well you understand it. Think about it, understand it, and all the things I teach you about investment will become as clear as a mountain stream."

John stopped speaking, breathless. He was very active, almost agitated, but tired as well. He knew these moods well, and he knew he would come crashing down and be exhausted the next day. He leapt up from the bench.

"Walk with me, Kate. I need to slow down, I need to relax. Please walk with me. Please walk with me and take me home."

4 *Principles of Investment*

4.1 *The successful approach*

Once again, several weeks had passed since Kate and John had discussed finance.

After each major section, John insisted on a few weeks' break, so that Kate could digest the things he had told her, and he could rest and enjoy the park.

The talks were helping Kate greatly, and John enjoyed them too, but they were a strain on both of them and neither person wanted to loose interest by spending too much time on the subject.

It had been late spring when Kate had first raised the subject of money, and they had talked through many warm afternoons and breezy evenings. Months had passed now, and the shadows of the trees were beginning to stretch out as the year grew older.

Autumn was John's favourite season. For him, autumn in the park was the most beautiful of the seasons.

Occasional rain, but generally fine, blue skies. There were many days when the air was cool, or even icy cold, but sun was bright and the sky clear. John loved the invigorating feeling of the cold air on his face, and the comforting warmth of his coat as he held it tightly around him. When the skies were bright and clear, the air cool and the wind wild, these were the times that he was happiest.

At these times, he felt young and alive, full of energy and happiness. He enjoyed the warm afternoons as well, and it was then that he relaxed the most, but it was only the bright sun and cold, cutting air that lit a fire in his soul.

Kate had noticed a distinct change in John's mood over the past few months. When they had started their talks, he had been a sweet, kind but tired old man.

Full of wisdom and kindness, but weak as well, his energy slowly leaving him. For a time, he even seemed to get worse from week to week, and Kate had become worried.

Then, without apparent reason, he had changed. Rather than decline, his energy actually increased with each passed week. Kate could not understand it. True, the hot summer days had drained his strength, and the slow change in the seasons had clearly had a positive effect on him.

Still, there was something more, some other change in him that Kate did not understand. Perhaps one day the pieces would fall into place, and Kate would understand the forces that drove the man.

After all this time, he was still a mystery to her. She trusted him with her life, but it was a trust based on instinct, not knowledge. She knew very little about the man inside, and yet she sensed that there was a great deal more to know.

John was watching a family of ducks on the lake. A handful of young ducklings were swimming excitedly, exploring among the reeds and the nooks and crannies between the rocks.

The mother swam slowly, occasionally leaning forward to fossick on the lake's bottom, her tail high in the air.

Her ducklings stayed close to her, sometimes venturing a short distance to explore, then scuttling back to the safety of their mother at the slightest hint of danger. It was a lovely sight, he thought. They were plain ducks, not a rare or special species, but their feathers shone and glistened in the sun.

The tiny ducklings were the most beautiful creatures he had seen, their tiny bodies soft and fury and brimming with eager excitement.

"Kate my dear," said John with a strong voice, "the time has come, the walrus said, to speak of many things. Of candles and sealing wax, and cabbages and kings."

"Please!" said Kate with mock disgust. She was guilty herself of quoting Alice in Wonderland, so she could hardly blame him for doing the same. Still, she was not going to miss the opportunity to have a friendly jab at her grandfather.

"My dear," said John ignoring her protest, "we have covered two major topics now, personal money management and the nature of our economic system. This seems to have helped you greatly, and you will be receiving my bill shortly."

"Bastard!" said Kate, slapping John's arm in mock irritation. "I should charge you for having to put up with your endless stories!"

John laughed.

"Only kidding my dear. Now, we have covered the first two major topics, and there are two major ones to go.

These are the principles of successful investment, and details of specific investments. Never let it be said that we finished half-way through."

"Go on, John," said Kate, smiling. Every time they had a long break, there was a nagging worry in her mind that they would never resume their talks on money.

She was actually quite relieved that he had brought up the subject.

"I am keen to learn more. I have thought about the things that you have told me, and I see that they are important.

I also see, though, that you are setting the scene for the next major topic, the discussion on investment. Let's start." Kate was quite excited.

"First, and most important of all, I will describe the attitude and approach that you should have to investment.

This is where most people go wrong. It is the most important factor in successful investment. If you have the right attitude and use a sensible approach, the rest will fall into place by itself.

Now, there are several approaches people take to investment. Only one is correct, and only one is consistently successful.

First, we have the abstainer. This person spends as little time as possible on their finances. They may have investments, but they spend little time reviewing them and learning about them, and simply hope for the best.

If they have money problems, they ignore them and hope they will go away. Sometimes these people are lazy, but more often this attitude is born of insecurity and lack of confidence.

This person believes that they know little about investment, and they could never understand it without a great deal of time and effort. They often believe that successful investment is a matter of luck, and there is no point wasting time worrying about it.

Some people believe they do not have the intelligence, the time, or the patience to become successful investors.

Others believe that they have no control over their finances, that their income is beyond their control, and that they will never have wealth because they need everything they earn to meet their expenses.

Don't fall into this trap, Kate. It does not take intelligence, education, luck or a large amount of time to become a successful investor.

It requires a modest amount of your time, and a certain desire to learn and improve your position, but anyone who is willing to make the effort can learn the required skills.

Abstainers are rarely successful with money. They make poor investment decisions, because of insufficient research and planning, they do not take the initiative to improve their wealth for the future, and they are easy targets for sharks.

Poor investments are often held for years, for once an abstainer has finally made a decision to buy, they try and forget about the investment, do not monitor it regularly, and avoid making another decision, the decision to sell."

John looked across at his granddaughter. Her face was a little flushed, and she looked quite embarrassed. She was, he knew, guilty of this particular fault, but John did not wish to embarrass her further, so he quickly moved on to the next item.

"While some people abstain from active investment, other people have different approaches.

One major trend in the modern world is the trend towards products.

Everything is a product. Ideas, machinery, political campaigns and insurance policies are all known as products. They are wrapped up in a neat little bundle, given a name and a price, and marketed as a product.

Many investments are marketed in this way, especially investments from large institutions like banks and insurance companies.

Some people take a consumer's approach to investment. They shop around for investments as they would shop for a lounge suite or a car.

Again, Kate, this approach is rarely successful. The consumer of investment products generally makes several important mistakes. First, they rarely have a long-term strategy, which they continually monitor and update.

The purchase of an investment product is treated like the purchase of new furniture; once the decision is made and the product is bought, no further thought needs to be given to it.

Consumers are often misled by marketing pitches, and rarely examine the true nature of the investment in critical detail. In fact, some products come with such limited information, that it actually impossible to fully understand how they work and what they really are.

These products should be avoided on principle. Never, Kate, invest in something you don't fully understand.

Although some packaged investment products are useful as part of a total portfolio of investments, they are no substitute for the investor managing and monitoring their own strategy as the years go by."

Kate was quiet, almost sullen. She had, she realised, made almost every mistake in the book. She hoped John would get to the positive steps soon.

"After the abstainer and the consumer, we have the speculator. The speculator is not actually a type of investor at all, he is a professional money manager.

His career involves speculating with money, much as your

career involves nursing and people. A speculator has several important qualities.

First, the nature of speculating involves taking large risks. A speculator expects to loose money on many deals, but hopes to gain even more money on other deals.

All speculators must be prepared to carry a fair number of losses and failures. Speculators put their money into things that have the potential for large, quick profits, but also carry the risk of significant losses.

Second, a speculator must put a great deal of time into their craft. Speculation should be a full-time job, or at least involve several hours' work a day. Like horse racing or any other form of gambling, the speculator's best friend is information, and the speculator that collects the greatest amount of accurate information is the one who will make a profit in the long term.

Speculation should be treated as a career or serious hobby, not as a form of investment. Some speculators make consistent profits from speculation, however many others loose a great deal of money.

Never, Kate, confuse speculation with investment. Many people believe they are investing their money, when in reality they are speculating with limited information and no experience. Speculation is best left to professionals, for like the young lamb, a naive speculator is quickly fleeced and left naked.

Investors look for steady reliable returns, with a minimum of risk. While an investor must be prepared to loose money on the occasional investment, this should be a small part of his total portfolio.

An investor avoids high-risk investments completely, and builds wealth through quality low risk and medium risk investments.

Investors do not need advanced skills or large amounts of time to manage their investments, and a few hours a month should be sufficient to prevent them from getting into trouble."

Kate was listening carefully. She was beginning to see investment in a different light, and it was true that she had confused speculation and investment herself. Investment was beginning to look much safer and more predictable than she had imagined.

"We have looked at the abstaining investor, the consuming investor, and the speculating investor.

Now, for the good news.

The wise investor.

The wise investor does two things to steadily increase her wealth. First, the wise investor builds a reserve of quality assets. Using her on-going saving, and income from her existing assets, the wise investor purchases more assets.

As her portfolio expands, the assets produce more and more income, and eventually it snowballs until she has a strong income from her investments, independent of her income from work.

Investment is largely about managing your assets. It is about selecting which assets to buy, and deciding when to sell them.

It is about improving the value of your assets, and using the income from them to buy more assets. It is about maintaining your assets, improving their value, buying at the right time and selling at the right time.

Through this, the wise investor builds her wealth, and keeps it in forms that will increase in value, not reduce in value.

The second step in wise investment is the management of financial risks. Some people keep all their money in the most secure places, such as a deposit with a bank or a government. They believe that they have reduced their risk to a minimum. However, this attitude is sadly and dangerously wrong.

In fact, the greatest risk of all, the risk of dying poor, becomes much more likely. The risk of inflation and tax reducing the person's wealth also becomes inevitable.

Wise investors manage their risks well. They spread their money into many different investments, so that a failure of any single investment does not seriously hurt them.

They keep their wealth in forms which are not vulnerable to inflation, and where taxation is simply a gentle annoyance.

Wise investors keep a mix of low risk and medium risk investments, so that they can protect their wealth and still increase its value. They understand the risks each investment is subject to, and take steps to reduce or eliminate them. Overall, Kate, wise investment involves two tasks. The management of assets, and the management of risk."

John stopped, looked at Kate, and waited for her to speak. She was staring across the park, deep in thought.

"You know, John, much of what you say applies to me." There was a touch of embarrassment in her voice, but she was making an admirable effort to remain business-like.

"I, too, think of the investment world as full of mystery and danger. I never believed I could understand it without a great deal of time and effort. I don't have massive amounts of free time, and if I did then I wouldn't want to spend it learning about investment.

I'm glad you say that it won't be too difficult.

It is also true that I saw investment in the same light as gambling. I thought of investment as waiting for a few hot tips, buying something, and hoping like hell that the value went up." Kate turned to her grandfather, a whimsical look on her face.

"It's too hit and miss for me, John. I will be very grateful if you can show me a better way."

John smiled, encouraged by Kate's words. "Of course, my dear. Believe me, if there wasn't a better way, then I wouldn't have the money that I have today. There was no luck involved. Now, I want to talk about three words. Greed, fear, and ignorance. First, let's take greed.

We all want things we don't have. This is natural, and the force of desire is the motivation the drives growth, achievement and success. However, the wise investor is always careful not to let greed control her thinking.

Many people fail financially because of greed. They

149

invest in high-risk investments, in the hope of gaining high returns. Although some investments may succeed, these investors will keep pushing for more and more money, until one day they loose the lot.

Greedy investors are not prepared to spend money maintaining their assets, and keeping them in good working order.

In their desire to keep every cent for themselves, they neglect the proper care of their assets, and loose far more than the maintenance cost as the value of their assets decline.

Greedy investors always demand the highest prices when they sell assets. Because of this, they take a very long time to sell, and usually loose more in lost opportunities and lost income than they gain from the slightly higher price. An investor waiting to sell an empty rental property, for example, should take into account the income that she is loosing each month that the property remains unsold.

Greedy people also loose their money in every boom in prices. When the price of shares or property rises, the greedy refuse to sell.

Higher and higher the prices rise, often to ridiculous heights, and still they will not sell. They wait for just a little more profit, then just a little more after that.

Finally, everyone sells at once, the price crashes, and the greedy are left holding assets worth half their previous value. A greedy investor cannot bear the thought of loosing money on an investment. When she has a bad investment, she holds on to it, refusing to sell, in the vain hope that it will recover its value.

Inevitably, the value declines even more, and her loss is even greater than it would have been if she had sold early and cut her losses.

Kate, we all want to improve our future, and after all that is the purpose of our talks. Do not let greed control you, though

. Keep a level head, and make objective, rational decisions. Be happy with a series of modest profits, rather that trying for a single massive one.

This strategy will always win in the end. The solution to greed is to develop patience and keep modest, realistic expectations.

Now, fear.

I have also seen many people fail financially because of fear. There is no such thing as a free lunch, and the more safe and secure an investment, the lower the return you can expect to receive.

I have seen many people's wealth whittled away by inflation and tax, when they could have been receiving healthy profits.

A carefully-managed portfolio of quality assets is just as safe as a bank or government, but your wealth will increase in time, instead of declining.

Do not let hysteria and fear of taking risks prevent you from practising wise investment. After all, there is risk in all investments, but if you are not prepared to take well-planned risks, then failure is a certainty.

The greatest risk of all, the risk of being poor, is the risk that you are embracing by spurning investment.

Unlike the speculator, the wise investor may receive a steady increase in his wealth. As the old saying goes, 'fortune is ally to the brave', or in other words, luck and success will come to those who are courageous and take positive action.

The best solution to fear is knowledge.

The only thing we truly fear is the unknown. You may feel dread, if something is unpleasant, but you should not feel fear. Fear prevents sensible, rational decisions.

Once we have finished our talks, and you understand how investment works, you will not be afraid. Listen, read, and learn, and you will not be worried any longer.

Finally, ignorance.

Many people have lost their money because they invested in things they didn't understand. Never do this. Ignorance, or a lack of knowledge, is behind many tragic stories.

Ignorant investors make poor decisions, since they have

limited information and knowledge with which to decide the best course of action.

People with a poor level of financial knowledge are easy targets for sharks. Unfortunately, the financial world is full of sharks.

Many of these people are not actually criminals, in the sense that they steal money illegally, but many are paid on commission, and will pressure people into investments which they don't need and can't afford.

Many people have ended up with their financial affairs in a mess, and lost thousands of dollars, because they were given poor or misleading advice by unscrupulous people in the finance industry.

There is only one person who is guaranteed to be by your side wherever you are, and that is yourself. You may have trusted advisers and family, but in the end your money is your own responsibility, and it is dangerous and unfair to expect anyone else to take responsibility for you.

There opposite of ignorance is knowledge. Don't invest in anything you don't understand, even if this means missing out on a wonderful opportunity.

It is simply not worth it in the long run. Learn all you can, for knowledge is the strongest safety net in the world."

John looked across at Kate. She was concentrating intently, listening to John's every word, and forming a picture in her mind of the image he was creating. He decided to continue, hoping that her concentration would last.

"Now, more about the wise investor.

The wise investor does not need great intelligence, wealth, qualifications, time or energy. The wise investor has a calm, logical approach to investment.

There is no room for emotion in investment.

The wise investor is never irrational, greedy or consumed by fear. The wise investor always fully understands the actions he takes.

There is no room for prejudice or personal preference. Every investment must be assessed on it's merits, there is no

152

room for a belief that one type of investment is the 'best way to make money', nor is there any room to believe that another investment is 'risky and dangerous - you're sure to loose everything'.

The wise investor has an open mind and assesses every investment on its merits. There is no room for excitement, fear, panic or hysteria.

The wise investor is calm and controlled. He takes every development in his stride, whether good or bad.

Should a major disaster happen, such as a fire or a crash in prices, the wise investor is not concerned, for he has planned for all these possibilities well in advance. The wise investor is always cautious.

He does not trust anyone blindly, and takes all advice with a grain of salt. He is, however, never paranoid, and is always prepared to act on the picture that the evidence paints for him.

The wise investor takes responsibility for his money and his actions. He seeks the advice of reliable professionals, but is always responsible for the overall strategy himself.

He never surrenders responsibility for his strategy to any person or any institution. The wise investor is assertive, and takes action whenever necessary. He demands all information that is rightfully his.

He never lets an unsatisfactory situation continue, and takes action to change it as soon as possible.

The wise investor collects all the relevant information he can. He never makes decisions under pressure or in a hurry, and refuses to take any course of action until he is satisfied that he understands it and has all the relevant information.

Sometimes, the wise investor misses opportunities because of this attitude, but he is never concerned, for he knows that his approach will win the day in the long run.

The wise investor often sees people boasting proudly about large profits, but he simply smiles to himself, for he knows that their great profits will be followed by great losses.

Once he has considered a possibility carefully, he never procrastinates, but takes positive action. A wise investor never becomes obsessed with money or investment, for this clouds his thinking.

He spends whatever time is required to manage his investments well, never any more and never any less.

The wise investor builds relationships with the professionals he relies on, and is prepared to work towards a healthy relationship for the benefit of all. The wise investor has a calm, rational and balanced view, an open mind, an independent and responsible attitude and a carefully planned strategy."

John looked at Kate and grinned. "Can you honestly tell me, that if you acted like that, you believe you would loose all your money?"

"Of course not," kate said angrily, annoyed at John's patronising words.

John grimaced. It had been an insensitive comment.

Kate turned to her grandfather, calm now, and said "It's not that easy, you know John. You make this person sound like a miracle-worker."

"Of course you're right," John said quickly. "I know it's not easy, and everyone would have trouble with some aspect or other, but it is a model to work towards.

The more you practice this attitude, the more successful you will be with investment. It is something well worth thinking about, as it is central to a successful approach.

4.2 Gathering and assessing information

John rested in the cool afternoon breeze while Kate thought over his comments on wise investment. She had listened to everything he had said, and the sense in his words was undeniable.

Kate had never thought about her attitude and approach to investment, and had never seen it as an important factor in success.

Luck, skill, money and other factors has always seemed more important. Now that John claimed that this was the single most important factor, however, she saw things in a different light.

After all, this was good news, as she could work on changing her approach right away. There was no need to wait for lady luck to come along, or depend on qualifications and experience that she didn't have. Overall, things were looking up.

"Tell me more, grandfather," Kate said. "I'm quite excited now that we are finally talking about investment. More money!" she said with a devilish grin.

John smiled. There was always the slight doubt in the back of his mind that Kate would tire of his talking, and they would never complete the things he wanted to say.

That would be sad, as he would have wasted a great deal of time and effort.

"Kate, keep my comments about attitude in mind while we are talking. It will be a constant theme through everything I say. Next we will discuss the gathering and assessment of information."

John adjusted his position on the park bench, sitting upright and making himself comfortable. He could feel a long talk coming on.

"The informed investor is the successful investor.

Of course, an investor must know what to do with the information he has gathered, but if he doesn't collect the information in the first place, then the race is over before it has begun.

Collect as much information about investments as you can. The most useful source of information is the major newspapers. Be sure to keep an eye on the business and investment sections. Their articles cover a wide range of ground, and are written in many different styles. Read them regularly, for this is the best way to develop a good general knowledge of investment.

Many articles may seem irrelevant, dealing with specific details which don't affect you directly, but you may still learn something from reading what the author has to say.

You will not understand many of the things that are discussed, or the terms that are used, but don't worry. An overall impression will filter through, and that is all you really need.

Newspapers will also give you a picture of the current state of the three major investment markets; property, shares and interest-bearing investments.

All three markets move in cycles, and reading the financial press for a while will give you a good picture of the stage of the cycle each investment market is currently in. Investment magazines also contain a wealth of information.

Do not restrict yourself to the major articles, either. Often letters and columns will teach you valuable things. There is no need, Kate, to become an expert on finance and investment. In particular, do not try and learn all the intricacies of tax rules or the law. This is the reason that you develop a strong relationship with your accountant and solicitor.

It is important, however, to develop an overall feel for the current environment. You should know whether the stock market is fairly high or fairly low compared to the past, whether interest rates are at a low ebb or have gone through the roof, and whether property prices have been rising strongly or are in decline.

I know that this may sound, but if you simply read the

156

business section of the paper each morning, then within a few weeks you will have a remarkably accurate impression of these things.

Remember, too, that at any given time, the majority of the public is quite wrong in their perception of the investment markets. Because of this, you will need to form a picture in your own mind, and not rely on the opinions of people that you might talk to.

When you begin to look at specific investments, such as shares in a particular company, or buying a house in a particular suburb, collect as much information as possible relating to the specific investment.

Companies issue annual reports, and real-estate agents often write articles about specific suburbs. Any investor who does not go to the trouble to read this basic information is taking a grave risk.

Although you are investing to make a monetary profit, is it often useful to read information that is not directly related to finance.

For example, you may come across an article dealing with a company's attitude to its staff. They may have recently introduced a bonus scheme, or some other initiative to benefit their employees. This is an excellent way to get a clearer view of the true nature of a company, and see where it is heading in the future.

Non-financial factors such as staffing policies can have a major effect on profit, but they do not show up in the figures for a year or two. Reading about these issues can be a good way to get a head start on the rest of the community and chose a company that has a strong future.

Overall, your aim should be to get the most accurate picture of the company that you can, using the most varied and accurate information.

Another example relates to property. Suppose you find an article in the newspaper that discuses the upgrading of a major highway through an outer suburb.

If this makes access to the city significantly faster, then

properties in this outer area may become more popular and so prices may rise. Everything that helps paint a picture for you will help in the choice of a property, company or other investment.

Often the non-financial information is the most useful, as may tends to tell you what will happen in the future, rather than what happened in the past.

Always remember that financial data relates to past events, not to the future. You will also find that few people, including professionals, go to the trouble of including these factors, and so you may be able to choose an investment that is not yet popular, and so is good value for money.

Many institutions, such as banks, insurance companies and even professional associations produce small booklets and pamphlets on specific topics.

These are usually free, and can be extremely useful. Because they must be small, they keep to the basic facts, rather than confusing the reader with complexities that cloud the main issues.

They are updated regularly, so they tend to be more accurate than books. They are also written in simple language that the layman can easily understand. Many professionals can pass these booklets on to you.

Books on investment, of course, can be useful. However, the details of tax and legislation change often, so be careful to check that the details are accurate. Overall, I suggest that you use these books to learn general knowledge, and consult with professionals about the details before a buy or a sell.

When you are gathering information about investments, there are two types of material you should be looking for.

The first is current information about the investment. This will allow you to form a picture of how it operates, and whether it produces a strong, reliable income.

The second relates to the future. This includes opinions and data that predict how the investment will perform in the future.

A word of caution here Kate.

Many people are seduced into buying investments on the promise that they are 'about to go up in value'. These people seldom look at whether the investment is solid at the current time.

Be careful not to fall into this trap.

There are no true get-rich-quick schemes in the world, but there is an abundance of ways to get-poor-quick.

The best way to ensure that your investments will hold their value is to buy investments that are solid at the current time.

If they produce a healthy, reliable income, then their future value will take care of itself. If an investment is a poor investment today, then it will never be a good investment tomorrow.

The next step on your information-gathering trail entails a visit to your friendly professionals. You should develop a good business relationship with an accountant and a solicitor.

Bank managers, investment advisers, real estate agents, insurance agents and stockbrokers can all be useful at various times. If you are not happy with the people who handle your affairs, then change immediately. Your future is in their hands, and you must have confidence in them. It is also worth spending a little effort to build a good relationship.

Professionals can be consulted to determine the details and specifics of an investment. The overall purpose and strategy is up to you.

After all, can you really expect your stockbroker to tell you that it is actually a bad time to invest in the stock market, and that you should give your money to the real estate agent at the end of the street?

Even an independent accountant or investment adviser can never understand perfectly your needs and plans, so the only person who can properly look after your strategy is yourself.

Now Kate, we should discuss the most important aspect of information gathering.

I have told you where to collect the raw information, but not how to assess it. We must also talk about what you should not do.

First, treat other people's opinions with scepticism. Ignore 'hot tips' altogether, as they almost never come true.

At the most, you can use a 'hot tip' as a reason to look at an investment in detail, but I recommend that you stay away from them completely. Why? Well, crashes in prices are the result of prices rising far beyond realistic values.

Prices may rise far above their true value when an investment becomes extremely popular. People may buy the investment in the hope that the price will continue to rise, and rarely examine the investment in detail on its merits.

As more and more people scramble to buy the investment, the price skyrockets, and eventually it crashes just as fast, leaving people like you holding the baby.

Whenever you hear comments like 'you can't go wrong with this investment', 'this is a red-hot tip', or 'prices are about to go through the roof', then stay as far away from the investment as possible. Many people will offer you advice.

However, very few people have the experience and ability to give you accurate predictions, and these people certainly don't spread their information around.

They are too busy keeping a low profile and making lots of money. The fact that someone offers you advice on an investment is almost a guarantee that they are not qualified to give it.

Comments overheard in a bar, the doctor's waiting room or the office should be treated with extreme scepticism.

Another common mistake is to assume that wealthy people know a lot about making money.

At first sight this seems obvious, but often the opposite is the case. Because wealthy people have money to spare, they do not need to be careful and they do not learn the lessons of careful money management and wise investment. When you meet a wealthy person, ask yourself this question. 'Where did they get all their money?' Perhaps they are a brilliant salesman, an expert in their profession, or perhaps they inherited their wealth.

None of these people will know any more about finance than you do, Kate. In fact, they are probably so busy pursuing their chosen vocation that they give even less thought to investment than you do.

If you meet someone who has become wealthy by being a professional investor, then listen carefully to what they say. Unfortunately, these people are as rare as hen's teeth, and when you do meet one they tend to keep their mouth shut.

My second comment on other people's opinions relates to professionals. One must realise, Kate, that every professional is making a living from his or her industry.

They have a strong vested interest in encouraging people to invest in their sector, especially if they are paid on commission. No real estate agent will ever tell you that it is a bad time to invest in property, just as no stockbroker will ever tell you it is a bad time to invest in shares. In fact, if you ever hear an agent say 'the market has risen strongly for several years, and we expect it to flatten out', run like hell.

This means there is about to be a crash in prices. When you consult a professional for advice, look for the facts in his comments.

Statements like 'the population growth has exceeded the building of new houses for three years in a row' are much more useful than 'this will be a great year for property'.

Listen carefully to all comments and advice, but form your own opinion based on the information you have read and heard.

Finally, we must look at assessing the information you come across.

When you read an article, look for the facts that are included in the article, rather than simply the opinion of the author.

Some articles are written by people who work in an industry. For example, an article on the property market may be written by a real estate agent.

You can expect these articles to have a positive bias.
In fact, making accurate investment predictions of any kind is

extremely difficult, and you should be sceptical of any predictions relating to future prices.

As children, we assume that everything we see in print must be true, but in fact very little written or spoken commentary is truly objective and accurate."

John stopped speaking and looked across at Kate. Sometimes he felt sorry for her. They had come a long way on their talks, and there was still a long way to go. The process involved a significant loss of innocence, and John could clearly see the effects in her slightly pale, flushed face.

"Go on, John," Kate said with a weak smile. "You weren't kidding when you said you would show me how to be independent and successful." Kate sat upright, took a deep breath, and a little colour returned to her face.

"All right," she said finally, "what is the next step?"

4.3 Trusts and companies

John decided to proceed, and discuss some more specific details of investments.

"Kate, my dear," he said, "now we should talk about the different forms of investment.

From our previous discussions, there are only two fundamental ways to invest money.

The first is to lend it to someone and charge interest.

The second is to buy something, or part of something. This item must produce an income, or rise in value, for you to make a profit.

Now, we should discuss the forms of investment that operate in the modern world.

First we have the company. The legal concept of a company has developed over several hundred years.

Companies have a name, own assets and employ people. A company acts like a person in its own right, and can do most things that an individual can do.

There are two ways that you may interact with companies when you invest your money.

First, you may lend money to a company. This is done in various ways, such as investing in debentures or unsecured notes. This is simply a fixed-interest investment, and is similar to a term deposit with a bank.

We will cover this in more detail when we look at interest-bearing investments later.

The second way you can invest with companies is to own shares in a company. If you own shares of a company, then you own part of the company, and part of all the assets that the company owns.

You are entitled to a share of the company's profits. If the company expands its business and operations, then the value of the company will increase, and consequently the value of each share will increase.

We will look at companies in detail when we look at investment in the stock market.

After companies, the next form of investment we have is a land title. We often speak of 'buying land', whereas we really mean we are 'buying a title to some land'. Ownership of the title gives us the right to use the land as we please, subject to certain restrictions of course.

Usually we buy a house, flat or other building along with the land title itself. In effect, we have bought two things, the title to the land and the buildings that are on it.

Should there be an increase in the demand for the use of the property, then the value of the property will increase as well, and we can sell it at a profit.

After companies and land titles, we have the investment trust. The concept of a trust has also developed in law over many years.

Many years ago, situations sometimes arose when a sum of money could not be controlled by the person who owned it. In these cases, a trusted person would be appointed to control the money, and use it for its intended purpose.

A common example is where a couple die, leaving young children. The parent's money could be kept 'in trust', and a family friend, 'the trustee', would spend the money on the children as the parents had intended.

The trustee had legal control of the money, however he could only use it in the ways that the 'trust deed' described.

The 'trust deed' was the document that the parents wrote to give control of the money to the trustee. This concept has been used for many years, in an endless variety of situations, and the law has defined the powers and responsibilities of each party involved.

In this example, there are three parties involved. First, there are the parents. The money was owned by them, and should they remain alive in a coma, for example, they would still own the money.

They were also the people that created the trust deed, the document that gave certain powers to the trustee. The second

164

party is the trustee.

He has legal control of the money, and may spend it in any way he sees fit, as long as he spends it for the purposes that the trust deed defines.

The third party is the beneficiaries, which are the children in the earlier example. Note that they had no control over the money, and their only connection with the arrangement was that the trust deed instructed the trustee to spend the money for their benefit.

In modern times, the concept of a trust has been applied to investment. There are two main ways that a group of people can pool their money together and invest it as a whole.

The first way is to pool the money together in a company. The company can then act as a single entity, and could purchase a large property for example.

Each investor would shares of the company, and consequently a share of the property. The second way is to pool their money into a trust, and the money can then be invested as a lump sum.

This raises many possibilities. For example, many small investors can pool their money together and purchase a large office building.

On their own, none of the investors would have enough money to contemplate the purchase. Investment trusts are one of the greatest success stories of recent times. They have given small investors access to a huge range of investments, which previously were only open to organisations or very wealthy individuals.

There have been a few problems, which I will discuss shortly, but overall the use of trusts has opened a whole new world of investment for ordinary investors.

Three parties are involved in an investment trust. First, there are the investors. These are the people that contribute their money. Second, there is the trustee. The trustee has legal control of the money, and is responsible for investing the money in the way that the trust deed defines.

However, the trustee is not generally an expert on

investment, so the third party comes into play.

The third party is the manager.

The manager is the person or organisation who makes the investment decisions. The manager makes the decisions, and the trustee makes the investments according to their advice. All assets are held in the name of the trustee.

The management company are experts in the investment field. Although legally the trustee has most of the power and responsibility and the manager has little, in practice the manager makes all the decisions and the trustee simply signs the relevant documents.

Although companies and trusts are both used to pool money into a single sum, there is a critical difference between the two.

While an individual and a company can act like a 'person', a trust cannot. A trust is simply a legal contract, it is not a new entity of its own.

A trust cannot own assets in its name. A trust cannot enter into contracts, it cannot employ people, it cannot be sued and it cannot sue others. A trust cannot be taxed directly. All the money and assets in the trust are held in the name of the trustee, not the name of the trust document.

Any tax or legal action that relates to the trust usually relates to the trustee. Whereas a company is an independent entity, a trust is simply a contract between several parties."

John paused, checking to see that Kate was still concentrating. She was.

"We have looked at the basic nature of investment trusts. Now, the most important part; getting your money back.

There two types of investment trust.

Although they are used for similar things, they are fundamentally different. This difference is so important that I will spend some time discussing it. There are a few pitfalls with investment trusts, and you can avoid them all if you understand the difference between the two types.

All investors that invest money in a trust own a share of the trust's assets. These shares are generally called 'units', and

166

hence the name 'unit trust'.

The unit represents a small share of the trust's assets, and is similar to a share of a company. An investor may buy and sell as many units as she wishes.

The difference between the two types of trust comes into play when the investor wishes to sell her units. Two schemes are used. The first is called an 'unlisted trust'. In this case, the manager of the trust calculates the value of the trust's assets, and so calculates the value of each unit. The investor writes to the trustee, informing him that she wishes to cash in a number of units.

The trustee then cancels the units and pays cash to the investor. Hopefully, the assets of the trust will have increased in value since the investor deposited her money, and the units will be worth more than they were when she bought them.

If a large number of investors wish to cash in their units, then the trustee will have to sell some of the trust's assets. This can create problems, as a long period of time may be required to sell a large asset.

The second scheme is called a 'listed trust'. In this case, the investor is not dealing with the manager or trustee. The investor simply sells her units to another investor.

The units are usually traded on a stock exchange, so the prices are commonly known and there can be active trading of units in the trust. The name 'listed' comes from the fact that the units are 'listed' on a stock exchange. In other words, they appear in the list of shares and units that may be traded on the exchange.

There is an advantage and a disadvantage with this method.

First, the trustee does not have to sell any assets of the trust to meet the investor's desire to cash in her units.

Regardless of the number of people buying and selling units, the assets in the trust remain stable and the manager and trustee have no involvement. This is a critical advantage of listed trusts.

In some cases, such as with large properties, it may not be

practical for the manager to sell the assets. If investors in an unlisted trust choose to redeem their units, then the trustee has no choice but to sell the assets as best he can. There can be significant costs and time delays involved in selling major assets.

With a listed trust, however, investors can buy and sell units at any time without affecting the assets of the trust.

There is, of course, a disadvantage with listed trusts as well. Because units are sold to other investors, the price will depend on supply and demand. If a trust becomes unpopular, then the value of the units may go down, even though the assets of the trust are still solid. In practice this is not a major problem, as the price of the units is usually a good reflection of the true value of the assets.

With an unlisted trust, the value of the units only depends on the value of the trust's assets, but in an unlisted trust, the value of units also depends on their popularity.

On balance, there is a simple rule to apply when choosing a trust. If the assets of a trust are easily sold, if they can be sold quickly, in small amounts, and for little cost, then an unlisted trust is safe. This applies to trusts that invest in shares or short-term interest-bearing investments.

If, however, the trust's assets are large items, if they cannot be easily sold, or if they involve long-term commitments then a listed trust may be safer than an unlisted trust. This applies to trusts that invest in large commercial property and long-term mortgages. The investor should generally prefer listed trusts to invest in these areas."

Kate was listening intently, absorbing everything her grandfather said. He had reached a more practical stage in their discussions, and Kate was learning even more than she had over the past few months.

"Remember the things I have told you about trusts, Kate. They are extremely useful, and properly used are very safe. Investment trusts will give you access to a whole range of different investments, with little cost and effort. They should become a major part of your investment portfolio.

Consider overseas shares, for example.

With a small amount of money, and no knowledge, an average investor such as yourself can invest in shares in every major country of the world. If you did not have access to investment trusts, this would not be practical.

Always remember, though, that a trust is simply a collection of assets, and you are really investing in the underlying assets. If the stock market goes down, then share trusts will go down. If property has a good year, then property trusts will go up. Always keep in mind the underlying assets that you are investing in."

John paused, took a few deep breaths, and relaxed. When they had first discussed money, he had been itching to give Kate as much practical advice as he could. He realised, though, that if she did not understand the principles, then there was little point in giving her specific advice.

At least if he gave her an understanding of what she was doing, then hopefully she would be able to handle any situation she came across. John decided that a quiet walk would soon be in order.

Although it was still early in the afternoon, they had covered quite a bit of ground already. He did not want to risk confusing his granddaughter, and after all they were there to enjoy the park as well.

It was a great shame, John thought, that basic money management was not taught in schools. He had seen a great deal of misery in his lifetime, and a great deal was due to money problems.

Even marriages, and some loving ones at that, had broken up after the constant stress of worrying about money.

A tragedy, he thought to himself. Even books were of limited use. John had seen limitless books on becoming an overnight millionaire, and countless texts on complex investment strategies.

What Kate really needed, though, was some basic knowledge, and her whole life could be different. Perhaps, he thought, he was doing something worthwhile after all.

"Grandfather!" Kate said with mock annoyance. "What on earth are you doing? I've been asking you questions for the last five minutes."

"I'm sorry Katie," John replied apologetically. "My thoughts were a million miles away. Let me finish the discussion on the forms of investment, then we can go for a relaxing walk."

"Very, well," replied Kate with exaggerated forgiveness. "But don't talk too long!"

John laughed, glad that Kate had broken the tension and brought them back on track.

"Companies and trusts are the main things that you should be aware of, but there are a few other issues to keep in mind as well. In your investments, you will find that you have many dealings with institutions, such as banks, insurance companies and investment houses.

Most of the money in the modern world is controlled by these institutions. Money you invest with these companies can take two main forms. First, we have the interest-bearing investment. This includes a traditional bank account, as well as many other investments.

In these products, you are paid interest at various times of the year. Interest is deposited in your account from time to time and so your balance increases.

In some products, it is possible to receive negative interest, in other words your balance can actually reduce.

This is generally rare however. The other category of investment is market-linked investments. These are similar to units in a trust, and often they actually use a trust deed like other investment trusts.

The key point is that when you invest your money, you purchase a certain number of units.

The value of these units may go up or down over time. Rather than being paid specific amounts in interest, your profit is represented by the increased value of the units and changes daily.

The main point to be aware of here is that the value of

your investment may go down from time to time, but in the long run you should still expect a positive return.

4.4 Assessing investments

Kate and John walked slowly through the park, taking a different path to the one they usually strolled along. It was a huge park, by far the largest in the city.

One could walk for miles along the paths without walking over the same ground, and at times Kate feared they would become lost.

She sometimes thought that her grandfather would see this as an advantage.

John, however, was never worried.

As they walked, she could almost feel his mind relaxing, his soul being refreshed. He had seemed a little distant lately, and Kate was worried that his recent increase in energy may begin to fade.

Suddenly, as they walked around an unfamiliar bend in the path, the couple came across a magnificent sight. Kate was dumbfounded. John, as one might expect, simply smiled, and absorbed the beauty that met their eyes.

Directly in front of them was a huge glass enclosure, filled with butterflies. Some were simple and plain, ordinary butterflies that one might find in the back garden.

Others were delicate and exquisite, the rich colours of their wings sparkling like diamonds in the bright sunlight. Kate was totally unprepared for such a sight. They walked further, and entered into the butterfly cage. Within the cage was a small bench. John led Kate over and they sat down together.

"My God, John," Kate said in wonder. "Did you know this was here?"

"I was only built recently, Katie," her grandfather replied. "I have been spending quite a bit of time here. Look at that one over there," he said pointing to a large, delicate butterfly. The butterfly sat on a leaf, opening and closing its wings slowly. With the wings closed, it looked like a plain, dark

172

brown leaf.

Then the wings would slowly open, revealing the brightly coloured splendour of the top surface of the wings. Kate and John sat there a long time, relaxing in the shade of the tropical trees in the butterfly cage, and watching the colourful insects fly gently around.

Finally, they returned to their customary park bench. John wanted to continue their discussions, and he explained that he needed the cool breeze on his face to stimulate his thoughts.

"The next step on the path," he said, relaxed now, "is the assessment of investments.

When you are considering an investment, whether it be a term deposit with a bank or the purchase of an investment property, there are several things you should consider.

The overall aim is to ensure that the investment is a good one, and that you buy it at the right time and sell it at the right time.

The first thing to do is look for the best quality investments. This particularly applies to assets such as property and shares, but also applies to investing with institutions.

Don't put your money with an institution if you have read worrying things about them. It's better to be safe than sorry. By high quality, I do not mean the most fancy, expensive or 'exciting' items.

On the contrary, it is far better to choose a property or share that is solid, reliable and will produce a steady income, rather than one that is currently in fashion or has exciting potential.

In investment, the word 'excitement' is usually synonymous with 'risk'. Our aim is to have steady reliable profits, not to take unnecessary risks.

Leave that to the professional speculators, Kate. When buying a property, for example, choose one that is well built and of common, reliable design. Avoid anything that is fancy or unusual, as it would be harder to sell, and the profits may be less predictable.

173

Your property may be quite plain, but as long as it is solid and maintained well then it will always fetch a good price. Just as 'exciting' is synonymous with 'risky', so a 'boring' or 'ordinary' asset can also be a 'safe' asset.

The very fact that it is common ensures an active market when you come to sell it. When selecting a share, stay with the solid, reliable companies such as manufacturers, banks and large mining companies.

These companies may produce a steady profit year after year. Avoid speculative companies, such as small mining companies which are hoping to make large mineral strikes.

Overall, you should be looking for the best quality investments you can find. These are the simple, steady performers, which produce a reliable income year after year.

If you keep to these assets, and avoid the ones with the chance of big profits or big losses, you will do far better in the long term.

Now, the second step.

Look at every investment, and reduce it to its basic components. If you look at all the financial transactions you undertake in a lifetime, there will be a huge variety.

However, at the end of the day, all investments come down to the same thing. All that really matters is how much money you put in, and how much you get back. It's as simple as that. The extra you get back is the increase in your wealth, also called your profit. Say for example that you have a retirement scheme with a life insurance company.

It may seem hideously complex, but it can be summarised in a single sentence. You may describe it as 'an investment managed by an insurance company, where the money is invested in shares, properly and fixed interest, where the government has special low tax rates, and I cannot spend the money until I retire'.

In one simple sentence, you have defined all the essential ingredients of a very complex investment.

You will find things much easier if you try and reduce each investment to the basics. Then you will understand it,

174

and you can proceed to examine it properly.

The next step is to brush the dust off your pocket calculator."

Kate groaned. "Oh no! I hate maths!"

"Don't worry, katie," John said with a smile. "All you need to do is to add, subtract, multiply and divide with an electronic calculator. Can you handle that?"

"Just," Kate replied with an exaggerated frown.

John continued. "The point I wish to make is that it is very important to look at some basic figures.

Many people buy expensive properties, and make long-term investments, without ever putting pen to paper. Say, for example, that rent on properties was returning about 4 percent a year, and money in the bank was returning 15 percent. Anyone who buys an investment property in that climate is taking a major risk.

Why would people want their wealth to earn 4 percent, when it could be earning 15 percent with higher security?

The answer is they wouldn't, and there is a significant chance that some people would sell their investment properties, and prices would stay stable or decline.

Remember, too, that stable prices are actually a declining wealth, as prices must grow to match inflation if you are to maintain your real wealth.

Unless you do a few simple calculations, you would never be aware of this risk. Now, I will get to the details later, but realise that you must be prepared to do a few simple sums to put your investment into perspective with the other possible investments.

Next, we have one of the most important issues of all.

The income that an asset produces is called its yield. If a property cost 100,000 dollars, and it returned an income of 12,000 per year, then the yield would be 12 percent. The percentage yield is equal to the income divided by the price, and multiplied by 100.

I cannot emphasise strongly enough, Kate, how important yield is as a factor in investment. Most investment assets are valuable because of their ability to earn an income.

The more income they produce, the more desirable they are, and the higher the price that people will pay for them. In the changing world of popularity, fashion and economic conditions, it is the ability of an asset to earn income that guarantees that it will be valuable.

Some investment assets, such as paintings, do not produce an income and are desirable for other reasons.

However, the vast majority of investments, including shares, property and bonds, are valuable because of their ability to produce an income.

If you own an asset that produces a strong income, then you can always be guaranteed of a good price when you come to sell it. Other times, you may choose to pay high prices for assets that produce little income.

This is the case when buying property in highly fashionable areas, as the prices may be way above the value of the rent they produce. Although you may be lucky, and the asset may continue to rise in value, I suggest that this is a high-risk strategy.

If the investment or area goes out of fashion, then there is nothing fundamental to give it any value, and the price may fall dramatically.

Always calculate the yield on any investment before you buy it. The yield can be compared to the interest rate that is available on bank deposits, and the yield that is available on other investments.

If the yield is low compared to other investments, think very carefully before proceeding.

This leads me to the next major point; valuations. Working out the true value of an asset can be quite difficult. Notice that I said the 'true value', Kate, and not the price. The 'price' of an asset is the amount that people are willing to pay for it.

Price is influenced by many things.

It is influenced by the true value of the item, by supply and demand, by how desperate the other party is to trade, by luck, and by the general public sentiment.

The 'true value', however, is what the asset is really worth, if all these other factors were eliminated. The 'true value' depends on the income the asset produces, and the future outlook for its value.

The difference between price and value is a critical one, Kate. One of your primary tasks in choosing an asset is to find one where the price is lower than the true value. How do you determine the 'true value'? There are several ways, depending on the circumstance, but there are two major ones worth knowing about. First, there is the 'market value'.

This is the price that similar items are fetching when they are sold. Take houses for example. By looking at different houses in the same area, and comparing them to the house you are interested in, it is possible to determine a quite accurate value for the home.

This method will still not determine the 'true value' of the item, as the general market price is subject to many factors, but it is a very useful guideline, and may give you a guide to the property's current value.

The second method is the 'yield method'. Imagine that bank investments and share investments where returning yields in the range of six to eight percent.

Based on this, we decide that we would be willing to pay a price for the property that would give us a yield of 7 percent or more.

Assume that our property is currently producing a rent of 14,000 dollars per year. If we wanted a yield of 7 percent, this would equate to a price of 200,000 dollars.

The value in this case is equal to the required yield multiplied by the income amount.

With one simple calculation we have arrived at a 'natural value' for the properly, completely independent of the current market prices.

The yield method of valuation is one of the major methods that is used to determine the value of an asset.

In simplistic terms, if this home was selling for 170,000,

then we would say it was a good deal, but if it was priced at 230,000 then we would call it overpriced.

I do not want to confuse you with figures, Kate, but I simply want to illustrate that the value of an asset can be determined by working backwards from the income it produces.

This is often the best way to compare investments that are very different."

John paused for a few deep breaths, but Kate was still listening so he decided to continue.

"We have now looked at quality, reducing an investment to its basic components, yield, looking at the figures and valuations.

Next, we must look at the expenses. All investments have expenses associated with them. These can range from virtually none, with some bank accounts, to thousands of dollars with some properties.

When you are looking at the income that an investment produces, you must allow for all expenses. All that matters is the income you receive after all the expenses are paid.

Keep in mind, too, that expenses are often fixed, but income can disappear when you can least afford it.

Commissions are a major expense with many structured investments. Always allow for any commissions when assessing the income that you can expect from an investment.

Next we have taxation.

Tax is often the biggest killer of all.

It takes a large proportion of the income and profits from investments, and can make the difference between a profit and a loss on an investment. One word of warning, however, Kate. As you become more involved in investment, you will come across many schemes and investments that are designed especially to save on tax.

I suggest that you avoid these completely. They are a licence for trouble, and if there is one organisation you do not want to get into trouble with it is the taxation office.

Even if the investment is legal and safe, there may be

other issues involved. Overall, your aim should be to generate a profit, with tax issues being a secondary consideration.

When you assess an investment, ignore tax initially and ensure that it is a solid investment on its own. If you decide that it is, then you should take tax into account, and see whether it is still profitable or whether it has lost its appeal.

Do not become obsessed with tax or inflation. They are very important, but each investment must be of good quality on its merits, without these factors taken into account.

Finally, after tax, look at the effect that inflation will have on the investment. As we have previously seen, wealth in the form of fixed assets is not greatly affected by inflation.

Cash, however, reduces in value at the rate of inflation. This can have a major impact on the real profits that are earned from interest-bearing investments, such as term deposits with banks.

In fact, once tax and inflation are taken into account, most money invested in fixed-interest investments is actually reducing in total wealth, not increasing. This may help explain why the saving you have done in the past has never seemed to get you anywhere.

The next step in analysing an investment is to write down all the risks. In other words, write down all the major things that can go wrong.

In the case of an investment property, for example, the would be four main risks.

First, there is major damage to the property, such as a fire.

Second, there is the risk of a decline in the general property market. Even if prices stay steady, this represents a decline in real wealth since the prices are not keeping pace with inflation.

The third risk is the possibility of the suburb or area going out of fashion.

Finally, the risk of an extended period of time passing without a tenant should be considered.

Once you have listed all the risks, look at ways to reduce them.

The risk of fire and damage can be managed with insurance.

The risk of a decline in the general property market can be managed by putting part of your wealth into other investments, such as the stockmarket and interest-bearing deposits.

The risk of a decline in the popularity of a particular suburb can be handled by owning several properties in different areas. If you cannot afford this, then the fact that you have money in other investments may help offset any loss on the property.

With an interest-bearing investment, there are two major risks. Interest rates may decline, leaving you with a lower income.

This is not a problem with fixed term deposits, however your money is locked away for a period of time in these deposits and you will miss out if interest rates rise.

The second risk is the risk of default, the risk that the institution will become insolvent and will not be able to repay your money. This is rare, however it does happen, so you should never keep your entire wealth with a single institution.

With every investment you consider, Kate, write down everything that can go wrong and look at ways to reduce the risks.

You will not completely eliminate the risks, but if you reduce the risks in all your investments than you will do much better in the long run.

The next step is to estimate the future potential of the asset. This is the hardest part to do, but it is not as important as you might think, as the best guideline to the future is an accurate analysis of the present.

If you can understand the present situation, then you have the best chance of predicting the future. Most people spend all their time thinking about the future value, and ignore the current factors.

Although it is important to look to the future, no-one can predict what will happen. The best way to ensure that your investment will do well is to consider the factors I have mentioned carefully.

If you consider the quality, the yield, and the risks, then you will be able to assess whether the asset is a solid investment.

If an asset is a quality asset today, then it will probably be a quality asset tomorrow as well.

The best way to ensure that your investment will have value in the future is to ensure that it is a good asset today.

If you judge it well, then the future will take care of itself. Finally, when you have looked at all these factors, you need to compare the investment with other investments.

If it is a property, do the same analysis on other properties, and compare it to the one you are interested in.

Make sure you also compare it with investments in the other sectors, such as the stock market and interest-bearing deposits.

For example, if inflation was low, property prices were stable and short-term deposits were returning 17 percent, then you may be better off keeping your money in the bank for a year and delaying the purchase of the investment house you were planning.

Always compare an investment with the other sectors, and be very wary if the yield and growth are much lower that other investments.

Kate was looking worried. "It sounds very complicated, John. I mean, I went to auctions last year when my best friend bought an investment house, and she just picked one that was about the right price.

I've never heard of anyone going to all this trouble. Where would I start?"

John nodded solemnly, then replied to Kate's question. "I understand how you feel, Kate. All you really need to do, though, is to spend an hour or two at the kitchen table with a pad, a pen and a pocket calculator.

In a single afternoon you could look at all the issues I have raised. You will be amazed at how writing it down on paper puts all the figures and issues into perspective.

In all the hype and excitement of making an investment, it can be very hard to keep a level head.

Don't worry, either, about how the other people invest. Many people and their friends believe they have made handsome profits in an investment, but if you did the figures, taking inflation, interest on loans, expenses and tax into account, often their profits are poor.

Others do make good profits, but it is a very hit-and-miss affair.

For every man at the pub who brags about making profits, there are ten others keeping very quiet about their losses and drinking their beer in misery.

A careful, thoughtful approach is your best weapon against chance and disaster".

4.5 The buy/sell decision

John rested for a short time, and regained his breath. He decided to slow down a little, and give them both time to rest.

Kate had been listening carefully, and although it was a great deal to absorb, he felt that she had kept up with his comments.

Many Sunday evenings Kate would write down the things that her grandfather had told her, and think about them at her leisure.

This was fortunate, since the discussions were becoming more practical and detailed. John's main aim had been to increase her understanding and widen her horizons, and this had been going well.

There was much practical advice that he still wanted to give her, though, and he was grateful that she was writing it down. There was a lot to remember.

"Now Katie, we come to one of the most important sections. Again, this is an area were many people go horribly wrong.

I would venture to say that if people only mastered this one single section, then most of them who have lost all their money in investments would still have it today. I am going to talk about the decision to buy or sell an investment, and how you should come to that decision. I use the term 'buy' loosely here.

You may buy an asset such as a house, or invest your money in a fixed term deposit. In both cases, you are putting your money into another form, and people in the finance industry would refer to it as 'buying a product'.

When I use the term 'buy' in this context, I mean investing your money. The term 'sell' is used for transforming your investment back into cash, either by selling an asset or retrieving your cash from the institution you deposited it with.

Now, you must try and assess the 'true value' of each

asset. There are no hard-and-fast rules for doing this, but comparing the yield with the yield from other forms of investment is a good starting point. All the factors I have previously outlined come into the 'true value' of an asset.

The price, however, is influenced by many factors, and rarely reflects the true value of the asset. In particular, an investment that is unpopular for any reason is usually priced below its true value.

Similarly, investments that are very popular, such as a house in a fashionable suburb or shares that have risen strongly over a long period of time, are often priced well above the true value of the asset.

After a slump in an investment market, such as property or shares, the investment may remain unpopular for several years. This unpopularity will remain long after the investment has started generating good returns again, and this is an excellent time to buy quality assets at cheap prices.

In the same way, investments remain popular long after they have risen well past their true value, and this is the time you should sell. Overall, you must compare the price of the asset with your estimate of its natural value.

If the price is lower that the natural value, then consider buying it. If the price is much higher than the natural value, then consider selling the asset. You may notice, Kate, that I have said nothing about the profit or loss you have made on the deal.

When you consider selling an asset, you should completely ignore whether you have made a profit or a loss. All that matters is what will happen in the future.

Consider the situation when the value of an asset has gone down. Many people refuse to sell, hoping that it will recover its value.

However, it may have declined because the quality of the asset has declined, such as a company with bad management or a property that has major problems. Consider the future, and ask yourself this: 'is it a high quality, strong asset that will produce a reliable income?' If the answer is 'no', then you

184

should sell.

I heave heard people say that they can't afford to sell, because they have lost half their life savings and they need all their money. The sad part, is that these people usually go on to loose the other half of their savings as well.

It is more important to sell at the right time than to buy at the right time. No-one makes a profit or a loss when they buy, they make a profit or a loss when they sell. Selling at the right time can make the difference between a healthy profit, or a modest loss, and disaster.

If an investment has a poor future, then sell it and put your money into an investment that has a good future. If an investment has a strong future, and the price is not well above the true value, then keep it.

In summary, there are two times you should sell an investment. First, if it is poor quality and its future is bleak.

Second, if the price has risen higher than the natural value. In this case, take the profit and look for a new quality investment.

John stopped speaking, as was his custom, and rested for a few minutes. Still it was early afternoon, the sun was bright and the air cool, and they were both enjoying the talk.

"I have spoken a little on selling, as this is the most important step to get right. Most people who lost all their money in investments saw the signs long before it was too late, but they hung on, hoping for the best.

One old business saying sums this issue up in the phrase 'last man out pays the bills'. This refers to failed institutions and failed pooled investments, where the last few investors are the ones who suffer most from the failures.

In other cases, investors held on to their investments after the prices had skyrocketed, hoping for even higher prices. Inevitably, the prices crashed and they were left with little or no profit.

Now, buying.

After assessing an investment carefully, comparing it to other investments, and ensuring that it complements your existing investments, you have decided to buy. This is where the final critical test comes in.

You have all the facts, and now you must make the decision as to whether to go ahead with the purchase.

There are two questions you must ask yourself, and only two questions.

If you answer these carefully, you will have more chance of success in the long term. First, look at the worst case scenario. This may be a stock market crash, a property price crash or the failure of the institution offering a fixed-interest investment. Ask yourself this: 'if the worst case scenario happened, would it be a major disaster?'. Of course it would be a problem, but the question you must ask is whether it would be a major disaster, whether it would completely derail your entire financial situation.

If you ask yourself this, and the answer is 'yes', then go no further. No matter how rare or unlikely the event, anything is possible, and the world is full of amazing surprises and astonishing events. Truth is stranger than fiction, as I am sure you have found Kate.

The easiest way to answer 'no' to this question is to spread your money into different investments. If, for example, you had one third of your wealth in property, one third in shares, and one third in fixed-interest, then you could answer 'no' to this for almost any situation.

Having survived the trauma of facing this question, the second question comes into play. This question is: 'are the odds of success in my favour?'. If you can answer 'yes' to this question, then you should complete the purchase or investment.

You may even pass by several investments until you find one where the signs are pointing strongly in your favour.

There are many bad opportunities for every good one, but there are still an abundance of good opportunities, so you should seek them out.

The safest way to assure success in investment, Kate, is to make many investments that fit these two rules; you could

186

survive if it went wrong, and the chances of success are excellent.

Finally, one last thought on making decisions. If you are going to achieve financial independence, then you must make investments.

Do not be afraid of the risks, for if you manage the risks carefully, then you will make steady profits.

If you don't ever buy assets, or invest money, then financial failure is certain. Action, too, must be taken when investments turn bad.

Sometimes you will make poor judgements, or there will be information that you weren't aware of, or perhaps it was a good investment at the time but things have changed.

The moment that you are sure you have a bad investment, and that its future looks uncertain, it is better to cut your losses and invest in something else.

Remember, Kate, that it's better to loose half your money than all your money. Anyway, if you spread your money in the way I have suggested, an occasional bad investment should have a minor effect on your portfolio."

4.6 Risk, risk management, protection

John was enjoying himself. Although he did not want to rush Kate, and risk confusing her, she seemed to be keeping up with the things he said, and they had frequent breaks to relax and enjoy the surroundings.

They had covered a great deal of ground each day, however, and John was grateful that Kate made detailed notes each Sunday evening.

Sometimes it took her several weeks to absorb the things he had said, and often she had to read over her notes many times. Still, they had the rest of their lives, and John was prepared to take the long haul and do the best he could to help her.

"Risk," John said thoughtfully. "Investment, like life itself, is largely about risks.

Money management and budgeting is about managing your cash, and investment is about managing your assets and your risks.

Managing your risks is essential to protect your wealth. It is also a big factor in ensuring that your profits are strong and steady.

Risk is the chance of something going wrong. It can be something drastic, such as a fire in a building or a stock market crash, or something more gradual such as the interest rate on a loan rising over time.

Any event that would have a negative impact on your investment is a risk. You should look at all your risks, and consider ways to reduce them.

Your primary goal in investment, apart from purchasing quality assets, is to reduce your risks as much as possible.

Life is full of surprises, and things never work out exactly as we expect. Even if something seems unlikely, such as a crash in property prices when all the signs point to the opposite, it is still possible.

You should prepare yourself for all possibilities, not

matter how unlikely.

More often than not, the events that actually happen will be the ones that you thought the most unlikely. No-one can predict the future. Do not be depressed, however, about the things I am saying.

I am showing you how to protect yourself, so when something bad happens to an investment, your overall wealth is not seriously damaged. As well as nasty shocks, you will have many pleasant surprises, and many investments that perform far better than you expected.

There is something I have mentioned before, Kate, but I wish to emphasise it once again.

In terms of your financial security and future, the greatest risk of all is being poor.

For this reason, placing all your money in secure, low-risk investments such as banks is not reducing your financial risk at all, in fact you are exposing yourself to the most dangerous and fatal risk of them all; the risk of not having assets and security.

Write down all the risks in your current and potential investments, and look at ways to reduce them.

Imagine, for example, that you currently have your entire savings in a single bank account. You are exposed to the risk of the bank failing, fraud by a bank teller, or a computer error with your account.

These events may all seem unlikely, but they are all possible.

Even if you recovered your money after one of these events, there could be expenses, long time delays and lost interest.

The first thing you should do is take half your money and put it with a different bank. You have now reduced the risk of loosing all your money, or suffering major problems due to mistakes or delays.

This may seem a trivial point, but if you apply this method to everything you do, then one day you will be thankful because you will discover that you have just avoided a massive disaster.

Now, let us talk a little more about the nature of risk.

The term 'risk' is widely used in financial circles.

Unfortunately, it is used with two different meanings. I define a risk as an event that fundamentally reduces the value of your investment. Risk is the odds that a bad event will occur.

This is the first definition of the word, however the word 'risk' is also used to mean 'volatility'. The price of a volatile investment may rise and fall by large amounts on a frequent basis.

However, in the long term, some investments with a high volatility can also be low risk. Some investments rise and fall in price on a daily basis, but still show a strong steady growth in the long term.

Consider the following strategy as an example. Imagine you invest money in the stock market, and spread the money evenly among the ten largest companies.

Over time, if a company falls out of the top ten, you sell the shares and buy shares in the company that took its place.

Overall, then, the companies may change, but you always have your money evenly spread among the top ten companies. Now assume that you keep to this strategy for ten years.

At the end of this time, you would be almost certain to have made a very healthy profit. This is a strategy that I would call a medium to high volatility, but very low risk strategy.

Never confuse volatility with the risk of loosing your money. They are related, especially if you are forced to sell an investment at a bad time, but they are not the same thing and it is well worth remembering the distinction.

My next point relates to the most famous truism in the investment world. This is the well known 'high risk, high return; low risk, low return' rule.

What this means is that investments with a low risk, such as fixed-interest deposits, generally have a low return, that is a low profit. Investments that have a higher risk may provide a higher return.

This saying is widely quoted, but unfortunately leads many people astray.

There are three important points I wish to make, and they stem from this saying.

First, given the choice between a safe investment and a risky investment, any sensible person would look at the safe investment first. To overcome this, the person offering the risky investment has to offer a higher profit to attract people away from the safe investment.

The laws of supply and demand operate, as always, and ensure that the risky investment will have a higher return than the safe investment.

No-one would invest in a risky investment if the profit was the same as a safe investment.

The person who chooses the safe investment is paying a price for safety, as they are missing out on the higher profit.

The person who invests in the risky investment is demanding a higher profit to compensate him for the risk he is taking on.

Risk is almost like a cabbage in the valley market, it can be bought and sold.

If you want to reduce your risks, you must pay a price, and in the opposite case, if you are willing to accept a risk, you may receive a profit from doing so.

In the investment world, risk can be traded like any other commodity.

In this way, the saying is completely correct; a risky investment may have a higher profit than a safe one.

The opposite case also applies.

There is no such thing as an investment that has a high return with low risk.

Investments that offer a high potential return generally involve a significant amount of volatility and risk.

On my next point, however, the saying is somewhat deceptive. As well as 'high risk, high return', the saying is also used to mean 'high volatility, high return'. This is a critical distinction.

An investment can be volatile, and still be very safe and low risk in the long term.

Investors hate uncertainty and instability, and so they demand a higher profit from volatile investments. In the same way as safety, a sensible person would always choose a stable investment over a volatile one if everything else were equal.

The laws of supply and demand ensure that volatile investments may provide a higher profit in the long term than stable investments. This means that people who are investing for the long term should choose safe but volatile investments, such as quality shares and quality properties, to gain the highest and most reliable profit over a long period of time.

Now, the third issue. On the surface, this saying implies that the investor is trapped. They can choose a safe investment, but this will lead to a low return. They can choose several risky investments, and these will each produce a higher profit, but since they are risky, the investor will loose money on some of them, and in total they are left with a low average profit for the whole portfolio.

It seems like a no-win situation. However, in reality the situation is very different. The missing link, the factor that this saying does not include, is the quality of the individual investment.

Take a trust or a company as an example. If the management is poor, the returns may be very low, and the investment is also very risky, as it may fail altogether. In this case we have a 'high risk, LOW return' investment.

Take the other case, where the management is excellent, and the people managing the investment are doing all the right things.

In this case, we will have a high return, but a low risk, as the investment will be very strong and have a secure future. Overall then, we come to the following conclusion. The saying 'high risk, high return; low risk, low return' or 'high volatility, high return; low volatility, low return' applies to the average investment across a whole sector.

On average, shares return higher profits but have higher volatility than property.

When we are considering a specific investment, however, the saying cannot be applied. Timing, quality and other factors are more important, and it is possible to assemble a portfolio of assets that have high returns, and are also relatively low in total risk.

There is one more comment I wish to make about the nature of risk, before we move on to discussing ways to reduce it. Every major financial transaction should be judged according to the rules of investment.

Often one will hear people say 'I have a mortgage, money in the bank, and some investments'. This is a dangerous attitude. Your home mortgage, your cash in the bank, and all other financial transactions should be treated as investments.

There are risks in all of them, and you should apply the same careful planning and rules to these things that you apply to all other investments.

Nothing is perfectly safe.

Never take any money or any asset for granted, or one day you might loose it."

John paused for a few deep breaths. It was mid-afternoon. The wind was strong and gusty, something that Kate found a little difficult, but John loved the sensation. Sometimes she wished he had chosen a more sheltered position, a place less exposed to the elements. John would have none of it.

"Having looked a little at the nature of risk, we should talk about the management of risks in your investment portfolio," he continued. "After that I will talk about ways to reducing specific risks.

First, there are several things you should consider. Your investment portfolio should contain many different investments.

Try to arrange your investments so that there is a mix of many different risks. Imagine that one investment is affected by falls in interest rates, and another is affected by the level of the stock market. For your overall wealth to suffer badly, two separate things must go wrong. Interest rates and share prices would both have to fall. If you only invest in one area, such as property, then a single event, a fall in property prices, could wipe you out completely.

Remember, we are not concerned about the chances of the event happening, as the future cannot be predicted.

Just when everything is looking perfect is when things usually start to go wrong. You can extend this idea even further, and have six or eight different investments that are subject to different risks.

One might be vulnerable to a fall in the value of the dollar, and another vulnerable to a low population growth in the outer suburbs.

Once you have six or eight different risks, then the chance of most of them happening at once is virtually zero.

You may have picked up, Kate, that the more investments and the more risks, the higher the chance that at least one will have problems. This is true, but because it would be a small part of the overall portfolio, the effect on your total wealth would be small.

Experience has shown that this is the most reliable and consistent way to make steady profits.

Next, you should consider the investments that you have in your portfolio. I will spend some time on this later, but there a few basic comments I should make now.

First, it is impossible to make money from a mix of low risk investments. You must have a mix of low-risk and medium-risk investments to make a healthy profit.

I suggest you avoid high-risk investments completely. They are exciting and glamorous, but I suggest you leave them to professional speculators.

It is a full time career to consistently make money from these investments, and requires a great deal of time and knowledge. When I say medium-risk investments, I really mean medium-volatility and low to medium risk.

If you choose quality assets carefully, then your overall

194

portfolio can be relatively safe. Next, there is a powerful method of managing risks that you should be aware of.

This method is excellent because it doesn't cost anything and it will give you steady returns in a variety of different circumstances. We have already spoken about mixing your investments, so that each different investment has a different mix of risks.

You can take this even further, and try and select investments that balance each other out. For example, one investment might reduce in value if a certain event occurs, and another might increase in value after the same event.

If you purchase both these investments, then you have eliminated the risk of this event, because a rise in one investment will cancel out a fall in the other.

Both investments, of course, must be strong, quality investments in their own right.

I will give you two examples, as this can be one of the most effective ways to manage your risks.

First, imagine that you have invested money in a trust that invests in the shares of an overseas country. You have several risks. One of the biggest, however, is the change in the value of the dollar. If the dollar rises by 10 percent, then the value of your investment in your own dollars will fall by 10 percent.

You are exposed to 'currency risk', also called 'foreign exchange' risk.

Now, what do you do about it?

You could, of course, ignore it, and hope that the investment performed well in the long term. Even better, however, is to reduce your exposure to this risk by making an investment that has the opposite behaviour.

You could, for example, buy some shares of a company that imports goods from that country and sells them to the public. As the value of the dollar rises, the imported goods become cheaper. In reality the importer would probably keep the prices constant and pocket a higher profit.

This, in turn, would increase the value of the shares and

would compensate for the reduction in value of your overseas shares. Another possibility would be to borrow some money in the currency of the other country, and use this money in your investment portfolio.

Banks can arrange foreign currency loans, although I would not recommend them for small investors. If the dollar rose, then the value of your overseas shares reduces, but the amount of the loan reduces as well, so overall you have less in the investment but also less to pay back on the loan.

I realise Kate that this all sounds very complicated. In practice you will not be able to cancel all your risks in this way, but it is something to be aware of.

When you are examining a potential new investment, look at your existing investments. If you already have three investments that reduce in value when interest rates fall, but the new investment increases in value when interest rates fall, then this is a point in its favour.

Something to keep in mind, Katie."

Kate looked exceedingly glum.

John laughed. "Don't worry, my dear. I want you to be aware of all the possibilities, and then you can choose the most relevant factors to consider. When we have finished our talks I will have given you a massive amount of information, and yet, the principles are simple."

Kate still looked flat.

"I tell you what, sweetie," John said as he hugged her, "When we have finished, I will give you a few simple rules. I will make them guidelines that a child could understand, and rules that you can apply in a few minutes. All you have to do is follow these few rules and everything will work out."

Kate brightened a little, and smiled at her grandfather. "John," she said expectantly, "do I really have to use everything that you have told me? I mean, hell, it's bloody complicated."

"Not at all, my dear. At different times, different factors will be relevant. As long as you have an overall picture of the things you should think about, that is the important thing."

John was unsure whether to continue, but a little colour had returned to Kate's face, so he decided to chance it. "Should we go on, Kate?"

"Of course," Kate said, straightening her back and taking a deep breath. "Hit me with it, grandfather."

"The next step is to look at all the variables in an investment.

With an investment property, for example, the main variables are the interest rate on the mortgage and the rent that you receive.

Every variable is a risk.

You should try and eliminate as many of the variables as possible. As well as making the investment more secure, it makes planning and budgeting much easier.

In this example, I would strongly recommend a fixed-rate mortgage. Choose a loan where the interest rate is fixed for, say, three years. The only exception to this is when rates are very high and you expect them to fall drastically. If they are at an average level, however, then it is better to choose a fixed rate loan.

Remember, Kate, you are investing in a house, you are not in the business of speculating on interest rates.

You may well pay slightly higher rates on the fixed mortgage compared to a variable mortgage. You are gaining safety and stability, and as we discussed you have to pay money to do this.

It is cheap insurance though if interest rates go through the roof.

Next, we have the rent.

This is harder to nail down, but offering a slightly lower rent than the market will attract reliable tenants who will take out long term leases and stay for extended periods of time. Overall, the more variables you can pin down, the more predictable and the safer your investment will be."

Kate was feeling much better. This was practical advice that she could understand.

"You may have realised that there are only two ways to

reduce a risk.

The first way is to pay someone else to take the risk for you.

This is the case with insurance, with choosing secure investments and with paying a premium for a fixed-rate loan.

The second method is to use careful planning. This is the case with choosing investments with counter-balancing risks, with spreading your money into different investments, and with choosing investments with a different mix of risks.

This brings me to remind you to insure all your assets. In some cases, such as a bank deposit, this cannot be done, but generally anything physical like a building can be insured.

This is essential Kate.

Finally, there are financial contracts called 'futures' and 'options' that can be used to reduce your risks. They are like insurance for financial events. For our purposes, the most relevant are contracts that insure against falls in the stock market, and contacts that protect you against movements in interest rates or changes in the dollar's value.

Like any form of insurance, you pay a premium and you receive protection for a certain period of time. One day, Kate, you may want to investigate these, but they are not necessary for the average investor.

One last tip on futures and options. While some people use them as insurance, the other side of the coin is the speculator, the person who takes on the risk in the hope of making a profit.

Never become involved in this Kate, it is a job for full-time experts.

Finally, as a reference, I will mention some of the more common risks.

Certain risks will apply to certain investments.

Remember, the rule is that anything that will reduce the value of your investment is a risk.

We have: changes in interest rates, falls in the share or property markets, physical damage, failure of an institution, lack of tenants in a rental property, failure of an individual company, changes in the value of the dollar, fraud and accident.

Note these last two points.

Most people, at some stage in their lives, will loose money due to fraud. They may not even realise it, if the fraud simply results in them getting a low return on an investment.

Accidents can also happen with lost paperwork and human or computer error. Stories of amazing coincidence and mistakes abound.

Overall, never forget the risk of fraud and accident.

It is present in every investment, even the safest ones possible. This is why you should never, under any circumstances, keep your entire wealth in one place.

4.7 Cycles and popularity: Contrarian investing

John sat on the park bench, staring thoughtfully into the distance. Kate leaned back and breathed in the cool air. It was amazing, she thought, how the weather in the park seemed more pleasant than the weather in the centre of the city, and yet they were adjacent to each other. Perhaps it was just the atmosphere of the place. John had been staring at the trees for some time, organising his thoughts. Suddenly, he spoke.

"Kate, today we have reached a milestone. We have not looked at any investments in detail yet, but we are finally ready to talk about strategies. This is where the real fun starts," he said with a boyish grin. "Shall I begin?"

"By all means, grandfather," Kate said brightly. Ninety-two years old and he looked like a kid in a candy store. Kate shook her head slightly, a bemused smile on her face. She couldn't believe that he was still like this at his age.

"The first investment strategy we will examine is called 'contrarian' investing. The name comes from the word 'contrary', which means opposite.

You should keep the contrarian strategy in mind when you buy and sell assets, however it should not completely dominate your thinking.

If you are building wealth for the long term, then the purchase of quality assets is more important than getting the timing right.

Now, contrarian investment basically means doing the opposite, buying when everyone else is selling. This may seem stupid, but let me explain how this works.

The three major investment markets; property, shares and interest-bearing, all move in cycles. Interest rates move in a distinct four year cycle, rising for two years and then falling for two years. They also have a very short term cycle of about a month, and a very long term cycle of many years.

200

It is relatively easy to determine whether rates are high or low compared to the past, and there are many articles in magazines and newspapers comparing the interest rates at the current time with rates in the past.

Overall, you should choose fixed-rate loans and mortgages when rates are fairly low. If rates are high, choose a standard variable-rate mortgage and wait for rates to fall.

This simple strategy can make a massive difference to your profit in the long term. When rates are high, invest your money in fixed-term deposits of a year or two duration. When rates are low, choose short term deposits so that you will not be trapped in a low interest rate investment when rates rise again.

When rates are low, you will often find that this is the same time that quality assets can be bought cheaply. This can be a good time to take some cash from low interest deposits and purchase some quality assets at cheap prices. This timing is due to the interaction of the cycles in the three markets, which we will explore shortly.

This brings me back to a very important point, and a cause of failure for many inexperienced investors.

The comments that I am about to make relate to the property market and share markets. We have already seen how a popular investment can rise well above its true value, and this is usually followed by a decline or crash in prices.

Most inexperienced investors follow the popular investments, the investments that their friends and colleges are purchasing. Unfortunately, this means that they often buy at the peak of the prices, and soon after that the prices decline and they are left with a loss.

This has been a cause of frustration and bitterness for many inexperienced investors. A wealthy investor once made the comment, that 'when a taxi driver advises you to buy shares, it's time to get out as fast as you can.'

By this he meant that when the average man in the street, such as an ordinary taxi driver, is excited about a particular investment, then it means that the prices have risen so drastically that they are ripe for a crash.

After the decline in prices, however, and a period of stability, prices inevitably rise again. The unwise investor is still bitter from his losses, and refuses to invest.

This is the point when the contrarian investor comes into play.

The contrarian investor buys assets after a decline in prices, and holds them until the prices rise again.

When everyone else is selling, and disillusionment is high, this is the time when the contrarian investor can buy quality assets at cheap prices.

As the prices rise, enthusiasm returns to the market, popularity increases, and prices continue to rise even higher. The cycle has come full circle, and everyone is buying once again. Suddenly, when everyone is buying and prices are high, the contrarian investor sells his assets.

He keeps the profit in cash, waits for the next decline in prices and starts the whole thing all over again. Kate, some people make a full-time system of this, but I suggest you simply include it as part of your overall strategy.

It is never easy to guess when a high or low point has been reached in an investment cycle.

The key point here is the basic principal, that successful investment sometimes requires going against the crowd, rather than following the same actions as everyone else.

One of your most difficult tasks is to outgrow the feeling that things will always be the same. During every boom, even seasoned professionals start to say that the good times are permanent and there will be strong growth for the long term future.

During bad times, there often seems to be no light at the end of the tunnel.

We are all affected by these feelings, and they are very hard to shake, but you must keep history in mind all the time.

As surely as summer follows winter, then winter follows summer again, every boom is eventually followed by a recession, and every recession by a boom.

It is only a matter of time. After each major crash or decline, there is a period of a year or two while things sort themselves out, and stability returns to the markets.

I suggest you wait at least this long before looking for quality assets. It can take another few years before prices start to rise strongly, but during this time the quality assets will start to produce a healthy income and slowly rise in value.

The fundamental cycle that drives all the markets is the cycle of economic growth and production.

This is affected by many things.

Inflation, for example, tends to rise for twenty years and then fall for twenty years in a regular pattern

. Interest rates, another important factor in the economy, rise and fall in different cycles.

Interest rates, the share market and the property market are all heavily tied to the economic cycle. As economic growth speeds up, the profits of companies increase, and so demand for shares increases and the share market rises. Much of the wealth that is poured into the share market comes from the sale of property, and so property prices remain steady or decline in real terms.

Time passes, and the price of shares reach high values.

Profit growth flattens out, so prices stop increasing or may even decline. Meanwhile, the price of property has fallen, and there are many good bargains around. Shares are sold to buy property, and so the share market declines and the value of properties increase.

When property is concerned, Kate, you must be very careful of the costs involved in buying and selling. Unlike shares, properties are large and expensive and cost a great deal to buy and sell. If you use property trusts, which we will look at later, then you may invest a small amount of money for a short time with ease.

If, however, you are buying a property yourself, then you should not consider selling it after a small rise in the market.

The costs are just too great.

If, however, there has been a massive rise, such as a 50

percent rise over two or three years, then you should consider selling as there will probably be many years of flat prices to come. Now, we have talked about the cycles in prices, but there is one more cycle that we should discuss.

This cycle is hard to measure, but it is the most important of all.

It is the cycle of popularity, the cycle of fashion.

All investments go in and out of fashion. There is usually a lag of a year or two before the public catches on to the change in an asset's true value. Take commercial property, in other words office buildings and other large properties, as an example.

After a strong rise in rents, commercial property will become a popular investment.

Prices will rise strongly.

Eventually, the economy will flatten out, new office buildings will be completed and demand and rents will stabilise.

Commercial property will remain popular for some time until it becomes clear to everyone that rents have stopped increasing. The popularity curve takes some time to catch up, and lags behind the curve in the true values by a year or two.

More time passes, and rents and demand may actually fall.

Commercial property then becomes very unpopular.

Finally, after more time, demand increases and rent will begin rising once again. People, however, are sceptical, and it will take a year or two of strong rises in rents before the popularity and prices begin to rise once again. The best time to buy an asset is when it has begun to return strong profits again but is still unpopular because of past declines.

This is the time when you can purchase asset with a strong future, a high yield, and a low price."

John looked across at Kate, wondering whether she was understanding his words. She looked a little confused. Finally, she spoke.

"How the hell do I work this all out, John?" she said. "I'm not an expert."

"True," her grandfather replied. "However, you don't need to be. All you need to look at is two things. First, has the investment had a bad time in the last few years, but does the future look better?

Reading the business section of any newspaper will soon give you an answer to this. Second, and most important of all, ask whether it has a good yield.

This one question will answer all the others for you. By definition, an investment which is strong but unpopular will have a high yield, that is a high income for its price.

An investment which is popular will always have a lower yield. This brings me to a very important point. Although you will need to have a reasonable idea of whether the prices are high or low compared to the past, do not try and pick the exact top or the exact bottom of the cycle.

Many people go wrong by waiting for the very top of the cycle, and then missing out altogether when prices decline.

No-one can predict the future and it is impossible to be sure when you are right at the top of the cycle. It is far safer to sell after a strong rise in prices, even if there may be a little more growth left in the cycle before the declines begin. As they say in the stock market, 'leave a little for the next man', and 'no-one ever went broke taking a profit'. It is better to sell after a healthy rise, than to try and wring the last little bit of profit from the investment.

Never sell an investment while the outlook continues to be positive, but always be aware that there will come a time when the outlook changes and it is time to sell.

The final point, is that even if you are wrong in your timing, as long as you buy an asset with a good yield, then you have a strong income which you can use for yourself or for purchasing other investments. Always, Kate, look for a reasonable yield when purchasing an investment. It is your best security against unexpected changes in prices. Be very sceptical of any investment where the yield is very low."

John stopped speaking, breathed deeply, and stared across the park. Minutes passed, and still he remained buried in a deep silence. Kate was resting, too, but as more time passed she became a little nervous. John was prone to these long silences, and she knew that he needed them, but at times she became uncomfortable. Many minutes had passed when John finally spoke. In a quiet voice, a strange voice Kate had never heard before, he began.

"There is a strategy, Kate, which I would like to tell you about. It must be combined with sensible purchases and wise management, and yet it adds a new dimension of its own. I do not use it myself, and few people would even recognise it as a strategy, but you should listen very carefully to what I say and learn from it."

Again there was a period of silence, then John spoke. "One night, many years ago, I was sitting alone in a bar, drinking. I was a young man then, and inexperienced in the ways of the world."

A tight smile spread over John's lips, but he continued with the story. "It was very late. I was very drunk, for I had many problems and I saw no way out of them. Many hours passed, and I sat in the corner, listening to the music and drinking.

Then, as I stared at the wall, thinking, an old man walked passed me. He must have seen my misery, and guessed that money problems had a lot to do with it. He walked over to my table, sat down and leaned towards me. I barely noticed he was there, but I could hear his breathing in front of me.

He, too, had been drinking, but he was enjoying himself and it was obvious that he had no problems that worried him, as mine worried me.

Softly, he spoke. "Do you want to know how to get rich?" he said. I was too drunk to answer, but I could hear his words clearly. He leaned towards me, almost whispering. "Never sell," he said.

John stopped speaking. Kate was perturbed. She didn't know what to say. John was still thinking back on his past, and there was a strange distance between them. She didn't understand, either, what he was trying to say. In the end it was he who broke the silence.

"I thought for a long time about the man's words, and finally the meaning of it dawned on me. Land exists forever, and land in a desirable place will still be valuable after a whole lifetime. Buildings last many years, and even when they finally need replacement, one can simply build a new house on the same land.

Companies, unlike individuals, are perpetual. Some companies have been in operation, in one form or another, for hundreds of years. Although companies sometimes go out of business and are wound up, this is rare for large, quality companies. One must remember, Kate, that selling something always involves costs. The very act of selling means that you loose a certain amount of your wealth in fees and expenses, and the sale of an asset often attracts various taxes as well.

The point that the old man was making it a good one. If you purchase high quality assets, then you may never need to sell them at all. You may patiently increase your portfolio of investments, using the income from the existing investments to purchase new ones.

You should give serious thought to the implications of the old man's words. I prefer a more active strategy myself, buying at various times and selling at others. This approach may lead to a higher profit in the long term, but also requires time and effort. The point about expenses is well made, too. Never forget to take tax and expenses into account when considering whether to sell an asset. The contrarian strategy involves selling assets when they are extremely popular and the price has risen well above the true value, but if the price rise has been modest and the asset is still of good quality then you may well be better off simply keeping it."

4.8 Gearing

Kate sat in silence and thought over the things John had said about Contrarian investing. She had to admit that he had a good point. Like most people, she assumed that a popular investment was popular for a good reason, and she would be inclined to invest in the same things as her friends and acquaintances. John, however, was suggesting the opposite. Although she could simply hold investments for many years and receive a good profit, she also saw the sense in selling when prices reached ridiculous peaks, and buying when an investment had returned to good profits but was still unpopular and cheap. She looked across at John, curious about what he would have to say next. "Go on, grandfather," she said. "What is our next strategy?"

John was pleased. He had feared an endless flurry of questions, but it seemed that Kate had accepted the sense in what he said and was ready to move on.

"Next, we have 'gearing'. This is something that all investors should be aware of, and a strategy that I suggest you incorporate into you own investment plan. Gearing simply means borrowing money and investing it. As long as the profit from the investment is higher than the interest on the loan, then you will make a profit on the overall deal.

Assume that you borrow money at 8 percent interest, and invest it for a return of 11 percent. Overall, your income is 11 percent of the amount, and your expenses are 8 percent of the amount, so your profit is 3 percent of the amount that you have borrowed. Now, the more you borrow, the greater your profit will be.

If you borrowed twice as much, then you would have a profit of 3 percent of the larger amount, and your profit would be doubled as well."

Kate looked extremely interested.

John smiled to himself. She was a very predictable woman in many ways.

"Of course," he continued, "there is a catch. Although gearing multiplies your profits, if things go wrong, it also multiplies your losses. In fact, the very name 'gearing' is an analogy with mechanical gears, in the sense that gears can multiply a force.

If you make a profit, then the greater your borrowing is, the greater the profit will be.

However, if you make a loss, then a large borrowing will lead to a large decline in your net assets. You may not realise this, Kate, but you have a highly geared investment at this very moment."

Kate looked at John in surprise.

"Most of us have to borrow money for our first home. You should treat your home, of course, as an investment, and it is the only significant investment that many people ever make.

Let us take an example where you have 10,000 dollars of your own money and borrow 90,000 from a bank. The house would, of course, cost 100,000.

Let's ignore all the expenses for simplicity. What you have done, is to invest some of your own money, and also borrow more money to invest in the house. You are gearing at a ratio of nine to one, since you have borrowed nine dollars for every one dollar of your own money.

This is a high level of gearing, and entails certain risks which you will soon see. Imagine that the value of the house rises from 100,000 to 110,000. If you sold the house and paid off the mortgage, you would have 20,000 left over. Since you started with 10,000, you would have doubled your money.

Now, the house only increased by 10 percent, but your profit was 100 percent. This illustrates how the gearing has multiplied your profit. If you have geared at twenty to one, then a rise of only 5 percent you have given you a 100 percent profit. I am sure you would agree that a 5 or 10 percent rise in a house's value is nothing unusual, and that a 100 percent profit on your own money would be something worth celebrating."

Kate was looking very excited now.

John's tone became cautionary as he continued. "We have not allowed for expenses or interest on the mortgage, so remember that in practice it would take a much larger increase to return the same profit. Still, the principle always applies. Now for the bad news."

Kate's excitement faded a little.

"Just as the gearing multiplies your profit, it also multiplies your loss if things go badly. Imagine that the house declines in value from 100,000 to 90,000 dollars. If you were to sell at this time, and pay off the mortgage, you would not have a single cent left to yourself.

Although the house has gone down in value by only 10 percent, quite a modest and possible decline, you would have lost the entire total of your money.

Your loss in this example would be 100 percent.

Things can become even worse, however. Should the value of the house fall by another 10 percent, then not only have you lost all your own money, but you are actually have negative net assets of 10,000 dollars!

It is important keep this in mind, Kate. This is why you should never gear highly if there is a chance that you could be forced to sell within a few years."

Kate pondered John's words solemnly. He had illustrated the concept clearly, and the potential for profits or loss was obvious.

"I have used an example of a house, as this is the most common example of gearing, and one that most people could relate to. Properly used, gearing can improve your profits for a modest increase in risk. The critical factor is the amount of borrowings. The higher the borrowings, the higher the risk and the higher the potential for profit.

As I have already said many times, though, we are not in the business of taking large risks. The wise investor takes modest, well-planned risks for a consistent increase in wealth, and avoids large risks altogether.

Companies also borrow money, to invest in equipment

and expand their operations. A rule thumb often used for businesses is one to one gearing, that is half the money is their own, and half is borrowed.

Depending on the company and the industry, it may be much higher or much lower, but this is a benchmark that is often used. I suggest that you follow the same approach, and borrow money on the basis of one dollar for each dollar of your own money.

If you have 10,000 to invest, then you should consider borrowing another 10,000 as well. You should only do this, of course, once you have gained some experience in investment, and feel comfortable that your portfolio of existing investments is solid and that you understand the risks and possibilities. This is quite a modest and safe level of gearing, and if you choose your assets well it should improve your profits significantly. Professional investors and companies sometimes gear at up to ten to one, so for every dollar they have, they borrow another 10 dollars.

This is clearly a high risk strategy, but with the potential for high returns. When we buy our first house, it is common to borrow up to 90 percent of the value of the property, so we are also gearing at a ratio of around ten to one.

In this case, however, it is virtually essential to keep the investment for at least a few years to allow the ups and downs in prices to smooth out into a steady long-term return. The gearing level of one to one is conservative and safe, and should increase the rate at which your wealth grows."

John paused to rest, and allow Kate time to absorb his words. This discussion was going well, which pleased him as it was an important one. Kate was deep in thought, considering the significance of the things John was telling her.

"Grandfather," she said at length, "what is 'negative gearing'? I have often heard this phrase, but I never understood what it meant."

"Negative gearing is a special case of the gearing I have just described. Say, for example, that you bought a house for

211

investment. Imagine that the interest on the loan was 8 percent a year, but the rent from the house was only 6 percent of the value of the loan.

Obviously, you will be going backwards. You are paying more in interest than you receive in rent. This is called 'negative' gearing, because you are making a loss each year.

Your cash flow is negative, your expenses are greater than your income. In a case like this, you would need income from another source, such as your job, to pay the extra amount for the interest on the loan. Now, you may ask, why would someone do this? The reason is that they expect the house to increase in value. If the income from rent was 6 percent, and the increase in value was 4 percent, then overall they are making 10 percent a year from the property. They still have to pay 8 percent for the loan, but they come out ahead in the end.

The major difference between this and previous examples relates to tax. Because, technically, they are making a loss in income each year, this can be claimed on the person's tax and it reduces the amount of tax they must pay. Negative gearing is simply an extreme example of gearing. It is used for two reasons.

First, there must be a very high level of gearing for this effect to come into play, such as a ten to one gearing level on an investment house. As we have seen, this has the potential for large profits.

The second reason it is used, is because it is very tax-effective, and the way the profits and taxes inter-relate means that the person ends up saving a significant amount in tax.

I must caution you with this Kate, and I will tell you a little about high levels of gearing. Any investment with a high level of gearing involves significant risks.

Anyone who claims otherwise is either foolish or deceptive. You may choose to gear yourself highly, and make large profits in the long term, but only if you can meet certain conditions. First, you must have a strong cashflow from other sources, such as your job or other investments. Ask yourself this: if you didn't receive any income from the investment, but you still had to pay all the expenses, could you survive comfortably? The best example is an investment property were you stop receiving rent, but still have to pay the interest on the mortgage.

Only if you can answer 'yes' to this question should you consider a high level of gearing. You must also consider the length of time you intend to hold the investment. As we have seen, even modest declines in values can have a dramatic affect on a highly geared investment.

Under no circumstances should you enter an investment like this if there is a chance that you will be forced to sell it at a bad time.

If you are able to hold on to it for many years, and ride out the bad times, and you also have plenty of spare income to cover the loans, then you could consider this type of investment. High levels of gearing, especially negative gearing, can be a good strategy for people on high incomes, as long as their income is secure. They may have to keep the asset for several years, while prices recover, until they can safely sell it.

During this time, disaster may happen, such as a fire or bad tenants. It is essential that they can survive without the rent for an extended period of time. Many people have lost money because they geared highly, and were forced to sell when prices were low because their income was not enough to meet the interest on the mortgage.

Make sure you never expose yourself to this risk Kate. Only gear to a level where you can meet all the expenses from your own income, and any rent or income you receive from the investment is simply a bonus. Now, my next comment on gearing relates to the loan itself.

The biggest variable here is the interest rate. I strongly suggest that you choose a fixed-rate loan, where the interest rate is fixed for several years.

The only exception to this is where rates are very high, and you expect them to fall. However, that would probably be a bad time to begin gearing anyway.

If you choose a standard variable rate loan, and interest rates rise strongly, then you will start to loose large amounts of money, and be forced to pay substantial sums from your own pay packet.

Although you may pay a little extra for the fixed rate loan, at least you will be assured that the rate will be reasonable for several years to come.

Remember, Kate, that if the profit from the property exceeds the loan interest, you make a profit, but if the loan interest is greater than the profit, you will loose money overall.

As well as avoiding the risk of rising interest rates, a fixed-rate loan makes budgeting and planning much easier.

The wise investor plans her expenses and income carefully. If you can secure a long term lease, and a fixed rate loan, then you can plan well ahead with relative safety.

One final comment on loans. You may also choose to take out an interest-only loan, instead on a standard loan where the repayments cover the principal as well as the interest.

The two loans are virtually the same for the first few years.

On a twenty-year mortgage with fixed payments, the first few year's payments are virtually all interest.

The final few years are virtually all principal payments, however this is irrelevant if you only keep the house for five or six years.

Interest-only loans make the calculation of profit a little easier, as you only pay the interest on the loan and the principal remains fixed. A standard loan is like an interest-only loan, where you also make small repayments on the principal as well.

You may wish to use this extra money in a different way in your investment portfolio.

After all, you have specifically gone to the trouble to borrow money for investment, so it would be pointless if you just pay it back again in a short time.

Overall, the choice is yours Kate, but I suggest that borrowing a fixed amount, and a fixed rate, and paying the interest only is a useful way to gear your investments and expand your portfolio.

John stopped to rest again, and breathed in the cool refreshing air. It was the perfect setting to teach, and the surroundings make him feel vibrant and alive. Had they been indoors, John doubted they would have come this far.

His energy would have been exhausted long ago. Kate was still listening carefully, so he decided to continue.

"My next comment relates to the asset that you purchase with the borrowed money. All the examples I gave you related to property, as this is the most common example of gearing.

Everyone who has bought their own home using a mortgage has geared an investment. It is just as possible, however, to gear with other assets as well.

Borrowed money can be used to purchase shares, as another example.

Shares have a higher return in the long run than property, but they are also more volatile. Whereas property prices tend to have sharp rises, and they stay steady or decline slowly, shares are subject to even sharper rises, but also significant drops.

Because of this you should not gear to the same level in shares as you would with property. Anything from one to one up to about three to one is more than sufficient for gearing with shares.

In fact, few bankers would be willing to lend you any more than this if the collateral was a portfolio of shares. In property, however, levels of ten to one are common. Some professional investors gear at ten to one or even twelve to one with shares, but this requires expert knowledge and nerves of raw steel."

The afternoon was growing old, and the sun was much softer now. Sunlight filtered through the huge trees in the park, and little shadows danced on the ground. It was John's favourite time of day, the late afternoon and early evening. He enjoyed the bright mornings and the wild winds during the middle of the day, but there was a gentleness to the soft evening light that appealed to him. The little children, with their excited games and high-pitched squeals had left for their homes, exhausted after an active day in the park. Soon they would move on to another topic, and then, perhaps, to home.

"One last thing on gearing, Kate. We should discuss some practicalities of borrowing.

I touched on this subject when we discussed your personal finance, but this is a whole new ball game, as you will be borrowing significant sums of money to invest for a profit.

First, we should recap the famous 'three C's' of credit and borrowing.

This is a saying in banking and credit circles which covers the three main factors that lenders look for in potential borrowers. They are 'Cash flow', 'Collateral' and 'Character'.

First and most important is the cash flow. Hopefully, the investment you are planning to purchase will produce an income of some description.

Properties produce rent and shares produce dividends.

If you are borrowing a modest amount, and using your own money for the rest, then the income from the investment may be sufficient to cover the interest on the loan. In this case, the lender will be fairly satisfied, and will have a quick check of your income to ensure that you have spare money in case something goes wrong.

If you borrow a great deal, however, then the income may not be enough to cover the loan interest. In this case, you are in a 'negative gearing' situation and you will have to pay the extra amount for the interest from your job or other income.

The lender will have a very close look at your income, to ensure that you have plenty of spare cash left over to pay the extra, and to cover the entire amount of interest if something goes wrong, like a period of time without tenants.

This should not be a major problem, however, as you should have done this analysis for yourself already. If the lender is unhappy with your situation, then there is a fair chance that they are correct and you are taking an unwise risk.

Second, we have 'collateral'. These are the assets that are used as security for the loan. In the case that you cannot continue with the loan repayments, the lender can sell the attached property or shares to recover the loan amount.

If you are borrowing a large percentage of the asset's value, or if the investment is something volatile like shares, the lender may be happier to see some extra assets as collateral.

Having extra collateral will also help you get a lower interest rate, because the lender sees you as a low risk and so is willing to offer a low rate for the loan. When you apply for a loan, be sure to list the combined value of everything you can possibly think of, even items you couldn't or wouldn't sell.

Finally, we have 'Character'. Lenders like to see a person with a stable history, without frequent changes in their jobs and homes. They like to see a steady income and assets in reserve. They like to see a sensible attitude, with a well-planned strategy.

They look for a general atmosphere of commitment, stability and responsibility. This is the image that you must project. Remember, bankers and lenders are human, and they are trying to assess you based on very little information. If you can show the lender a carefully thought out plan, then you are more likely to get a loan, and your interest rate may be lower.

4.9 Portfolio construction

Once again, Kate and John had taken a long rest. The afternoon light had begun to fade, and the air had become quite chilly. It was late autumn now, and winter would soon be upon them.

John looked forward to the sight of the pure white snow lying heavily on the tree branches, and children playing joyfully in their heavy winter coats.

Even so, he was always glad when spring came again, and the young green shoots burst through the freezing snow, little sparks of life battling bravely against the fierce elements.

All through the summer they would grow, until autumn came once more, and the seasons would give way to gentle warm afternoons and cool evenings.

"Kate," John said as puff of mist blew from his mouth, "we should be going soon. While we are still here, though, there is another important topic I would like to cover. This involves the planing and management of your investment portfolio."

Kate looked on in curiosity. Although she had little money of her own, after all these talks about investment she almost imagined that she actually had a whole range of different investments herself. Perhaps, one day, she would.

"Firstly, as I have said many times, the three primary investments are interest-bearing deposits, property and shares.

People invest in many other things, from gold to rare coins, but these all have problems

Later I will go through a few of the more common ones, and why you should avoid them.

Their main flaw is their lack of income, which gives then no intrinsic value at all, apart from the desire of other people to posses them. Desire, as you well know Kate, can be a fickle beast.

Overall, I very strongly recommend that you keep your

218

investments to the three major sectors. Other investments can be profitable, but you can also loose your money and the only consistent long-term performers are the three major sectors.

The only exception to this is where you have a serious hobby or career that earns money. You should treat that as a serious business, however, not as part of your investment strategy.

Now, the starting point for your portfolio should be one third in interest-bearing, one-third in property and one-third in shares. If you keep to this, then it's almost impossible to go wrong.

Over time you will be almost certain to make steady profits. Think of all the people you know who have lost money in investments, and I bet you that they never had anything close to this split between the sectors.

Overall, they probably had their money in a single investment, or at least in a single sector. During different times of your life, you will want to vary the proportions in each of the three areas. When you are in the early and middle part of your life, you should be looking to build your wealth in the longer term. You should lean towards the long term, growth investments such as property and shares.

If your income is strong, then you should also consider a modest level of gearing. Later in life, and after you have retired, income will become more important than growth, and you should lean towards the interest-bearing investments to provide you with a good income, and have less in property and shares.

Only do this when you really need to, though, as inflation and tax are usually much harsher on income-based investments than growth-based investments.

Growth investments like property and shares are a good shelter against tax and inflation, and you should keep a substantial proportion of your wealth in these forms unless you have a strong need for income.

I caution you, also, to always keep a minimum of 10 percent of your money in each of the three sectors. In this way, you will catch every boom in shares, property and interest rates, and make a profit from each.

By maintaining a minimum of 10 percent in each sector, you will avoid many problems.

Having money in short-term interest-bearing deposits will mean that you always have cash available when you need it, and having money in shares and property will protect your wealth from inflation and ensure you still have a decent income when interest rates fall through the floor.

My next point relates to gearing. During the early and middle stages of your life, when you are building your wealth, I suggest you invest all your money, plus an equal amount of borrowed money.

This is a modest gearing level of one to one.

Take an example where you have 30,000 to invest. Ideally, should borrow another 30,000 for a total of 60,000. You could then invest 20,000 in interest-bearing instruments, 20,000 in shares and 20,000 in property. Depending on the opportunities that arise, you will not be exactly equal to one-third in each sector, but you should use this as a benchmark and be wary of moving too far away from it.

On the subject of borrowing, some people would claim that you should take your money from the interest-bearing deposits and use it to pay off the loan. On the surface, they would have a valid argument, as the interest you pay on the loan would normally be higher than the interest you receive on your deposits.

The difference between the two rates is the profit margin for the bank. However, there are several flaws in this argument.

First, you would no longer have ready access to cash. It is essential to have a fair proportion of your wealth in an easily-accessible form, to handle any unexpected problems or opportunities that may arise.

Second, this argument does not allow for the timing of the rises and falls in interest rates. You should always take out fixed interest rate loans when rates are low, and variable rate loans when rates are high.

In this way, over time, your average interest rate can be lower than a person who simply uses a standard variable-rate loan.

The opposite applies to deposits. When rates are high, put some of your money into long term deposits of a few years' duration. Not all of it, of course, as you may not be able to access this money until the term is completed.

With some investments we will look at later, such as bonds, you can sell the investment and retrieve your money, but you will suffer a loss if interest rates have risen.

Overall, then, I suggest your starting point should be using half your own money and half borrowed money, with one third in interest-bearing, one third in property and one-third in shares.

This is a safe and secure long-term strategy. If you want to spend a little more effort and increase the returns, then we can incorporate a bit of contrarian thinking into our strategy.

Read the papers, and you will soon get a good picture of what stage the three markets are in their respective cycles. You can decrease your investments in the markets that have risen strongly and are close to their peak, and increase the investment in markets that have had a rough time but are gaining steadily in strength.

Perhaps you may want to move to 10 percent fixed interest, 30 percent property and 60 percent shares at one stage, and a few years later move to 20 percent fixed interest, 60 percent property and 20 percent shares.

Don't worry about how you would do this in practice, as it is quite easy and I will explain some ways to do this later. It is your choice, Kate, as to how much effort you want to put into managing your portfolio, and whether you are willing to increase your risk slightly by putting more money into some sectors and less into others.

Whatever you do, as long as you keep substantial amounts in all three sectors then you can't go too far wrong.

Now, I have some comments on diversification. We have

spoken about spreading your money into the three sectors, but you should go even further and spread your money into several actual investments in each sector. Your investment in the stockmarket should be spread into at least three or four companies, as your investment in property should be spread into several forms of property investment.

More on this later.

Within each sector, there are a great variety of sub-sectors. Let's look at property first. We have 'residential property', with houses, flats and other residences, from inner suburbs to outer suburbs and low price brackets to high price brackets.

Even here there is a great variety.

Do not be fooled, either, into thinking that their prices all rise and fall together.

Prices in each group are related, but they all rise and fall in their own different patterns. As well as residential property, we have 'commercial property' such as large office buildings, 'retail property' such as shopping centres and 'agricultural' property such as farms, orchards etcetera.

Through trusts and companies, even the small investor like you can participate in all these different sectors.

In the stock market, we have mining companies, both large and small, we have banks and insurance companies, manufacturers, oil companies, retail stores, service organisations and shares in every other type of business imaginable.

The variety is endless.

Overall, then, once you built up a reasonable store of wealth, say a year's salary, then you should invest it in a dozen different investments. Try and spread your money into the different sectors within the property market and the stock market, so that you have the widest spread of investments possible.

Always, of course, always look for high quality, reliable investments. Avoid the speculative areas like small mining companies and new holiday resort developments.

Stable, long-term performers are the assets you are looking for."

John paused for few deep breaths. They were progressing faster than he had expected, and there was still a substantial amount of daylight left in the afternoon.

"When you choose your different investments, don't simply consider the income and profit that they provide. You should also consider other factors. Try and balance out the risks, as we spoke about previously.

If you invested in all three sectors in a foreign country, for example, then you would be heavily exposed to changes in the value of the dollar and it is unwise to be too exposed to any single risk.

Look for flexibility as well. Property trust units and shares can be sold in a single day, whereas a two-year term deposit may be locked away for two whole years.

Sometimes, the flexible or inflexible investments are not the ones that you may expect.

Look for a mix of volatile and stable investments. Shares provide the greatest long-term profits of the three sectors, but they are also the most volatile.

If you have a mix of investments, then you will benefit from the high returns, and you will not be forced to sell at a bad time as you will have access to money from other, more stable sources.

The first thing you should do, Kate, is to make a list of your investments and your investment loans. Do not include items like a car or a boat, as these decrease in value and so they cannot be considered investments. Your family home, however, should increase in value and is most definitely an investment.

Any loans that you use for investment should also be listed. This list is your investment portfolio, the assets and liabilities that are part of your investment strategy.

Once again, only include items that will increase in value. Loans that you take out for a car, boat or other leisure and personal items should be ignored.

They are not part of your investment strategy, they are part of your spending and your personal finance.

As we spoke about earlier, loans for spending and personal items should be avoided as much as possible. The general rule is that if the loan is used to purchase assets that rise in value, then include this loan in your description of your investment portfolio. If you rent a home, then the process of listing your investment portfolio is relatively straightforward.

You will have a list of assets that increase in value, and a list of loans that were used to purchase them. Your personal finances, which are separate from your investment strategy, contain all the assets that decrease in value, and the loans used to purchase those assets.

In your personal finances, use loans as little as possible. Once you buy a home with a mortgage, however, the picture may become a little muddier. Your family home may be subject to special tax rules, and does not fall into the same category as an investment asset or property.

Interest on investment loans in treated as a business expense, and so is tax deductible. Income from investments is added to your tax, interest on loans is subtracted, and you pay tax on the difference.

The difference is your actual profit, the increase in your wealth and the amount of money that you have available to spend.

However, interest on the mortgage for your own home is not tax deductible, which means that you have to pay the whole lot yourself, rather than is being tax deductible.

The next result of this, is that if you have a very large mortgage, then the best investment you can probably make is to make extra payments onto the loan.

The quicker you reduce your loan, the more interest you will save. There is a flaw in this strategy however.

If you channel all your savings into paying off your house, you have broken the golden rule of spreading your money around.

You are completely exposed to the changes in property prices. Things may work out all right if prices rise, but if prices fall and you are forced to move for unexpected reasons, then you may loose all your hard-earned money.

You will also, of course, miss out on any boom in share prices, which rise by thirty to 50 percent a year quite often.

Overall, I suggest the following strategy for someone with a large mortgage and few other assets. Save every cent you can, and pay half the money on to the mortgage and invest the other half.

While this may not be the optimum strategy from a purely mathematical point of view, I suggest that it is the best compromise between profit and flexibility.

Now, let us consider a person with little or no mortgage on their home.

What they have is a large property asset. This should be listed in their portfolio of investments, as it will increase in value and is probably their largest store of wealth.

Along with their other investments, they will probably be heavily weighted towards property.

When your portfolio is unbalanced, you should consider moving closer to the one-third split, with one third of your wealth in interest-bearing, one-third in property and one-third in shares.

A person who owns most or all of their home has a valuable asset, which can be borrowed against to invest in the other two sectors. They should do this, and move as close to the one-third split as possible, with half their own money and half borrowed money.

Remember, Kate you should keep at least 10 percent of your wealth in each of the three sectors, and the closer you are to the one-third split, the more stable and reliable your profits will be.

Now that you have a list of your investment assets and loans, you should list the income and expenses associated with each.

Your main cost will be interest, particularly if you have

taken out a large mortgage for an investment property.

Most of you investments will produce income, such as rent from houses, interest on deposits and dividends from shares. Now look at the worst case scenario, where your sources of income dry up but your expenses continue.

Should there be a fire in your investment property, for example, it may be many months before you have tenants in the property again and you are receiving rent.

Companies may have a bad year, and may cut their dividends to a low amount or perhaps cancel them entirely.

Fixed term deposits will provide guaranteed income for a period of time, but this does not last forever, and interest rates can fall dramatically.

Make sure that this worst-case scenario would not cause you serious problems.

If it would, then you may have borrowed too much money and you should use some investments to reduce your debt.

Now, looking once more at your income and expenses, make sure you are comfortable with the proportions.

A person on a high income may choose to negatively gear, and keep a portfolio where the expenses are greater than the income.

In retirement, the opposite applies and the portfolio should be structured to maximise income.

In short, the level of income is dependent on two things.

First, the greater the borrowing, the less income that is available to the investor, as interest costs will be higher.

Second, leaning towards the growth investments, shares and property, will reduce income, whereas leaning towards income investments, such as fixed-interest, will increase income.

Choose the balance that best suits your current needs. Look carefully at the possibilities, too, because in certain periods of history, particularly at the end of recessions, shares and property actually return more income than interest-bearing deposits, not less.

4.10 Protecting your wealth

Kate sat patiently on the park bench, watching the soft light flicker through the trees and the ducks swimming around on the lake. Spending time with John required a certain amount of patience, as he was a person who needed frequents rests from speaking,

Somehow, Kate believed that it was not just his age that made him this way. When John spoke, he put all his energy and thoughts into the conversation.

John was not a man who was prone to idle chatter.

Everything he said, he meant, and when someone asked him a question, he thought seriously before answering. This could be frustrating at times, for Kate was a woman who greatly enjoyed conversation. Still, she had learnt to grant John his rests, and in some way she had even understood his words more deeply through having time to contemplate what he said.

John watched some small animals playing by the lake. Their fur was soft and their tails bushy, their faces petite and their claws sharp. They danced and jumped, rolled over, and played about with each other. It was a beautiful sight. John was very happy, relaxed and peaceful as he watched the little beasts scurry about. He wished there was no need to speak, but he had promised to help Kate, and their journey was only now reaching the point of practical advice. John had begun to teach Kate, in the hope of helping her improve her life, and he was not prepared to leave the job half finished.

"Kate," he said eventually, "there is an important topic which I have been considering, and now seems as good a time as any to bring it up. I wish to speak about protecting your wealth."

"Go on, John," Kate said with encouragement. This sounded like and important and useful topic.

"There are two aspects to protecting your wealth.

First, we have the obvious risks such as theft, fraud, failed investments and legal conflicts.

Secondly we have the ravages of inflation, tax and social change, which can whittle away your wealth as surely as the world's finest cat-bugler.

Let me look at the second type of problem first, as the solution to these lies in the things that we have already discussed. There is a saying that is applied in many fields, from the intelligence of old people to the maintenance of industrial machinery.

The goes like this: 'use it or loose it'.

Kate, I cannot emphasise strongly enough, that if you simply sit on your wealth, and do nothing with it, then you will loose it year by year. Your saving and sacrifices will come to nothing. All wealth in cash or interest-bearing investments is subject to inflation. Although interest-bearing investments may return a profit at times, the combination of inflation and tax make it almost impossible to maintain the value of your wealth if it is kept in the form of cash.

Before worrying about profit, your first battle is to ensure that you are not going backwards, and that your wealth is not actually reducing in value. The solution to inflation is to store your wealth in non-cash forms, such as ownership of assets like shares and property.

As the saying 'use it or loose it' goes, only the person who takes an active approach to managing their wealth can hope to maintain and increase it.

My next point relates to the risks of particular investments. When you consider an investment, try to determine who bears the ultimate risk if things go wrong.

Sometimes it is obvious, in simple cases like owning a property, where you bear all the risk of failure yourself. Other times, however, the answer might surprise you. Sometimes institutions, such as banks, offer products like investment trusts to their customers.

The investment product has the same name as the bank, but this can mean little more than coincidence. One would assume that the bank would guarantee the investment, but often this is not the case. In many cases, the investment is totally self-contained, and it could quite possibly fail while the bank was still operating profitably.

With products offered though institutions, you should find out who is actually guaranteeing the investment if things go wrong.

In some cases, no one really knows the answer to this question, and there have been lengthy court battles about which party is responsible for which parts of a failure.

Needless to say, all the parties deny responsibility for the failures and refuse to pay the investors any money. This is not a major reason to reject an investment, but it is important to have your eyes open and be clear about what the risks are and where the buck stops if the whole thing falls apart

Now, on to the more practical aspects of protecting your wealth.

As I have said many times, insure all your major physical assets. Insure your income with 'disability income insurance'.

Always remember that your skills, labour and time are your greatest money-earning assets. Be organised in your business affairs, and keep records of everything that you do.

Some of us choose to have a relaxed and dis-organised attitude to our lives, but when it comes to money management and investment, self-discipline is essential.

If an organised and business-like attitude is not taken then disaster has a ready foothold in the door.

I have spoken about the need to be responsible for your own financial affairs, and the dangers of relying on someone else to manage these things for you. Many people have placed their entire affairs, records and papers with a trusted accountant or adviser, only to find that the person betrays their trust.

Often the embarrassment and shame that they feel is even worse than the monetary loss itself. Even if the person is honest and trustworthy, they may make poor investment decisions or mistakes that you are not aware of.

Always keep all records, receipts and decisions to yourself, never let another person do these things for you.

All business transactions should be in writing, even agreements with family or friends. This may create a little embarrassment at first, but it is not necessarily a sign of mistrust.

Recording agreements in writing ensures that everyone is clear as to what the agreement is, and what the conditions and rules involved are.

Studies have shown that people often come to a verbal agreement, and both believe that they have agreed to completely different things.

The only way to be clear, formal and organised about agreements is to put everything in writing.

This brings me to a very important point about protection. Although it is important to put everything in writing, you must also be aware of how the modern legal system operated.

The simple truth of the matter is that the famous quote, 'possession is 9/10th's of the law', has never been more true than in the modern world.

Consider an example where a man has an old, broken down lawn-mower. His neighbour offers to repair it, and puts a great deal of effort into the repair and renovation task.

Finally, the lawn mower is restored and in working order. Now, the dispute arises. The neighbour claims that the lawnmower is now rightfully his, as it was completely useless before and has been repair with his expense and effort.

The first man, however, claims that the lawnmower still belongs to him, and the fact that the second man offered to fix it for free is irrelevant. Now, Kate, listen very carefully to what I tell you. In this situation, whoever has the lawnmower physically in his possession, has at least 9/10th's, that is 90 percent of the advantage.

In the modern world, there is simply no way to settle disputes quickly and cheaply.

For the average person, the legal costs are often greater than the amount of money being disputed.

It can take years to settle even minor disputes. This is very, very important Kate. If something is rightfully yours, or you have a signed piece of paper that proves a certain fact, this is of limited use if the other person has physical possession of the item.

Never give something to a person unless you receive a receipt at the same time.

When you are trading something, try not to give anything away on the promise that the other half of the deal will be completed shortly.

Even written proof is useless if the other person disappears.

I do not wish to scare you, but simply to encourage you to be careful.

Never be too trusting, and remember that the person who has physical possession of the money or item has a great advantage. Try and ensure that it is you, Kate, and not someone else who has this advantage. Once you have handed over the money, you have lost much of your power, so check out as much as possible before you actually sign on the dotted line."

John paused for a short rest. Kate looked a little pale, and he hoped he had not spooked her too much.

It was important, though, that she did not reply too heavily on formality and legal rights, and understood the practicalities of dealing with people and getting what she wanted.

If she was careful in her business dealings, then many nasty problems could be avoided.

"Finally, I can summarise the protection of your wealth in three basic rules. Manage your affairs yourself, be careful and cautious in your business dealings, and invest your money wisely."

5 *Specifics*

5.1 Interest-bearing investments

John sat on the park bench in stony silence.

Autumn had long since passed, and winter had fallen on the park. Snow fell softly, and Kate pulled her coat tightly around her to keep out the cold.

Although the air was very cold now, Kate and John continued to meet in the park. Winter brought its own character to the park, and small animals scurried through the snow around the edge of the lake.

Eventually John spoke. His voice was very quiet now, and Kate worried that their discussions were talking a heavy toll on her grandfather.

"Kate," John said at length, "we have finally come the point of discussing specific investments.

First we have the interest-bearing investments. These are the most familiar investments to many of us, and the simplest to understand. There are a great variety of interest-bearing investments to choose from, but they are all essentially the same.

You are simply loaning your money to a person or organisation, and receiving interest for doing so. Most of the money invested on an interest-bearing basis is done for a fixed term and at a fixed interest rate.

This includes examples like a two-year term deposit with a bank, or a three-year government bond. This sector is often called the 'fixed-interest' sector, rather than the more general name of the 'interest-bearing' sector.

Fixed term investments fall into two categories. Firstly, there are the 'non-tradeable' deposits like bank term

232

deposits.

Once you commit your money to these investments, you cannot get it back until the end of the term. There are often clauses to allow the money to be paid out in cases of extreme hardship, but these are very rarely exercised.

In general, once you have committed your money then it remains there for the full term of the deposit. This may cause you problems, as the term may be several years long and your circumstances may change unexpectedly.

The other type of fixed term investments is the 'tradeable' contracts. This includes government bonds and company debentures. These investments may be treated in exactly the same way as a term deposit with a bank, and the money can be left on deposit until the term expires.

However, there is a way to get your money back early if you wish to. Although the party who originally borrowed the money, for example the government, will not pay it back early, you can sell the bond or debenture to another investor.

In fact, there is an active trade in the major interest-bearing investments like government bonds. Institutions will often buy and sell ten-year government bonds on a daily basis, and may only keep them for a month or two, rather than the full ten years.

Bonds and other interest-bearing contracts are may be traded on stock exchanges, in the same way that shares are bought and sold.

Your stockbroker is the person to talk to if you wish to sell some government or company bonds. There is an important issue that you must be aware of, however.

Virtually all of these interest-bearing contracts have a fixed interest rate. Imagine that you invest in a ten-year government bond with a 6 percent interest rate. A year later, you may need the money for something else so you decide to sell the bond to another investor.

However, during the year, interest rates have dropped to 4 percent. You have in your possession a bond, a commitment from the government, to pay 6 percent interest for another nine years.

Since rates have fallen to 4 percent, investors would be very keen to purchase your bond.

Because the rate on the bond is so high, they would be willing to pay more money for the bond than the amount you initially invested.

As well as the interest you received during the year, you can actually sell the bond for a higher price than you paid for it, and make a profit.

Unfortunately, the opposite situation can also occur. Imagine that rates have risen instead of falling. Your bond has a rate of 6 percent, but the new bonds being issued carry a rate of 8 percent.

Investors will not be willing to pay the full 'face value' of the bond, which is the amount you originally invested, as they can invest the money at a higher rate by buying a new bond.

You can, however, sell the bond for less that you paid for it.

The bigger the change in interest rates, the larger the difference in the price.

If rates rise strongly, then you may loose money overall, even after the year's interest is taken into account.

Always remember, though, that it is your choice to sell, and you can always keep the bond until it expires and treat it like a normal bank term deposit."

John stopped talking to take a few deep breaths, and check that Kate was still listening. She was.

"It is also interesting to note, that if you purchase a fixed-interest bond or debenture, and later consider selling it, then you will make a profit if rates have fallen, rather than rising.

When your money is deposited at call, you have a higher profit when rates rise and are high, rather than falling.

There is another distinction between the different fixed-interest investments that I should mention. When we come

234

to the practical aspects of investing your money, there are two ways the paperwork is handled.

The first is called a 'bearer' investment, and the second is known as an 'inscribed' investment. The name 'bearer' comes from the fact that the bearer of the contract, in other words the person physically holding the paper, is the one who owns the investment. In this way, 'bearer' investments are like a cash note.

If the note is lost or stolen, then you have lost your money. The contract simply states that the 'bearer of this contract will be paid a certain amount of money on a certain date.'

If you invest money in this type of contract, Kate, I strongly suggest that you keep the paperwork in a secure place such as a safety-deposit box in a bank or a 'clearing house' which is created for this purpose.

The second type of contract, 'inscribed' investments, is named after that fact that the organisation borrowing the money from you has 'inscribed', or 'written' your name down in a central register. Your name is recorded as the owner of the contract. The paperwork you receive is simply a record of the transaction, and has no value of its own. If the paperwork is lost or stolen there is no harm done, as you are still recorded as the owner of the investment.

Shares in companies are recorded in this way. Now that we have covered some of the practicalities, we should talk a little about trusts.

We have spoken about investment trusts, and how they can be used to pool investor's money together for investments such as purchasing a large office building.

There are several types of trust that relate to interest-bearing investments. First, we have the 'cash management' trust. These trusts go by various names, but they are all designed for short term deposits of money.

Interest is calculated daily or weekly, and often paid monthly. Some trusts even have chequebook and electronic transfer facilities. The investor's money is pooled together and invested in short-term fixed-interest investments, often ninety-day government notes.

Contracts with a term of less than twelve months are often called 'notes', rather than 'bonds'. These trusts have been a great success, and rightfully so. They have low administrative overheads, in contrast to bureaucratic organisations like banks which must charge large amounts to cover their huge expenses.

Cash management trusts allow the small investor to access interest-bearing products that are otherwise only available to professional investors and institutions.

In theory, they are actually safer than a bank, as all the money is invested in very short-term, highly secure investments. Banks, on the other hand, lend out your money to the general public on long-term mortgages, and hope that their customers do not want their money back in a hurry.

I recommend these trusts as a vehicle for storing your short-term cash, Kate, but of course you should never break the golden rule and put all your money in a single place. As well as 'cash management' trusts, you should also know about 'bond trusts'.

As the name suggests, these trusts invest in bonds of varying terms. As they are a medium-term investment, there will be some fees to pay, but these are usually a minor expense.

We discussed earlier how bonds may be brought and sold, and there is a very active trade in government bonds and other fixed-interest securities. Prices rise and fall on a daily basis, in line with changes in interest rates and expectations of the future.

The management of the trust will buy and sell bonds daily, in the hope of making a profit from movements in the prices. They also operate with many different types of bonds, and some trusts even invest in bonds from foreign countries. Overall, the managers of these trusts are reasonably successful, and you can often receive an extra one or two percent interest rate from investing in a bond trust, compared to buying the bonds themselves.

Investigate the various trusts that are available, Kate, and you may wish to incorporate one or two as part of your portfolio. Although the underlying investments are highly secure, being guaranteed by a government, bank or large corporation, there is some potential for volatility in the returns due to the rises and falls in the value of the bonds.

Overall, though, you can expect a steady return that is in line with current interest rates. One final point on bond trusts, and selling bonds in general, relates to the changes in interest rates.

Obviously, when rates are steady and high, bonds will return high rates, and when rates are steady and low then bonds will return low rates of interest.

However, we saw previously how a fall in interest rates leads to a profit on a bond. Because of this, when interest rates fall steadily over a long period of time, the profits of bonds and bond trusts will be boosted, and when rates rise steadily for a long period of time, the profits will be cut.

The end result of this is that you should invest in bond trusts when rates are high.

When they fall in the future, you will maintain a healthy profit from the investment."

Kate considered John's words. She had imagined that this would be the easy part, the discussion on interest-bearing investments. Like everything else John had described though, it was both simpler in principle and more complex in practice than she had imagined. "Go on, grandfather," Kate said encouragingly.

"I began with fixed-term, fixed-interest rate deposits, as these are the ones where most of the money is deposited, and most of the trading takes place.

There are, of course, the more familiar, variable-rate products such as standard bank accounts. Any investment, Kate, where you earn interest, is simply a loan from you to another party."

This made Kate feel a bit better. Banks were something

she could understand.

John watched his granddaughter, and he sensed the thoughts that were passing through her mind.

"I have mentioned several alternative investments, and there are some more we will cover in a moment, but don't panic Kate. I will tell you about all the major interest-bearing investments, but all you need to understand initially is how to put money in the bank."

Kate brightened significantly. Although it was true that she spent a lot more time taking money out of the bank than putting money into it, the concepts behind a term deposit and an ordinary savings account were things that she could readily understand.

"Interest-bearing investments are either for a fixed term, such as a term deposit or a government bond, or at call, like a savings account or a cash management trust. I suggest, Kate, that you initially use the banks, and keep some money at call and some money in term deposits.

You should, however, investigate the other products over time as the interest rates are better and they are more flexible."

Kate was reassured now, and keen to hear what else her grandfather had to say. "Go on, John," Kate said with enthusiasm.

"There is another type of interest-bearing trust I should mention, but one which you should treat with caution.

This is the mortgage trust. As the name suggests, money is pooled together and loaned out for mortgages on property. As there are large amounts of money involved, the mortgages are usually for office buildings, hotels and other large properties.

I caution you with mortgage trusts because they suffer the same fundamental flaw as banks, but they have far less public confidence than banks to act as a buffer in hard times.

The money is lent on loans with terms of several years, however investors require access to their funds at short notice.

This problem, and some very shady operations, has lead to problems in some mortgage trusts.

There are some good ones around, however, so you should not discount them entirely. Interest rates can also be good, as the risk is higher with mortgages than with government and corporate bonds and so rates are also higher.

If you invest money in one of these trusts, make sure it is a small part of your portfolio and watch it closely.

Look for a trust with slow but steady growth over several years, and managed by a reputable organisation with operations in other areas as well. This brings me to give you some special advice about trusts, banks and other financial institutions.

Sometimes you will come across an investment or organisation that has had very rapid growth over the previous few years. Treat this as a strong warning sign Kate.

In business, particularly in finance, there are ways that one can achieve rapid growth in the short term by sacrificing the long-term health of the company.

This high growth leads to praise and large bonuses to the people running the organisation, and attracts many new customers. The public loves a winner, and people assume that a company that grows strongly is successful and good at what it does.

Sometimes, this is true, but more often it is the result of some very damaging practices. A few years down the track, things fall apart at the seams and the management is long gone with their bonuses in their pockets."

Kate was intrigued, and listening carefully.

"I will give you an example from a manufacturing company. A successful man was offered the position of chief executive of a medium sized manufacturing company.

The company was very profitable and had grown strongly over the past year. The salary was excellent, and the man was very pleased to be offered the job. He readily accepted, although it seemed too good to be true.

Unfortunately, it was. When he began the job, the man was told that he would have a hard time filling the previous chief executive's shoes.

Although the previous man had only been in the job for a year, he had greatly improved profitability and had left the company with the respect and thanks of the board.

As he began learning about the company, however, the new man discovered the truth of the situation. The previous man had simply cancelled most of the maintenance on the machinery.

Maintenance is a major expense for a manufacturing company, and so the profits improved immediately.

However, a year or two later, the machinery began to break down, and the company's most valuable assets were in a serious state of disrepair.

By this time, however, the previous chief executive had moved on to greener pastures."

John turned to Kate. She was thinking deeply.

"This is an extreme example, Kate, but unfortunately this sort of thing happens all the time. In the finance industry, the most common example is the use of high-pressure sales methods to sign up as many clients as possible.

This leads to rapid growth in the size of the organisation, but many of these clients are low-quality clients who can't pay their debts and don't have any money.

The rapid expansion also puts a severe strain on the infrastructure of the organisation. Its training methods, management structure and personnel practices all go out the window in the mad flurry to keep up with the new business.

The end result, Kate, is that organisations who have several years of very rapid growth often have several years of very difficult times afterwards, with shaky foundations and poor profits.

If you come across an organisation that boasts of rapid growth, such as doubling in size over two or three years, then treat this as a warning sign, not an advantage.

The best organisations and investments are ones that have consistent and steady growth, through good times and bad, rather than rapid expansion followed by problems."

Perhaps she was naive, Kate thought to herself, but she had not believed that people would be able to get away with the things that John was suggesting. His implication that it was not only possible, but actually common, was worrying.

John's strategy of spreading one's money around was looking more sensible every day.

"If there is one rule of finance, one factor that has applied since the dawn of time, Kate, it is this: everyone wants to borrow money.

Banks, governments, individuals, companies and every group you can imagine borrow money.

There are limitless possibilities for people who want to lend their money in return for interest. Remember, though, that they all come down to the same thing. I will try and summarise the most common examples into a few categories.

Governments issue bonds and notes, with wide ranging terms. Ninety days, one year, three years and ten years are common examples. These are fixed-interest, fixed-term investments, and are obviously extremely safe.

Banks offer accounts with money at call, and fixed-term deposits of various terms.

Companies issue 'debentures', which are the same as bonds. These are fixed-rate, fixed-term investments. Bonds and debentures can be traded on stock exchanges, so you can retrieve your money early and make a profit or a loss. Companies also issue 'unsecured notes'. These, again, are fixed-term, fixed-rate investments. The only difference between debentures and unsecured notes comes into effect if the company fails and is liquidated.

Debenture holders have first rights to the assets of the company to get their money back, and holders of unsecured notes may only be paid back after the debenture holders have been repaid.

In other words, the holders of unsecured notes do not have any specific security from the company's assets.

Because of the higher risk, unsecured notes have a slightly higher interest rate than debentures. Finance companies are in the business of borrowing and lending, and they also issue debentures and unsecured notes.

Various other organisations, such as insurance companies, offer bonds and deposit-based investments.

Investments in these different organisations are sometimes subject to special tax rules, so check this out carefully before deciding if they will fit into your portfolio. Finally, we have the trusts, the cash-management, bond trusts and mortgage trusts.

These are all useful as part of a portfolio, especially the cash-management trusts. There is one final avenue of interest-bearing investment which you may like to consider. This involves lending money to family and trusted friends. Effectively, you are cutting out the middle man, which is the bank. This can cause tensions within relationships, and there is the risk that the person will be unable or unwilling to repay the loan, so this can often cause more harm than good.

There are times, however, when the benefits can be very significant. If you do this Kate, then I suggest that you take a very business-like approach. Put everything in writing.

Stress that this is not a sign of mistrust, but simply to make sure that the terms of the agreement are clear to everyone involved.

This will help to avoid any tension and misunderstandings.

Be clear about the interest rates, when the payments will be made, and set a fixed date for repayment.

Never leave things open-ended, Kate, such as not specifying a date for repayment. This causes tension and embarrassment when the parties cannot agree on the repayment of the money."

5.2 Stock market

John's voice was barely a whisper now, but he continued speaking.

"The time has come," he said, "to talk about the stock market in detail."

Kate grimaced. She had not been looking forward to this. Ever since John had identified the three major sectors as property, shares, and interest-bearing investments, Kate had been dreading the discussion on shares.

She could understand a bank account, and there was nothing complicated about a term deposit. Property, too, was not too daunting, as she had bought her own home already, and the concept of buying a house as an investment seemed straightforward.

Shares, however, were a mystery to her. She had always relegated the share market to the same category as mythical flying beasts and fairy stories, a place where spectacular profits and losses were made, and only the brave or foolish dared to tread.

A place of mystery and intrigue, and a place best left well alone. She knew, however, that John would be the last person to accept this view, so she gritted her teeth and remained silent.

"On the whole," John said as his voice regained some strength, "the public has a very poor understanding of shares and the stock market. This is sad, as it is actually very simple in concept, and properly used will return good profits with high security. Let me dispel a few of the myths about shares for you Kate. First, the stock market is not just for the wealthy. In fact, it is far simpler for the ordinary person to invest in shares than it is for them to invest in property. If you saved one month's salary, you would have enough money to buy some shares and begin your investment in the stock market."

This surprised Kate a little, as she already had more than

a month's salary put away for a rainy day, but she never imagined that she had enough money to be a serious investor.

"You do not need any great skill, knowledge or effort to invest in shares. If you simply spread your money into half a dozen of the best-known companies, the household names that you hear about every day, then you are likely to receive a good return over the long term.

A little knowledge, however, may improve the returns and make your investments more secure, so I will describe the essentials shortly.

Many people have the view that the share market is a gambling casino, where your chances of profit and loss are based on luck.

This is completely false.

There are two causes for this misconception. First, the prices of shares are subject to large rises and falls. At certain times in history, the value of shares has fallen by half in a single day. This is extremely rare, but it is possible.

The simple solution to this problem is to invest in shares for the long term.

If you spread your money into different companies, and are prepared to hold on to the investment for at least three to five years, then the peaks and troughs should smooth themselves out and you should make a consistent profit.

In the long term, the majority of companies make steady profits and their shares increase in value.

The second cause of the misconception about risk relates to the types of companies chosen.

I suggest that you invest in large companies, with a long history of consistent profits. Large mining companies, banks and large manufactures are examples of these types of companies. Small companies have the potential for greater expansion, but they are also more risky.

Choosing solid companies is a safer form of share investment, in comparison to speculating in the shares of small companies. For example, occasionally a small mining company will announce that they have made a new mineral strike.

The company may have nothing more than a handful of employees and the mining rights to some land, but a mineral discovery could be worth millions. Shares in the company may go through massive rises and falls until it is clear whether the discoveries are valuable or not.

Another classic example of risky shares involves high-technology companies. Companies will announce that they have made a major breakthrough, perhaps a new drug or a new industrial technique.

Again, the share price will move through massive rises and falls until the true value of the discovery has become clear. Avoid these speculative companies, Kate, they are simply not worth it. Keep to the steady, consistent performers."

Kate was listening with interest. John had only just begun the discussion on shares, but already her dread was beginning to fade. There was a great deal that she didn't understand, but she had confidence in her grandfather to explain it clearly.

"Now that I have set the scene, let us begin at the beginning.

What exactly is a share?

Quite simply, if you own a share, you own part of a company. The more shares you own, the bigger the percentage of the company that belongs to you.

In owning part of the company, you own part of the assets of the company, and you are entitled to part of the profits.

In practice this means two things.

First, each year the company will, hopefully, make a profit. It will keep part of this profit to expand the business, and distribute the rest to the shareholders, in other words the owners.

This is you Kate.

Each year, or more commonly every six months, you

will receive income from your shares. These payments are called 'dividends', and are your part of the profit that the company makes.

Over time, if things go well, the size and value of the company will increase. Should you wish to sell your shares, then another investor will buy them.

The price that he is willing to pay will depend on several things; the assets of the company, and the profits and dividends that it generates. Over time, these things should increase, and so the value of the shares will increase also. This, Kate, is the fundamental nature of shares."

Kate had to admit that it sounded simple. She was still not convinced, though, that this was all she really needed to understand.

"Let us spend a little time talking about what it means to be a shareholder.

In theory, being a shareholder gives you the right to vote at the Annual General Meeting and exercise some control over the company.

In practice, however, corporations in the modern world have become so large that the small investor like yourself has no control whatsoever. It would be quite common for someone like yourself to own 1000 shares in a company that had a total of five million shares on issue.

You can imagine, Kate, that your vote would be insignificant as a percentage of the total. In the modern world, companies are controlled by their board of directors and one or two large shareholders.

The small shareholders have to live with their decisions. This means that you should read the newspapers and the annual reports of companies that you invest in, and if things start to look shaky then you should consider selling the shares.

Now, I spoke before about how profits are distributed. A young company, or a company that is rapidly expanding, will retain a large part of its profits to expand its business, and distribute a smaller part as dividends to shareholders.

Some companies even have a policy of not paying any dividends at all. In this case, the profits of the company will be reflected in your shares having a higher price, rather than you receiving income from dividends.

An older and more mature company may pay out most or all of its profits as dividends, giving you a steady income stream and a smaller increase in the share price. By choosing the company, you can lean towards a growth investment, with little income, or an income investment with little growth.

Finally, we have assumed all along that the company makes a profit each year.

The word 'profit' means that the total wealth of the company increased, and generally means that its income was greater than its expenses.

A company can also make a profit from increases in the value of its assets.

Some years, however, a company may make a loss. This means that the total value of the company actually declined during the year, and may mean that the expenses were greater that the income. In this case, the company may not pay a cash dividend to the shareholders.

The value of the shares will also drop, because the value of the company is less, and its future looks uncertain.

Although many companies make a loss occasionally, this is not necessarily a serious problem. When a company makes a loss, this puts the fear of God into the board and senior management.

They fear for their jobs and reputations. This normally leads to drastic changes, and many projects that are long overdue may be completed with impressive haste.

This can greatly increase the health of the company, and within a year or two they are back to steady profits.

When a company hits bad times, reading the press will give you an impression of whether it is a strong company that has been a victim of low prices for its products, or whether the management is abandoning the company like rats from a sinking ship, leaving a rotting hulk that is useless to anyone."

Colourful language, Kate thought to herself, but John painted the picture remarkably well.

"Finally, we look at the worst-case scenario. The company has been badly managed, it has borrowed too much and cannot pay it back, and the market for its products is in a coma.

When a company cannot pay its bills, Kate, it is 'wound up'. The term 'bankrupt' applies to individuals, not to companies, but the concept is the same. Note that the critical point is whether the company has cash to pay its bills when they are due.

A company may still have large assets, such as property, but if it does not have ready cash then it cannot continue to operate. Conversely, a company may have debts that exceed its assets, so technically it is worth nothing, but as long as it has cash to continue paying interest and bills as they are due, then it can continue to operate.

The process of 'liquidating', or closing down a company works like this: first, the assets are sold. Then, all debts and borrowings are repaid.

Finally, if there is any money left over, this is distributed to the shareholders.

If, however, there is not enough money to repay all the debts, then the remaining debts are cancelled, and the shareholders are not required to contribute any money to repay the debts of the company."

Kate looked glum. She could not believe that John was suggesting that she invest money in something like this.

John watched his granddaughter, and the doubts on her face were obvious.

"We have covered the major rights of shareholders, Kate, and I have shown you the worst-case scenario.

However, the good news is that it is rare for companies to fail, particulary large ones. If you restrict your investments to the larger companies, then you may go through your entire life without owning shares in a single company that is wound up.

The price you pay for the high returns on shares, though, is a certain element of uncertainty and risk. It is this risk, and the laws of supply and demand, that guarantee that shares must return a higher profit in the long term than other investments.

The risk can be managed by spreading your money into several companies. After all, the wealthy people who invest in the stock market can afford the best advice, and they wouldn't be doing it if it did not lead to even greater wealth."

A fair point, Kate had to admit.

"We have looked at the ownership of shares, and disposing of them.

Now it is time to look at the beginning of the road, the acquisition of shares in the first place. There are two times when new shares are created.

When a public company is first created, shares are issued to the public in return for cash. This process is called 'floating' the company or 'listing' the company.

Sometimes, the company is completely new, and it then uses the cash to carry on the purpose that it was created for. This is often the case when an existing company wants to enter a new field, and creates a whole new subsidiary company to carry on this task for it.

At other times, an existing private company will be 'floated', or converted to a public company. In this case, the cash contributed by the new shareholders is used to pay the existing private owners for the business.

During the life of the company, there are times when a major opportunity exists to expand the business, but the company does not have sufficient cash to take advantage of the opportunity. At these times, the company may choose to issue new shares.

This increases the number of shareholders, but it also increases the size of the company, due to the cash that is contributed to purchase the new shares.

Overall, then, the effect on the existing shareholders is small. They own a smaller share of the pie, but the pie is larger. The company can use this new cash to undertake a major project and expand its business."

John stopped, as he tended to do from time to time, and rested briefly. Kate was still listening intently.

"New issues of shares are relatively rare however Kate, and a company will only issue new shares once every few years. A stable company, without major plans for expansion, may operate for many years without having a share issue.

The other way to acquire shares is to purchase them from another investor.

This is done through a 'stock exchange'. The stock exchange is simply a place where people can buy and sell shares with each other. In practice, the public does not deal directly with each other, but must go through a stockbroker. Stockbrokers have some similarities with real-estate agents, in the sense that they act as an agent between two parties.

However, the stockbroker also handles the actual purchase and sale of the shares, and advises his clients on companies. All you need to do is telephone your broker, tell him how many shares you want to buy or sell, and he will make the trade for you.

The cash you receive or pay is settled within a few days. Overall, is it an extremely simple process."

The more John explained about shares, the more comfortable Kate felt about them. It was clear that there were some risks involved, but then John was not suggesting that she commit the majority of her money to shares anyway.

For the first time, the thought of investing in shares did not terrify her.

"Let us look a little at the factors that affect the price of shares," John said with renewed vigour. "Firstly, we have inflation.

Inflation, as I have said before, is a phenomenon that affects cash only, not real assets such as buildings and businesses.

If a company maintains its share of the market it operates in, then any increases in prices should also be reflected in increased share prices and dividends.

The first factor that affects share prices, then, is inflation.

Over time shares will rise in price to compensate for inflation.

The second factor that affects share prices is the expansion, or occasionally the contraction, in the operations of the business.

If the company grows and expands, increasing its share of markets and spreading into new markets, then the value of the shares will increase also.

The shares represent a portion of the assets and profits of the company, and if the value of the company rises, then so will the shares. Sometimes a company will actually contract in size, and this leads to a reduction in the share price.

Third, we have the earnings. This is the key factor in the changing prices of shares, and the reason why the prices change so drastically. People buy shares to receive dividends, and also so that the value of the company and the shares will rise over time. It is quite possible, however, for a company to make a profit of 100 million dollars one year, a loss of 100 million dollars the next, and then a profit of 100 million dollars the year after that.

Contrast this with property, where rents only change by small percentages each year.

As long as a property has tenants, then the rents are quite predictable from year to year, hence the greater stability in property prices.

The earnings of companies, however, are much more volatile, and hence share prices are also more volatile than property prices.

Large and diversified companies have the most stable earnings from year to year, but even these companies are subject to large changes in their profits as the economy goes from boom to recession and back to boom.

There is one final factor that affects share prices Kate. This is the infamous 'popularity' factor, which I have mentioned previously. Popularity of investments tends to take some time to catch up with changes in their true value.

After a recession, earnings and dividends will rise strongly, but it will be a year or two before shares become popular again and the rices rise accordingly. Prices may actually start to rise about six months before the profits increase, but the rises do not become strong and steady until there is a clear pattern of increased profits, and this may take one or two years. Towards the end of a boom, popularity reaches hysterical levels and people will continue to buy shares when the prices have risen well above their natural values.

This often ends in cold water being thrown on the party by a crash in prices."

John was beginning to warm to his topic.

"The easiest was to assess the level of share prices is to compare the dividend yield of shares with the interest rates of cash deposits," he said.

"If interest rates are much higher than dividend yields, then share prices may be over valued. Conversely, if dividend yields are similar to interest rates, then prices are probably at sustainable levels."

"There are a few other comments I would like to make, Kate, about investing in shares. Share prices are volatile. This is a fact of life, and one that you must take into account when planning your strategy. Never invest money in shares if you know you may need the money for something else in the near future.

You must take a long term view when investing in shares, and be prepared to maintain your investment in shares for five years or more.

You may change the companies that you invest in, but do not withdraw from the market completely if you have only recently invested and prices have fallen.

If you spread your money into many companies, as I have suggested, then you may have one or two that perform badly. Again, this is a fact of life that you must accept.

The companies may not fail completely, but they may perform badly and their share prices may fall. All this, however, is the bad news. The good news, is that there are only two golden rules of share investment.

First, invest for the long term, and second, spread your money into several different companies.

If you follow these two simple rules, then your portfolio of shares will be safer than a bank, and far more profitable."

Kate was pleased. She had been afraid that John would venture into all sorts of complex terminology and strategies, but the guidelines he had given her were quite straightforward. Now that she understood more, she was feeling more comfortable about the stock market.

"Go on, John," she said brightly. "This is very interesting."

Kate's grandfather smiled. He had been confident that her fears would pass once she understood how things worked, but there was always the slight element of doubt in the back of his mind that she would still not be convinced.

John's confidence increased, and he continued speaking.

"I should tell you, Kate, a few of the terms used for describing the finances of companies. These are the basic methods used to evaluate companies, and compare them with others.

You may not want to go into detail with this, but a basic understanding is useful. When you begin investing in shares, I suggest that you purchase a simple book on the stock market. This will explain the different terms used, and give you a better idea how to assess whether your companies are doing well or not."

"Which book should I buy?" Kate said with curiosity.

"The smallest one you can find," John replied dryly. "This is the one that will have the most useful information, and the least complicated rubbish. A simple guideline, I agree, but one I have found to be remarkably accurate."

John returned to the topic at hand, keen to continue their progress.

"When we have finished discussing the details, I will describe some trusts and other methods of investing in shares where you can avoid the complications of choosing companies yourself.

You should still be aware of the terms though. First, we have the word 'equity'. The word 'equity' means ownership. This word is widely used in the financial world, in many different contexts.

A company's money and assets come from two sources. First, there is the money contributed by the shareholders, and the money retained from previous profits. This is called equity, as it is the portion of the company that is owned by the shareholders.

A company can also borrow money, which gives it the 'debt', its other source of money.

This is the same as the gearing that I described for you Kate. Companies vary greatly in the amount of debt they have, but half debt and half equity is a good benchmark.

Virtually all personal and company failures are related to borrowing too much money.

A company that has a high level of gearing may return higher profits, but it also has a higher risk of failure. I suggest that you avoid companies that are highly geared.

Newspaper articles will often discuss the financial health of the major companies, so you do not have to work this out for yourself.

If a company is in the business of making plastic spoons, then I would prefer that it concentrate on making plastic spoons and leave the gearing arrangements to me. At least I can control it then, and I know what I am getting involved in. Gearing for companies is often expressed as the 'debt to equity ratio', and a company with a debt-to-equity ratio of three to one has borrowed three dollars for every dollar of its own money.

Besides the 'debt-to-equity' ratio, another major statistic is the 'price-earnings ratio', often written as the PE or P/E ratio. You will remember, Kate, when I talked earlier about the yield on investments. A 100-dollar investment with an income of 14 dollars per year has a 14 percent yield.

When we are speaking about shares, the yield is often expressed in a different way. The 'price-earnings' ratio is the price of the shares divided by the earnings of the company. For example, a PE ratio of twenty means that the share price is equal to twenty times the earnings.

If a PE ratio is turned upside-down by dividing it into one, it becomes the "earnings yield". This figure can be directly compared with the yield on other investments.

For example, a PE ratio of 20 is equivalent to an earnings yield of 5%. This is a very important statistic.

As I spoke about previously, every investment should be considered on its merits, and the yield that an investment generates is one of the most important factors. If a share generates a lower yield than other shares and other investments, it may have trouble maintaining its share price and there is a risk of a decline in the price.

Another important figure is the 'dividend yield'. This is the dividends that the company distributes, as a percentage of the cost of the shares. A dividend yield of 4 percent means that you will receive the same income from the share as you would from a bank deposit at 4 percent interest.

However, a low dividend yield is not necessarily a bad thing, as the company may be retaining much of its profits to expand the business and increase the value of the shares.

Look at the PE ratio, also expressed as the earnings yield, to determine if the share is over priced. Also look for a high dividend yield if a high income is important to you.

Finally, read everything you can about the company, to get an impression of the quality of the company. In the long term, this is more important than the current figures. Remember, too, that the figures are generally based on previous profits and dividends, but what matters is the future."

John stopped for breath, and relaxed while Kate thought over the things he had said. She had been waiting for the technical part of the discussion, but it had not been as bad as she had expected. She could not remember all the ratios, but John had promised to summarise them later so this was not a problem anyway.

Kate did not feel confident playing around with figures, but perhaps she didn't need to. If she read the newspaper reports, as John suggested she should, then they would analyse the companies for her.

All she needed to do was understand the concepts behind the points the author made in his analysis, and she would be able to get an impression of the health of the company.

Perhaps John was right, she thought. Perhaps a little reading on the subject would be worthwhile.

"This is going well, Kate," John said confidently. "I know it is new to you, but write it down tonight and read over your notes later.

After a little thought and contemplation, the pieces will fall into place. When you choose companies, select companies from different sectors within the stock market. If you chose a major bank, a major mining company and a major retail chain, and buy shares in each, then you have already spread your risks significantly.

Each of these businesses is subject to quite different problems, and while a recession would affect them all in some way, the risk of them all having major problems at the same time is far less that it would be with a single company.

Now for the good news.

You may choose to invest in shares directly, but it does require some attention to ensure that one of your companies has not run into major difficulties.

This is not an onerous task, and an occasional check of the newspapers and the share price should be sufficient, but it is still a job which must be done. An alternative is to invest your money in a trust which then invests in shares.

This minimises the effort involved, and spreads your money into many different companies. In addition, you have experts working full time to assess and choose the companies that the money is invested in.

Overall, it is a good system, and one that many investors should consider. Many institutions offer these trust investments to their customers.

Do not, however, be fooled into believing that you will get a higher profit because you have experts choosing the companies.

For some reason, these trusts rarely perform much better than the average share, and in fact some perform worse that a totally random selection of shares.

Perhaps this is because the trust managers always look for short-term gains, attempting to make profits from changes in the share prices, or perhaps because the are so close to the day-to-day price movements that they forget the long-term basics.

Whatever the reason, you should consider these trusts for their convenience, rather than hoping for superior performance.

As well as the general trusts, there are also trusts that invest in certain sectors of the stockmarket. These include trusts that invest in small companies, trusts that invest in certain sectors, such as mining companies, and trusts that invest in the largest companies, often called the 'leaders'.

Once you are familiar with the basics of share investing, Kate, it is well worth investigating these other trusts.

Look for at least five years' consistent performance, without excessively sharp rises and falls.

I suggest that you avoid any very new products. They always promise great things, and sometimes they deliver, but other times the returns are very flat.

On your search for trusts and other investment products, I suggest you restrict yourself to ones that have a proven track record, such as five years consistent performance.

You may want to incorporate some of the specialist trusts into your portfolio, but restrict each one to a small part of your overall wealth.

Finally, there are the international trusts. These trusts invest in shares of companies in overseas countries.

There are always countries that are developing faster than your own, and overseas trusts can show strong growth, although they are often highly volatile.

Even a small investor like you can easily participate. Overseas investments are vulnerable to changes in the value of currencies, but if it is highly profitable investment then this will not be a problem in the long term.

If the entire country is growing strongly, then its currency will rise and this boosts your profits even more. I suggest that you include an overseas share trust as a small part of your portfolio."

5.3 Property

Kate sat on the bench and looked out over the park. It was mid-winter now, and her breath condensed into a mist that floated away on the cold air as she breathed. Children played in the snow and a thin layer of ice covered the lake.

She though over the past few months. She had never imagined that her request to John would lead her down a whole new path in her life.

It had seemed a simple request, all she had asked for was a little financial advice from a respected and successful friend. Now, she had learnt so much that her life would never be the same again. It was more that just knowledge, too.

Kate had begun to view things in a different light, to see success and failure differently and look at her life in a new way. John's message was deeper that just financial advice, it was a cry of hope, a belief in a better future and a happier life.

Kate thought back over the journey they had walked together, and she was suddenly infinitely grateful that her grandfather had taught her so much. She sensed that he, too, was happy in the task he had undertaken, and had gained something from their talks.

"Property," John said suddenly. "Today, Kate, we will talk about property. We have already covered the interest-bearing and stock market investments, and this is the last of the three major sectors."

Kate's grandfather made himself comfortable on the park bench, and settled down for a long talk. He was used to their discussions now, and while he had been nervous in the beginning, after all this time it had become second nature.

"When you invest in property, you are really investing in two separate things. You are purchasing land, and you are purchasing buildings. This is obvious, of course, but it is worth keeping in mind.

Often we forget this, and speak about investing in 'a house', forgetting that the purchase price covers two things, the land and the buildings.

This distinction will become important later when we discuss the assessment of an investment property.

Depending on the location, a greater or lesser proportion of the cost is due to the buildings themselves. In an expensive inner-city location, for example, the cost may be almost entirely due to the land. The buildings may be almost incidental to the total cost of the property.

In some locations, one can simply calculate the area of land, multiply by a cost for the area and arrive at an accurate price for the property. Beware of buying a beautiful house on a small area of land in one of these locations, as it may not hold its value as well as a poor house on a larger block. Remember, you can always improve the buildings, but you can't change the size of the land.

In other areas, such as sparsely populated country areas, land may be very cheap. In these areas, almost the entire cost of a house may relate to the building itself, and the cost of the land may be minor. If you keep in mind the two factors, buildings and land, then the variations in prices between different properties becomes much clearer.

Like all other assets, properties have value because they are useful to people. There are three main uses for land and buildings.

First, we have farmland. I doubt that you will ever consider investing in a farm, Kate, but if you do, then subject it to the same evaluation that you would apply to any other investment.

Look at the yield you can expect to earn, consider all the risks, learn about it and ensure that experienced farmers are managing the project for you.

Rural investment is a specialised area and I would not recommend it unless you are experienced in this area, or you are simply a 'silent partner', contributing money while someone else does all the work.

Besides farming and agriculture, the second use of land is for living space. When a person is lost in the wild and living in hazardous conditions, it is said that they can survive for three minutes without oxygen, three hours without shelter, three days without water and three weeks without food. This saying highlights the critical need for shelter and a place to live.

More than anything else, it is this fact which gives property investment its fundamental value.

The third use of buildings and land is for commercial purposes, such as office buildings, factories and shops.

Let's spend a little time looking at the factors which affect the prices of property.

There are four major factors which affect property prices.

First, we have inflation. Inflation is a phenomenon which results in cash reducing in value over time.

As a result of this the price of real assets such as properties and shares increases. Note that the actual value has not increased, just the price when expressed in dollars.

It is a small consolation to own a property that has doubled in price if everything you want to spend the money on has doubled as well. The price of properties, then, tends to rise over time to compensate for inflation.

The second factor is the growth in population.

All prices are determined by supply and demand, and the demand for housing is largely related to the increase in population.

If the population increases strongly, then demand for houses will rise and prices will increase.

Population growth results from two things, the birth of babies and the immigration of people into the country and the area.

Country towns are particularly susceptible to large rises and falls in population.

The third factor relates to the number of new homes that are built. This is the supply side of the equation. If there is a high rate of building, then after a few years there will be an excess of homes and prices will remain steady or fall. The excess of empty buildings is called the 'vacancy rate', and is a very important statistic when evaluating commercial property such as office buildings.

A vacancy rate of 10 percent means that one in every ten buildings is empty.

The higher the vacancy rate, the more buildings a tenant has to choose from and the greater the chance that rents and prices will fall.

Finally, we have the fourth factor affecting prices, and one of the most significant.

It is our old friend, popularity.

Like all investments the property market goes through cycles in popularity, and these normally lag a year or two behind the true value of the properties.

Properties are large and difficult to sell at the best of times, so forget about selling one in a slump if you can avoid it. Different areas also change in popularity, and the choice of location is one of the most critical factors in successful property investment.

If you buy a property in an area that is increasing in popularity, then you may make large profits. The purchase of a property in an area of declining popularity, however, may prove to be a very poor investment.

The best way to assess the state of the overall property market is to look at the rental yield on properties. If the yields compare favourably with the past and with other investments, then consider buying, otherwise leave it alone and wait."

John paused for a break. There was a great deal that he wished to tell Kate, and it was difficult to organise it into any sort of logical order.

Perhaps, when he had finished, Kate would be able to look back over his comments and fit the pieces together.

"You have several options for investing in property, Kate. There is your own home, of course, and I will say a few words about that later. There are two avenues for property investment that I can recommend.

First, you may buy a house or flat and rent it out. This has the advantage that you can choose the property carefully, and you can make improvements to it if you wish. We will speak about this shortly.

The second approach is a property trust. You should avoid unlisted property trusts, as it is difficult for the managers to sell the buildings if there is a sudden rush of investors who want their money back. Quality listed trusts are quite safe, however, and have several advantages over owning property directly.

Most important of all, is that you can invest small amounts of money, and withdraw it at short notice.

Purchasing a house is a major step for the average investor. There are many heavy costs, and the property must be kept for many years to ensure a reasonable return.

Property trusts allow you to avoid the work involved in managing a property, such as dealing with the tenants, maintenance and paying all the various expenses.

Property trusts generally invest in large properties, such as office buildings or shopping centres. Although these sectors of the property market provide good returns, they also tend to be more volatile than the private residential market and you should be prepared for falls in values from time to time. Finally, there are the forms of property investment that I recommend you avoid.

First, don't purchase vacant land. You will not receive any income from the investment, and the tax situation is normally against you. The value may increase over time, but you are better off owning land with a home on it or investing in something else so you can receive an income from your investment.

Be wary of holiday houses or properties in unusual areas. Choose properties in popular areas where you can be assured that there will be many tenants willing to rent your property all year round.

You can also build houses as an investment, and this has the potential for large profits.

However, I caution you with two rules for building homes. First, realise that it takes quite a deal of time and effort to manage a project like this, and it will always cost more than you expect.

Only do it if you can afford to devote a significant amount of time to the project.

Second, don't do it when prices are flat. It is unlikely that you will make a profit once the building costs and interest are taken into account.

Building can, however, be a profitable strategy in a strong and rising market."

John stopped speaking, took a few deep breaths and relaxed. Kate was listening to everything he said, and building up a picture in her mind of how to invest successfully in property.

"Next we have the assessment of properties.

Let us assume that you have decided to buy a house and rent it out. In the real estate market, they say that there are three critical factors in successful property investment.

These are 'location, location and location.' A trite saying perhaps, but one that is often quoted and one that illustrates the importance of the issue.

Everyone needs a place to live. What is more, everyone must purchase this home from their wages and savings. This factor ensures that property, more that any other investment, should remain constant in real value over time.

If the price of properties kept increasing for ever, then we would soon be living on the street because not-one could afford a house.

People do make great profits in property, however, and this is largely because the choose the correct area to buy in.

Although the average price of a house may stay steady in real terms, some areas will increase in value and other areas will decrease in real value.

By choosing a location wisely, you will have an investment that is in strong demand and commands a healthy price.

This brings me, Kate, to explain two special features of property investment that are not found in other types of investment.

They are both the result of the fact that properties are very expensive, and can only be purchased in large amounts, unlike fixed-interest or share investments. You will remember when we spoke earlier about gearing. I showed you how gearing increases your profits, and also increases your losses if things go badly.

When you buy an investment house, it is quite possible to use your own money for 10 percent of the value, and borrow the other 90 percent. This is a very high level of gearing, of around ten to one. You would not dream of gearing to this level in any other investment.

This high level of gearing is the first reason that good profits can be made in property.

If the prices increase at a faster rate than the interest on the loan, then you can make large profits from a small outlay of cash.

There is a second unique factor in property investment.

Because of the large size of the properties and the loans, you are virtually forced to save a large percentage of your salary.

The mortgage payments could easily equal one quarter of your salary, as an example.

Imagine if you were to save one quarter of your salary, and also gear your investments at a level of ten to one. Under these conditions, almost anything you invested in would return a massive profit, assuming of course that the return on the investment exceeded the loan interest.

When you consider you own home, the picture is a little more complex because you are avoiding the cost of paying rent, but the principles still apply.

We have raised the location of the property as a critical factor. As well as choosing a suburb that is growing in popularity, look at the location of the individual property as well. Noise is a significant factor, and a property in a quiet location will always fetch a better price that one near a railway line or a major road.

Good access to services like transport and shops is also important. The basic question you must ask yourself when you assess the location of an investment property is this: 'would I want to live there myself? Is it a good, convenient location and a good place to live?'

This is the question that potential purchasers will be asking themselves when you want to sell.

Having looked carefully at the location of the property, we come to assess the building itself.

Choose a building that is of sound, solid construction.

A building that is poorly built will cost a great deal in maintenance and have difficulty keeping its value.

The building does not have to be exciting or inspiring, but as long as it is simple and solid it will maintain its value.

This brings be to the second golden rule of property investment, after you have chosen a good location.

This is the improvement of the property. You should improve the property you have purchased.

Your building must be structurally sound when you purchase it, but it may be in a state of disrepair.

It may need new carpets and a fresh coat of paint. This can be an advantage, as it is a chance for you to buy cheaply and improve the value of the property.

In general, minor work such as paint and carpets that has a highly visible affect will pay for itself when you sell the property. It is essential to keep the property in a good state of repair.

Major renovations, however, are another story. These come into the same category as new buildings. You should only attempt them if you can afford to spend considerable time on the project, and if the prices are strong and rising.

266

You may not get back the cost of major renovations if you sell in a weak market when prices are low. When we consider improvements, Kate, you should be aware of the word 'overcapitalisation'.

Kate had been listening carefully, but she could not contain herself when John mentioned this word. "What the hell is 'overcapitalisation'?" she said is anguish.

John smiled. "A big word, I grant you, but the concept is simple. Basically it means that you shouldn't spend too much improving a property. If you buy a property in a poor area, and install every luxury feature you could ever imagine, then you will still not find a rich person who wants to live in that area and you will not get back the money you have spent on the house when you sell it. Now, you may ask, how much improvement is too much?"

"A very good question," Kate said with emphasised solemnity.

"There is another saying in the real estate market, Kate, and it goes like this: 'it is better to buy the worst house in the best street, than the best house in the worst street.'"

Kate pondered this, trying to understand what John meant.

"Listen a little longer, and the reason for this will become clear. When a person decides to buy a house, whether for investment or for their own home, they generally choose an area to live in first. This is critical Kate.

Before anyone comes and looks at your house, they have already decided that they want to live in your area.

They know what price they expect the houses to be, and they know the size and features that they expect in their new home.

This is where the improvement comes into the picture. If you want to be a passive investor, then you may choose to buy a property in good repair and simply maintain it.

However, if you are willing to put a little more effort into your investments, then before you buy you should get a clear picture of the condition, size and facilities of the

267

average house in the area.

Then, look for a house that is structurally the same as the other homes, but is in poorer condition and with less facilities.

Buy it, and then improve the house until it matches that same level as the other homes in the area.

Do not improve it any further, as you will not get a good return on the extra money you spend. Remember that when you sell, the people coming to see your house have a fixed amount to spend, and this will be related to the average price in your area.

This is what the saying about the 'worst house in the best street' means; you should buy in a good area, and choose a house that is in worse condition that the other houses, and then improve it to be equal to the standard of the area.

Improving the property is the second golden rule of property investment, and one of the best ways to make money in real estate."

John paused briefly, but the wind was chilling to the bone and he was keen to continue talking.

"We have looked at the location of the property and the condition of the buildings. The third factor that you should consider is the yield that the rent would return.

This is a very important factor. The best way to compare a property with other properties and with other investments is to compare the yield that you would get if you rented it out at the current market rental rates.

Although there are many ways to compare a properly with others, the yield is the primary way to determine whether the property market as a whole is priced too high. If the yields on other investments, particularly shares and fixed interest, are higher than the yields on properties, then there will be limited scope for property prices to rise.

Be very cautious at times like this. When you compare yields between investments, remember to allow for inflation and tax otherwise the comparison will be deceptive.

Having considered the location, the condition and the

yield, you decide that the price is reasonable and you decide to buy. Your problems have only just begun."

"Thanks for the encouragement," Kate said dryly.

"Only kidding, honey," John said a little red-faced. "If you are careful then you will avoid any major problems. Property investment is the most complex of the three investment sectors, and the expenses are the largest and most numerous.

It does have, however, a good balance between profits and stability, and the ability to gear with property investments is second to none. Now we come to some practical aspects of owning a property.

First, keep it in good condition and never neglect the maintenance.

If you do, you will loose much more than the maintenance cost when you come to sell.

Many people purchase a home to live in themselves, and few buyers are willing to pay high prices for a property in disrepair. If you wish, you may improve the property in the ways we spoke about. I mentioned the buildings, but never forget the garden as well, as a good garden can be inexpensive to establish and puts the whole house in a much more attractive frame.

Now we come to the tenants."

John paused for several minutes, and his expression became thoughtful.

"I have never understood, Kate, why so many landlords treat their tenants so poorly. Perhaps, in some dark corner of their mind, it is a superiority and contempt born of fear.

Although the tenants are probably far poorer than the landlord, deep down inside the landlords realise that they are largely at their tenant's mercy.

The tenants are often their lifeline, and they are at their mercy in ways that few people understand.

You will remember when I spoke about the legal system earlier. In the modern world, the legal system is of little use to the ordinary person. The person who has physical possession of an item has the great majority of the power.

In the case of an investment property, this is the tenants. Make no mistake, Kate, if you have major problems with your tenants, then it will cost you a great deal of money to solve them.

I doesn't matter if you are legally or morally right, and although you may win in the end you will loose money overall. I suggest that you take the following approach.

First, determine an accurate rent for your property, based on the rents offered for other properties in the area. Then, reduce it by ten to 15 percent."

"Reduce it?" Kate said, confused. This seemed stupid.

"Yes, reduce it. Once you take tax into account, you will find that this makes a negligible difference to your overall profits, but it has several important effects. First, you will be greeted by an avalanche of people wanting to rent your house.

Already you may be better off financially, compared to a landlord who goes without rent while waiting for a tenant. More importantly, you can now choose a tenant yourself from the hopeful applicants.

Ask for references, and check them out carefully.

Few landlords do this, but I believe it is essential.

It used to be said that 'an ounce of prevention is worth a pound of cure', but it has been my experience in the financial word that an ounce of prevention is worth about ten tons of cure."

John was beginning to make his point.

"Choose a tenant with good references and a stable history. The lower rent will have other benefits as well. It is amazing how much more care the tenants take of a property if they feel they are getting a good deal, and the rent is more than fair.

Let the tenants know that you are looking for someone who will stay for a long period of time and look after the property well, and you are willing to offer them a lower rent in return for this.

They may even be willing to paint or improve the garden, and make sure you encourage this and pay for the materials.

It is every tenant's dream to have a landlord with this attitude.

The harsh reality is that the tenants will be living in the property every day, and the condition of the property when they leave will be the result of how well they treat it. If the tenants leave the property in poor condition, then in practice there is little you can do about it.

Anything that you can do to encourage the tenants to look the property well will pay for itself many times over in the long term.

If the rent is a little lower than the market, this also encourages the tenants to stay for a long period of time.

This saves you the costs and risks in changing over tenants, and encourages the tenant to see the property as 'home' and look after it well. Treat your tenants well, and they will be more likely to treat your important investment well too.

Finally, you should choose a good agent to manage the property and the tenants for you. Do not deal with the tenants directly.

Agents have a wealth of experience is handling tenant problems, and they will look after the details of collecting rent and dealing with maintenance issues.

They charge a fee for this service, of course, but this is money well spent and if you run into problems you will be very glad of their skills and resources."

5.4 A comparison of the three sectors

We have looked at the three sectors in detail," John said, "and a brief comparison of the three will be useful.

First, we have the long-term profits from the three sectors. Interest-bearing investments have the lowest returns, property has moderate returns and shares have the highest long-term returns.

This relationship does not always hold at a particular point in time, but historical records show a clear long term pattern in the profits from the three sectors.

It is not only history, either, which shows us the difference in the returns, it is related to the fundamental structure of the economic system.

Take property first. Everyone needs a place to live, and so the value of property tends to remain fairly constant in real terms over time.

Some areas will increase, and others will decrease, and the growth in population tends to drive all prices up. Overall, however, the real value of property tends to remain stable or increase at a very modest rate. If it didn't, then people would soon be unable to buy a home, and the laws of supply and demand would ensure that prices returned to affordable levels.

The very nature of property, then, tends to tie down any extreme increases and decrease in value. Always remember, though, that even if the price remains constant in real terms, an investment house will still return a profit from the rental income.

Now we look at the interest-bearing investments.

One of the major reasons that money is borrowed is to purchase property.

People would not borrow for investment unless the returns on the property were greater than the cost of the loan. Thus, in the long run, supply and demand for mortgages will adjust themselves so that the interest on loans is less than the returns on property.

Because of this, we can be sure that over long periods of time the returns on interest-bearing investments will be less than the returns on property investments.

This is a simplistic explanation, but history has shown that the principle does apply in practice.

Interest rates are lower than the returns on shares and property in the long run, because the reason that money is borrowed in our economic system is to invest in business and property and make a higher return than the interest on the loans.

Finally, we have shares. Shares, as we have already seen, have much more volatile prices than property.

Given the choice between a volatile investment and a stable investment that both have the same returns, every sensible investor would choose the stable one. Because of this, volatile investments must return higher profits than stable ones. If they don't, then their prices will fall until they reach a level where the profits are greater than the profits from less volatile investments. Over time, then, shares must have higher returns than property.

Finally, you can see that the relationship between the returns on interest-bearing, property and shares is built into the nature of our economic system. Examination of returns over more than 100 years shows that it happens in practice, and not just in theory."

John stopped to let Kate ponder his words. She was intrigued. Although she was not surprised about the investments that earned the higher profits, Kate had never considered why this actually happened.

For all she knew, it was simply a coincidence, or a historical fact without any clear reason. John's explanation put the three sectors into a common perspective, and the relationship between the returns became obvious.

"Keep talking, grandfather," Kate said with interest. She was enjoying their John's explanations.

"Next, we have the issue of volatility of prices. Shares are the most volatile of the three sectors, followed by property which is less volatile, and then interest-bearing deposits which have no volatility at all.

Share prices are volatile because the profits of the companies vary drastically from year to year, and property prices are more stable because the rental income is fairly stable from year to year.

Remember that the prices are largely based on the income and profits that the investment returns, and if the income changes drastically, then so will the price. One final point on volatility.

We have discussed how some fixed-interest investments can be bought and sold before their term expires. Ten year government bonds are a classic example of this. The prices of the bonds, however, vary daily with changes in interest rates and expectations of the future.

If you buy and sell bonds or other fixed-interest investments, Kate, then you should realise that the prices can be quite volatile.

If you simply keep your deposits for the full term, as I recommend that you do, then the returns are fixed and the volatility is zero. The next issue I would like to canvass is the minimum amount required to invest in each of the sectors.

This is a significant issue for small investors such as yourself. Before we look at each sector, however, we should revisit our old friend the investment trust.

By investing in trusts, the small investor such as yourself can invest in any sector she wants to. This includes a whole variety of specialist trusts that invest in particular sections of the different sectors.

If you have saved a month's salary, Kate, then you should be able to invest in anything you want to by using a trust.

This the first major advantage of investment trusts.

The second, is the easy access to your money, which we

will cover shortly. Now, the interest-bearing deposits.

You can begin earning interest with a single dollar in a bank account, however the interest rates will be terrible.

As you save more money and invest it, and your wealth grows, you will find that you will have access to higher rates of interest from banks and other institutions.

Practically speaking, there is no minimum amount of money required for fixed-interest investment, but you will get higher interest rates if you have more to invest.

Next we have shares. A single share is usually very cheap, perhaps costing only a few dollars. However, they are generally sold in small parcels, not as individual shares, so you should have a few weeks' salary saved if you want to buy some shares. Contrary to popular belief, all you need is a small amount of money to begin investing in the stock market, and a few week's salary for an average person like you is more than enough.

Finally, we have property. Unless you use an indirect method of property investment, such as an investment trust, then property investment requires a large sum of money. The fees and expenses are high, and you would probably save a minimum of six months salary to buy an investment property directly.

Even with this much cash, you would have to borrow a substantial amount. Be careful not to over-stretch yourself Kate, and I would not recommend buying an investment property directly until you have built up a substantial portfolio of other investments and you can purchase the property without stretching your budget or exposing your portfolio too much to the changes in property prices.

Now that we have looked at the minimum investments required, we come to the issue of liquidity.

This is the difficulty in selling your assets, or retrieving your money from an investment. Shares are easy to sell. The prices are quoted each day in the newspapers, so you know exactly how much your shares are worth.

A telephone call to your broker is all that is required to

sell your shares. With some smaller companies you may have to wait for a buyer, but the shares in the larger companies are traded so frequently that you will be able to sell them in a matter of minutes.

Next, the interest-bearing investments. Money on deposit at call, such as a bank account, can be accessed at any time.

Money in fixed-term deposits must be left there for the full term of the deposit.

Because of this, I would not recommend any fixed-term deposits of more than a year or two, unless there is a facility for accessing your money early such as selling the investment to someone else.

'Negotiable' investments, that is bonds and other fixed-interest investments which can be bought and sold, can be sold at any time to retrieve your money.

However, the price of the bonds will change and you may loose money if you do not hold the investment for the full term.

Properties may take several months to sell. In addition, the property must be sold as a whole.

If you own shares, then you may sell some of the shares and keep the rest, but you must sell all or nothing of a property.

There are significant costs in buying and selling properties, so it is something that should not be done frequently or without careful thought.

Property trusts avoid this problem, and you may sell some of your trust units, and keep the rest.

The units can also be sold at short notice, and the price is known in advance, in contrast to a direct property where the value can only be estimated.

A disadvantage with property trusts is that you cannot improve the value of the buildings yourself.

Next we will look at the issue of gearing.

There is no point in borrowing money to invest in interest-bearing investments. In general, the interest you pay on the borrowed money will exceed the interest you earn on your investments.

Although it is possible to make a profit from doing this, by borrowing at fixed rates when the rates are low and rising, and investing at a higher rate later, the difficulties and risks involved mean that you should not even consider this idea.

You may borrow to invest in shares, but because of the volatility of share prices you should be conservative in this. I suggest that the average investor should not gear at more than three to one with shares, or in other words don't borrow more than three dollars for each dollar of your own.

Even this is too much for some investors, however in the long term the profits can be very good.

It is very common to gear with property, and to borrow substantial amount of money to buy properties.

This is for two reasons.

First, properties are so expensive that many people find it essential to borrow if they want to buy a house.

Second, the prices of property are more stable than shares, and while share prices have large rises and large falls, the pattern in the property market is to have moderate rises, followed by steady prices or modest declines.

The more stable the price of an investment asset, the higher the percentage of the price that you can borrow money for.

Finally, the issue of cash flow.

Interest-bearing investments generate income of one sort or another.

Property returns rent, and shares return dividends.

However, much of the profit from shares and property comes from the growth in the value of the investment, rather than the income that the investment provides each year.

In general, interest-bearing investments provide the highest income, followed by property and then shares with the least. The opposite applies to 'capital growth', the increase in the value of the investment.

Interest-bearing investments have no capital growth,

property has modest capital growth and shares may have high capital growth. A word of caution however Kate.

All these differences show up over the long term, but they may not apply over short periods of time, such as a year or two. It is possible, for example, for the dividends on shares to be higher than the income from fixed-interest investments at certain times.

You should understand the relationships between the three sectors, but never assume that they happen to apply at the current moment.

Always check out the current situation carefully when choosing your strategy.

Sometimes, the investments that are the most appropriate for the current time are the ones you would least expect.

This particularly applies to retired people living from the income from their investments."

John paused for another rest. He was a little breathless, and although he was more used to speaking now, his body was still old and he was easily tired. After a few minutes rest, his energy was restored and he continued.

"There is one important conclusion you should draw from this comparison Kate.

There is no single 'best' investment. Everyone has a favourite investment, and the surest sign of an unwise investor is the person who speaks endlessly about the virtues of a particular sector, and denigrates the other two.

All three sectors have their strengths and weaknesses, and there are good times and bad times to be exposed to each of the sectors.

The very question, 'what is the best investment?' Betrays ignorance and a lack of understanding of the nature of successful investment.

Only by combining all three sectors in appropriate proportions does the wise investor guarantee steady returns in all circumstances, and secure wealth for the future."

Kate's face turned red. She was not going to admit it, of course, but this was the very question she had been dying to ask when she had first discussed finance with her grandfather.

Luckily for her pride, however, she had remained silent and hoped that John would raise the issue himself.

"From time to time, Kate, you will meet people who have made large amounts of money by investing in a single sector.

It is certainly possible to build wealth by concentrating on a single sector, although the risks are much greater. Overall, you will find that these people have several things in common.

They were usually lucky with their timing, and bought assets just before a strong rise in prices. Second, they often invested substantial sums of cash, and rarely took into account all the money they poured into the investment when considering the profit they made when they sell.

The profit may seem impressive, but the percentage return on the money they spent may be quite modest.

Finally, these people often spend substantial time and effort on their investments. This time and effort increases the profits for any investor, regardless of the sector they choose.

When you meet these people, Kate, the first thing they will do is try to convince you to do exactly the same as they have done.

This boosts their pride and self-esteem and helps convince themselves that they have done the right thing. Resist the pressure Kate.

For every successful investor who speaks loudly, there are ten unsuccessful investors who are saying very little.

The strategies I have outlined are the safest and surest ways to wealth, and I strongly recommend that you keep to them.

Invest in all three sectors, and you will not make money at the fastest possible rate, but your wealth will be secure and your returns will be steady and strong.

5.6 Managed and pooled investments

"The world, Kate, is full of people who want to manage your money for you.

They come with promises of expert, skilled management, high returns and secure strategies.

Naturally, they charge a fee for their services. These people may be accountants, investment advisers or even institutions.

The first class of managed investments we will look at are often called 'portfolio management services'.

These are called various different names, but the basic operation is the same.

All individual investments are owned in your name, but someone else makes the decisions on what to buy and when to sell.

I suggest you avoid these services, even though many work well, because the benefits provided do not outweigh the disadvantages.

I have spoken many times about the need to manage your affairs personally, and I cannot stress this highly enough.

Your financial future is simply too important to trust to anyone else but yourself. Some people cannot be bothered managing their investments, and would rather pay someone else to do it.

Others suffer from a lack of confidence, and believe that only an expert can invest their money successfully.

Both these attitudes are highly dangerous. Even if the person or institution you choose to manage your affairs is trustworthy and successful, and many are not, then they can never fully understand your needs and plans.

You will find, too, that the person you deal with may change often and there will be no continuity in the investment strategy over your lifetime.

Surprisingly, wise investors generate the same returns as professionals, and in many cases better.

Ask yourself this, Kate: if the person you are considering to manage your money was really an expert in the field, then why would they be working for you, instead of lying on a beach somewhere with a fortune in profits in the bank?

The very fact that they need to manage your money to earn a living, means they are probably not successful in managing their own.

The sad fact is that many people who make their careers in the financial field are very unwise investors, and often produce poor results for their clients.

People performing this task for you as employees of institutions may be paid a fixed salary, and the success or failure of your particular investments may have little impact to them.

This does not mean, of course, that you should not seek the advice of professionals on the details of an investment, but it does mean that you should choose the overall strategy yourself.

Now, there is a second class of managed investments that we will look at.

In these investments, you make a single payment or group of payments and this money is invested into the different sectors.

This can be done in several ways, through banks and insurance companies, and through trusts and investment managers.

From your point of view, it is a single investment, however the money in spread into the different sectors.

In some products, you can choose the spread yourself, but in others the manager of the fund makes the decision for the investors.

These products have certain advantages, however there are pitfalls as well.

On the positive side, this is probably the simplest way to invest in a variety of sectors.

The paperwork is simple, the legal and tax considerations are fairly straightforward and you usually have access to your money at short notice.

There are two primary disadvantages.

First, there will be fees involved in the exercise. No-one performs any business service for nothing, and you will be charged money for the service, in one form or another.

You may even pay fees to the manager, and more fees again on the purchase and sale of individual investments within the fund.

In this type of investment, it can be very difficult to determine who gets a cut of your money, and how much of the money actually goes into profit-producing investments for yourself.

The second disadvantage is the lack of control. You cannot, for example, choose your own shares or buy a property and improve its value.

In some products you can vary the proportions among the three sectors as conditions change, but this can be cumbersome and expensive.

The lack of control limits your potential profits.

Overall, some of these products are quite good, and you may wish to consider investing some of your money in one of them.

However, do not break the golden rule, and never put all of your money in one place. This includes never putting all of your money with one institution, person or management company, even if the underlying investments are spread around.

One final point on institutions and management investment funds Kate.

There are only three major sectors, property, shares and interest-bearing.

All your money is invested in these sectors, the only question is how many middle-men there are between you and your investments, and how many people get a cut of your money.

If you deposit money in banks, then the money is loaned out for loans so you are effectively investing in the interest-bearing sector.

If you invest money with an insurance company, then the money will be invested in shares, property, and fixed-interest so you are indirectly investing in these sectors.

All investments, including money deposited with institutions, eventually ends up in one of the three sectors.

This brings me to discuss a much-maligned term in the investment field, the word 'guarantee'. One of the oldest tricks in the book of unscrupulous sales methods is to give naive investors the impression that an investment it guaranteed in a particular way, when in fact it isn't.

Some people even tell blatant lies on this issue. When you see the word 'guaranteed' in relation to an investment, be extremely sceptical. Often it is not what it seems.

The guarantee may last for a specific period of time, or only apply in certain circumstances.

The next question, of course, is who is actually offering the guarantee. Often there is an implication that the government is guaranteeing the investment, that the money is legally protected and cannot be lost. This is almost always false.

Usually the term 'guaranteed' means that the institution offering the product has promised to give a certain return, or promised that the value of the investment will not actually decrease.

This is of no use, however, if the institution itself fails. A 'guarantee' in these circumstances means nothing at all. When you see the term 'guaranteed' applied to an investment, Kate, investigate the true nature of the guarantee.

Find out who is providing the guarantee, whether it be the institution itself or perhaps a parent company.

Ask for a confirmation of the information in writing. Overall, I would tend to ignore the term 'guaranteed' completely, as it often has little meaning in practice.

In fact, it may even be a disadvantage, and this brings me to the final point on guaranteed products.

There is no such thing as a free lunch in the investment world, and if you want something then you have to pay for it. If institutions offer a guarantee, then they must put aside money to support the guarantee in case things go badly.

This reduces the returns on the investment, and so your returns may be reduced because of the need to fund the guarantee.

Indirectly, you pay for the guarantee, and the long term returns on a guaranteed investment will generally be lower than the returns on an equivalent non-guaranteed investment."

5.7 Other investments

John and Kate sat in the park, as they usually did on a Sunday afternoon, and watched the huge green trees sway in the wind. The wind was icy cold, and they both held warm coats around themselves as shelter from the wind.

After they had rested, relaxed and soaked in the peaceful feeling of the park, John returned to the subject of finance once again.

"We have covered the three major sectors now, Kate, and I have also made some comments on the benefits and pitfalls of managed investments. There are a few other issues that we should cover before we move on to the next major topic for discussion.

First, I wish to talk about an investment product that works in the opposite way to most investments.

These products go under various names, such as 'annuities' and 'allocated pensions', but they all have the same basic nature. Imagine that you have a large sum of money, and you wish to live from the income that the money generates when invested.

Most people in this position are elderly people who are entering retirement.

You can give this money to an institution, usually an insurance company, and they will invest it for you and pay you a regular income, derived from the profits on the investments and part of the original capital.

When we spoke earlier, Kate, I recommended against having someone else manage your investments, whether it be an individual or an institution, as I believe that the fees and restrictions outweigh the benefits.

Annuities, however, are an extremely useful method of investment for retired people.

All the investment issues are handled by the insurance company, and the investor simply receives a payment each month in the same way as a salary payment.

Additionally, there are many options that the investor may choose from for his annuity. The payments may be fixed, or automatically increased each year in line with inflation.

The annuity may operate for a fixed period of time, or last for the whole lifetime of the investor, whatever that may be.

Although the wise investor can manage his investment portfolio competently, the payment of a regular salary from a portfolio of investments is far more complicated.

It takes a great deal of effort and calculation to determine how much of a salary the investor can afford to draw from the capital invested, and how long the money will last. In the case of annuities, Kate, I suggest that the convenience and benefits outweigh the disadvantages.

Never, of course, give your entire life savings to a single institution.

I also recommend that you keep part of your wealth in other forms and manage it yourself.

This will give you ready access to money when you need it, and alleviate the risk of problems due to mistakes or accidents with the annuity.

Remember Kate, that the aim of the wise investor is to protect herself, and reduce her vulnerability in any situation.

If you deposited every cent you had into a single annuity, then you would be very vulnerable if there was a problem with your payments.

There is one final advantage with annuities, and one that only a life insurance company can provide. This is the sometimes called a 'lifetime annuity', and it means that the insurance company agrees to take your money and pay you a certain income for the rest of your life, regardless of how long you life.

In this case, there is no need to fear that the money will run out, as the payments continue for as long as you live.

If you only live a short time, then the insurance company

286

would do well, and if you lived a long time then they would make a loss.

When their returns are averaged out over their clients, however, the company makes a profit.

This is an excellent idea, as you have the security of knowing that you will have an income for as long as you live.

One of a retired person's greatest fears can be running out of money.

With a lifetime annuity, however, the person is better off financially the longer they live, in contrast to the usual sad case where the longer they live, the poorer they become."

Kate thought carefully about John's words. The annuities he described did sound like a very convenient idea, and she made a mental note to investigate them more thoroughly when she came closer to retirement herself.

"The next topic I would like to investigate is 'superannuation'. Again, this goes under several names, but they all relate to money that is saved for retirement.

In order to encourage people to save for their retirement, the government offers tax advantages to people who save money in superannuation.

However, the disadvantage is that you cannot spend the money until you retire, and your control over the investment of the money may be limited.

The first thing to realise about superannuation is that it is simply a form of investment, nothing more and nothing less. There are several special features that distinguish superannuation from other investments, but fundamentally it is simply saving money and investing it until retirement.

The money that is deposited in a superannuation account is invested in the three major sectors, in the same way as any other investment.

This money is then used to support you during retirement.

The first special feature of superannuation is the taxation treatment. This can be complex, but the key point is that the tax is less than the tax on other investments, and there are various benefits and reduced taxes to encourage people to save.

When we looked at investments earlier, I stressed the importance of tax in determining the overall return.

However, I also stressed that investments must be of a high quality and good profitability on their own merits, without taking tax into account.

All money contributed to a superannuation fund is invested in some way. If it is invested in a sector that provides low returns, such as the fixed-interest sector, then it may be possible to get higher returns by investing the money yourself, rather than putting it into a superannuation fund, even after tax is taken into account.

The second special feature of superannuation is the rules relating to the spending of the money. In general, the purpose of superannuation is to save for retirement, and it will be difficult or impossible to spend the money any earlier.

This is the primary disadvantage of superannuation. We all have times in our lives when things are particularly difficult, and some extra money could put us back on our feet. I have seen people with huge amounts of money in superannuation, but struggling to survive because they have little cash that they can actually spend.

There is a risk that I have not mentioned which applies to all investments, but it is critical to superannuation. This is the risk of changes in the law and tax rules.

No one can predict the future, and there will be times when the government will change the rules so that a good investment that you have made becomes a poor investment.

There is little you can do to avoid this, except to spread your money into different investments. Since the money in superannuation is locked away for up to fifty years, the rules can change many times over this period.

On balance, Kate, I suggest that you avoid superannuation in the early and middle stages of your life.

You should save, invest and build your wealth in the other ways that I have described.

You must always keep control, and be flexible and ready to adapt to changing circumstances.

This is the best way to ensure a secure financial future, including your retirement.

As you approach retirement, say within the last ten years of your working life, then you may wish to consider transferring money into superannuation schemes to gain the benefit of the tax advantages.

You should still control the money as much as possible, and choose a superannuation scheme that gives you choices as to the sectors that your money will be invested in.

There are benefits to superannuation, Kate, but you must always remember that the wise investor keeps control of his money, and builds his wealth for his future security, and superannuation is only one tool to be used within an overall strategy."

Kate had often thought about her retirement, and indeed the fears of being old and poor had been one of the driving forces that had brought her to speak to John in the first place.

After all their talks, however, she was not afraid any more, and she began to view her investment options in a logical and objective way. Superannuation, she now realised, could be a part of her portfolio and her investment strategy, and was an investment that would be examined on its merits at each stage of her life.

"Now," John continued, "we come to an investment product which has trapped many people, and been a factor in many struggles and financial disappointments.

I am speaking about savings plans. People use savings plans for many purposes, but especially for saving for their children's education. Any investment which is offered by an institution, where you make small regular payments over a long period of time falls into the category of investments I am examining here.

You should avoid these plans completely Kate. They usually have very high commissions and expenses, they are inflexible and it is almost impossible to calculate the real rate of return that you are getting, to compare it with other investments.

Remember, too, that some of these expenses are justified.

One of the reasons the institution charges you fees is to cover the cost of administering the investment.

It costs them the same amount of money to process a payment of one thousand dollars as it costs them to process a payment of one hundred dollars. The person who makes ten payments of one hundred dollars is costing the institution ten times as much in administration costs as the person who makes a single payment of one thousand dollars.

Eventually, in one way or another, you are the person who pays these costs.

You must save a regular amount from each pay packet, and invest it wisely.

Some people claim that they do not have the self-discipline to do this, and they need to have the regular demands of a formal savings plan.

Unfortunately, Kate, these people are doomed to financial failure. It can be difficult at times, but it is essential to have a certain discipline when saving.

If you carry out the ideas that I gave you earlier, then you will be able to save substantial amounts without missing out on your personal pleasures.

However, you must still be willing to live within your means.

If you find that you are unable to save steadily, then you must do two things immediately. First, you must reduce your expenses.

This involves planning ahead to purchase things more cheaply, and at the end of the day you may have to spend less on your non-essential activities and purchases.

The second step is to take action to increase your income in the future, such as learning new skills or studying.

You do not need to suffer to save, Kate, but you do need some self-discipline and a desire to improve your position.

Without it, you will surely fail. Remember, though, that it is your own choice, and if you have a strong desire to improve your position then you will be able to save."

John's words seemed a little harsh, Kate thought, but then he was clearly right. She had used some of these plans herself when she was younger, and although she had made many contributions, when she finally received the money back it hardly seemed worth it.

"Now we come to examine a few miscellaneous investments.

Although there are only three major sectors, there are an endless variety of investments built around them.

There are also investments outside the three sectors, which I will examine shortly.

We have spoken many times about investment trusts and products offered by institutions, and there have been some very strange investments launched from time to time.

I suggest you examine these investments in the usual way. Look at their yield and their risks, and write down the basic nature of the investment in a single sentence.

Once an investment is reduced to its bare essentials, it becomes much clearer and easier to understand. One example of an unusual investment is an 'ethical investment share trust'. This is a trust that invests money in shares, but the manager chooses companies that perform in line with current social concerns and take an 'ethical' approach to business.

This is a difficult term to define, and in practice the choice of companies is determined by the opinion of the managers.

However, they have certain rules and will reject companies completely if they operate in certain areas which are considered irresponsible and socially undesirable.

Other trusts include the 'manager's selection', a type of trust where you contribute your money, and the mangers of the trust invest the money in anything they think is worthwhile at the time.

There are enumerable examples of unusual investments. On the whole, I suggest that you keep to the simple, tried-and-true investments in the three sectors. You may wish, however, to include some of these investments as a small part of your portfolio."

John paused, exhausted from speaking. Even after all this time he was still not accustomed to speaking for long periods. It was a skill he had never mastered, being a person who preferred to listen than to talk. At least, be mused to himself, he had learnt a great deal by taking this approach. After a few minutes rest, however, he felt invigorated and felt an urge to move on. As usual, they had covered a great deal of ground, and John was enjoying speaking.

"We have covered most of what I want to say about specific investments.

There are, however, a few other investments I would like to discuss. I will choose some of the more popular investments that I believe you should avoid, and explain why.

First, we have gold.

Gold has been used as a store of wealth since the earliest days of civilisation. It has always been in demand for jewellery and ornaments because of its rarity and beauty. Gold is one of the most chemically inert metals, it does not rust and will not react with most substances.

A bar of gold will still be a bar of gold in a thousand years. The only other possession a human being can have with this longevity is ownership of land, but even that is at the mercy of changing social systems, governments and laws.

Gold, however, remains gold. Let us now consider the price of gold.

This is subject to two things, the same as every other

price in a market-based system. The price is subject to supply and demand. The demand is based on the demand for gold for jewellery, and also the demand for gold for industrial uses.

The supply is dependant on the amount of gold produced from mines.

Here lies the great risk in the price of gold. If mining technology improves, or major new gold deposits are discovered, then the production of gold will increase and the price may fall.

Gold is often described as a hedge against inflation, and this is true in the sense that any form of wealth that is not based on cash is not subject to inflation.

However, there are two fundamental flaws in the use of gold as an investment.

First, it does not produce any income. You should reject it immediately for this reason, as it is simply not worth using your money to purchase assets that don't produce an income.

The second flaw, is that the price is dependant on the supply and demand, and if the supply increases then the price may actually decrease in the long term."

John paused, resting for a few moments, then continued.

"This brings me to another class of investments that naive investors often choose, and an area where I have seen many people loose money and almost none make real profits.

These are the art and collectibles investments. Paintings, antiques, handmade rugs, rare coins and sculpture all fit into this class.

Kate, on this issue there is only one conclusion I can come to. Forget about these investments completely.

They produce no income, which is their first fatal flaw.

The lack of an income means that they have no intrinsic value.

Second, the prices are highly subject to fashion and changes in public taste, and these factors are fickle and

293

unpredictable.

Third, it requires expert knowledge to properly select items and care for them correctly.

Fourth, they are subject to physical deterioration and damage.

Overall Kate, these investments may seem seductive, and many people will sing their praises, but for the average investor it is simply not worth it. Implement the strategies that I have described, and your wealth should steadily increase."

5.8 Insurance products

"Now that we have covered the specifics of the main investments," John began, "there are some other issues I would like to raise.

Actually, I use the word 'like' very loosely here Kate," he said with a grimace.

"We should talk a little about insurance. This is a topic that few of us find interesting, but it is an essential part of financial success and security so it deserves some attention.

Consider the policies and products offered by life insurance companies.

These companies offer two basic services; insurance and investment.

Some policies have an insurance and an investment component, and others only have one or the other.

Pure life insurance is often called 'term' insurance.

This is similar to insuring your car or house.

You pay the premium, and you are protected for a specific period of time. If you die within that period of time, then your dependants or your estate is paid a certain amount of money.

The concept is quite simple.

The premiums are dependent on your age, which in turn is related to the probability that a person of your age will die within the period of cover.

For a young or middle-aged person, the premiums are quite reasonable.

This type of insurance is essential for a person who has dependants, such as young children.

If anyone is financially dependent on you, then you should have life insurance.

Some life insurance policies also cover you against being permanently disabled, but the definition is very strict and you must suffer horrendous injuries to qualify for this condition.

Payments are rarely made under these clauses so don't rely on it to protect you against illness and injury.

This insurance simply covers you for the unhappy chance of a fatal accident or disease.

The next question, of course, is how much cover you need. If you have young children and few assets, then I suggest that insurance equal to three times your salary would be appropriate.

This may sound like a fortune, but if the person who raises the children after your death was to invest this money and use the income for the children, then it would still be less than the income you provided when you were alive.

Some will suggest that more or less is appropriate, but this is a good place to start. Insurance companies also offer many investment products. The variety is quite wide, from products that allow you to choose the underlying investment sectors to ones where you have no control at all.

Some of these products are quite good, but remember that you are paying substantial fees to the company for something that you could be doing yourself.

Some policies combine insurance and investment, such as the famous 'whole of life' and 'endowment' policies that were popular in earlier times.

Unfortunately, the fees in many of these policies are hidden within a single premium amount, and it is almost impossible to calculate the return you are getting on your investment.

I suggest you avoid these type of combined policies and handle your insurance and investment separately.

This is the easiest and most cost-effective way to do it. Next we have the 'disability income insurance', a policy offered by life insurance companies that we spoke about previously. This policy will pay you your usual salary if you are unable to work for any reason, due to illness or accident.

This is an excellent idea and I suggest that everyone who works should have one of these policies. The only possible exception is the people who have substantial assets and are not reliant on their income from working to support themselves.

Having covered life and disability insurance, we come to health insurance.

In fact, insurance is a bit of a misnomer here. Since we all have various medical treatments throughout our lives, it is really more of a savings plan than real insurance.

The premiums are simply a form of saving up for medical treatment that we will inevitably need. Like all savings plans, however, there are commissions and expenses, which means you never get back the value you put in.

Health insurance is also expensive, in fact it may be the most expensive form of insurance you have.

However, there is always the chance of a serious illness, where expensive treatment is required which you can't afford to pay for yourself. I cannot give you clear advice on this issue Kate. It is something you will have to investigate personally.

You must protect yourself against problems that you can't afford to pay for, and yet health insurance is expensive and poor value for money. If you are poor and vulnerable, then you may have to have it, but as soon as you can build your wealth to the point where you can cover major health costs yourself then you should look very seriously at whether you should continue the plan or not."

Out of breath and a little tired, John paused for a rest. His speeches had begun with general advice and methods, and had become increasingly practical as they had laid the groundwork together. John enjoyed this stage, as he was finally able to give Kate practical suggestions that she could understand and place in the proper perspective.

He did fear, though, that at times it would be too much for her and she would miss out some of the things he said. John wanted to avoid this if he possibly could, for each thing that he said was like another brick in a wall, and the wall would only be strong if every brick was in place.

Every part was important.

Kate, however, still seemed fresh and interested, so John decided to continue their discussions and rest later in the afternoon.

"This covers the main insurance issues related to your body: health, life and disability."

"Honey," Kate said in a lusty voice, "there are many issues related to my body that you haven't even touched on".

John laughed out load at Kate's banter. It was beautiful how she always made him laugh when he was the most serious and worried, and John saw for the first time how much he now relied on her. They had known each other all Kate's life, but their talks over the last few months had brought them closer than ever before, and the relationship was having a positive effect on him.

"Now," Kate's grandfather said as they settled down once more, "we come to the insurance of physical assets. This includes your home buildings, the contents of your home, your car, boat and other possessions.

All major assets should be insured. The rule you should follow, is that if you cannot afford to replace an item, then you should insure it.

Usually you will pay a premium and the insurance cover will last for a specified period of time. There a few points here that are worth mentioning.

People often speak of 'house and contents' insurance, but in fact this is two separate insurance policies rolled into one.

First, there is the insurance on the actual home buildings. This covers damage due to fires or accidents.

The cover usually specifies a fixed amount of money, and the insurance company will spend up to that amount to build you a new home if the building is destroyed.

Contents insurance covers the possessions in your home. If they are stolen or destroyed, then the insurance will replace the item.

You must specify a total value for the possessions in

your home. Use the guidelines that the company gives to and estimate the value of your possessions accurately.

If you choose a figure that is too high, then you will be paying an unnecessarily high premium for the policy.

However, if you choose a premium that is too low, then the company will penalise you if you need to claim the full amount and you have not insured the full value of your possessions.

For these reasons it is important to make a fair and honest estimate of the value of your home contents.

Include everything, such as clothing and kitchenware, as you will need to start from scratch if a fire burns your house to the ground.

Another point to watch with these policies is the amount that is paid out when an item is lost or destroyed.

This may be based on several different values, commonly the 'replacement value' or the 'market value'. The 'replacement value' will pay for a new item, which is what you really need.

If your washing machine is stolen, then you need to buy a new washing machine.

The 'market value' is the value of the item if it was sold second-hand. Even if the item is quite new this figure will be well below the cost of replacing the item. Make sure you are clear as to which type of policy you have, how much you will be paid for an item if it is stolen, and what the conditions are on the policy.

Next we have insurance on major items such as cars and boats.

Again, you pay a premium based on the age and value of the item, and this premium insures the item for a certain period of time.

Like home contents insurance, the issue of valuations is an important one here. The amount that is paid to you if the item is stolen or destroyed is usually based on either the 'market value' or an 'agreed value'.

The 'market value' is the value that the insurance

company believes the item would be worth if it was sold.

Kate, I can guarantee that this will be less than the amount that you believe the car or boat is worth.

Although the value will be within a reasonable range, one of the ways that insurance companies save money is to use the lowest reasonable estimate of the value of an item when paying out a claim. In practice there is little you can do about this.

The other type of policy, an 'agreed value' policy, operates differently. In this case, a fixed sum of money is agreed between yourself and the insurance company when the policy is taken out.

If the item is stolen or destroyed, then this sum is the amount that you will receive.

If you have an expensive and valuable item, then I suggest that you chose an 'agreed value' policy, even though it will cost a little more. If the asset is of lower value, however, then a standard 'market value' policy will be sufficient."

John paused, rested for a few moments, then continued.

"My final point on insurance relates to the complexities of insurance.

There are many pitfalls in insurance, and it is important to read the fine print carefully.

Let me tell you a brief story to illustrate some of the pitfalls.

Two women lived in similar houses, and had similar possessions.

Both women insured their contents for 20,000 dollars.

The first woman took out a single policy, but the second took out two separate policies for 10,000 each with two separate insurance companies.

One day, a massive fire raged through the street and both houses were destroyed.

The first woman had her possessions replaced in full.

The second woman, however, soon discovered that both insurance policies had clauses that prevented a payment if there was any other insurance policy involved.

The woman was forced to ignore one policy and simply claim on the other. However, her problems had only just begun. This policy was only for 10,000 dollars cover, of course, but her possessions were actually worth 20,000. She was told that the policy also had a clause that penalised her if she had under-insured the contents, and because of this the woman was only paid 5,000 on her claim.

Both women had paid the same amount in premium, but the first woman received her entire claim of 20,000 dollars and the second woman was left with only 5,000 dollars.

The lesson from this story is that insurance can contain a number of pitfalls, and you should ensure that you are familiar with the details of any insurance policies that you take out."

5.9 Taxation

Once again, Kate and John sat in the park on a Sunday afternoon, and John prepared to speak about money. It had been many months since they had first begun, and the seasons had moved from spring through to late winter.

It had been a long time, and a long journey of discovery for both of them. John was tired. The experience had drained energy from him, and although the cool air and the beautiful, natural surroundings invigorated him, there was something missing. The sparkle that had been in his eyes had faded a little, just a touch, but it was something that he could not recover from.

Sometimes, they did not discuss finance for several weeks while Kate thought over a major subject, but even then the tiredness inside John remained. It was almost as if he had permanently lost something, as if some inner reserve of energy had been used up and could never be replaced.

Still, though, he persevered, determined to finish what he had started. Kate worried at times, and yet she was very grateful to her grandfather and hoped that he would finish the things he wanted to say.

He was, she realised, and old man. Not just physically, either, but the strain and suffering of a long and difficult life was clearly evident in his nature. John sat back on the park bench, breathed in deeply several times, and gathered his energy.

"Kate my dear," he said brightly, "we come to one of the most boring topics that I must cover, but an essential one just the same. Don't worry, for we won't spend much time on this. I am speaking about taxation."

"Yuck," Kate said with exaggerated disgust. "Do we have to discuss this?" she asked, hopeful that they would not spend hours on any complex details.

"Unfortunately, yes," John replied. "Tax is a very

important element of successful investment. I mentioned previously that you should never consider a scheme or investment if its only purpose is to reduce your tax, and that every investment must be strong on its own merits before tax is taken into account.

However, once you have considered the basic merits of an investment, then you should look carefully at the tax issues as this can make or break the investment.

The tax rules are so complex in the modern world that no human being can completely understand all aspects of taxation law.

A good accountant is essential when it comes to issues relating to tax. You must, of course, have a basic understanding of the major taxes and how they work, but always consult an expert on the specific details.

I could sit here for a year and talk about tax, Kate, and by the time I had finished the rules would have changed anyway, so I will just give you a few guidelines."

This put Kate's mind at ease a little.

"Before we begin, we should revisit the purpose of taxation. You will remember the people in the valley, and how they formed a community group to manage affairs that affected all the people, such as the use of the river and the building of roads.

This group became the government, and of course it needed money to perform its tasks and this money was contributed by the people in the valley.

Things are the same in the modern world.

This community group is the government as we know it, and the money that the valley people contributed is the taxes that we pay today.

Our population is so large, and our society so complex that the government has many expensive tasks to perform.

In fact, there are so many tasks that a government must perform that in some countries the government employees half the entire workforce.

The taxes that we pay are used to support this massive

structure. Now, let us consider tax in detail. Although tax is simply a payment to the government, there are two ways to view it.

First, tax can be viewed as an expense. Consider an investment house. You have income from rent, expenses for maintenance, agent's fees and tax.

Whatever is left over is your profit, the money that is yours to spend. This is the first view of tax.

The second view sees tax as a share of your profits. Your house has income from rent, and expenses for maintenance and agents' fees. The money left over is the profit.

This profit must be shared, with part of it paid to the government and part of it kept for yourself.

Both views are correct, and it is useful to keep each in mind for different circumstances. For example, an increase in your tax payment may seem like a bad thing if you view it as an expense. However, it is actually a good thing if you view it as a share of your profits, as it means that the total profits and your own share must be larger as well.

Keep both views in mind, Kate, and it will help you understand many things in business and investment."

Kate pondered John's words, and made a mental note to consider this more carefully at a later date.

"Now, as we have already seen, there are two ways to increase your wealth, two ways to make a profit.

First, you can receive income.

Second, you can own an asset that increases in value.

Lets look at income first. Income includes the salary you receive from working, and also any income which your assets generate, such as dividends from shares and rent from properties.

There are special tax rules for different types of income, such as dividends, and you should read about the basics of these at another time.

For now, just consider all the payments you receive as income.

Now, the term 'income tax' is a little deceptive. In fact, it is actually 'profit tax', as it is a tax on the profit from work and investment, not the total income.

Income tax is the most common tax in the world, and the basis of most modern tax systems.

Let me illustrate with an example using an investment property.

Imagine that you receive 10,000 a year in rent, and your expenses, such as maintenance, amount to 3,000 a year. You will pay tax on the 7,000, as this is your profit.

In this way, the tax is applied to your 'net income', which is the income minus the expenses. This is your profit, the increase in your wealth.

This system raises a few interesting points. First, as we saw, any expenses related to the property are deducted from the total income before tax is calculated. This makes these expenses 'tax deductible'. If you spend a dollar on maintaining a property, then this expense will be deducted from your income before tax is calculated, so the tax you pay will be less.

In short, you pay a dollar, and you will also reduce your tax by part of a dollar, so it costs you less than a dollar overall.

Remember, Kate, that any legitimate expenses that are tax deductible will cost you less than the cash that you have to hand over.

However, it still costs you money, so don't fall into the trap that some people do and throw money around just because it is 'tax deductible'.

Things still cost you money.

The question of which expenses are deductible is a difficult one, and there are many grey areas and inconsistent rules. Any expense that directly relates to an investment, and is necessary to keep it operating, will generally be deductible.

Take an example based on manufacturing. Imagine that a woman operates a commercial knitting mill that makes clothes from wool.

She purchases a large and expensive machine to increase the output of her factory.

This machine has an expected lifetime of ten years, after which it will be worn out and useless.

Although this machine is a necessary expense for the successful operation of her business, she cannot claim the entire price as an expense on her tax. However, the machine gradually wears out, and at the end of ten years it will be useless. The reduction in value of the machine each year is called 'depreciation'.

Various schemes are used, but the simplest method in this example is to assume that the machine reduces in value by one tenth of the purchase price each year, so that after five years it is worth half as much and after ten years it is worth nothing.

This depreciation may be claimed as an expense against her tax.

The profit, then, would be the income from the machines minus the depreciation. Each year, the machine returns income, but the value of the asset also declines. The difference is the increase in her wealth, and this is the amount that she pays tax on.

This example may seem distant to you, Kate, but many investors are able to claim depreciation as a tax deduction at some time in their lives. In general, any asset that you own that produces income and reduces in value is said to depreciate, and you can claim this depreciation as a deduction against your tax. The best example is an investment house. Although land lasts forever, buildings wear out over many years and you may be able to claim depreciation for your investment buildings."

John paused for a break, and breathed in the cold air. It worried him that Kate would become lost when they discussed more complex concepts, but it was important that she have exposure to all the major issues. He hoped she would spend some time later that evening thinking over the things he said, and absorbing the concepts he was trying to teach.

"That covers income tax, in a very basic way. Income tax is a percentage of your 'net income', which is your income minus your expenses.

The income is your wages, rent from properties, dividends from shares and any other payments you receive.

Expenses are costs that directly relate to operating your investments, and the depreciation in value of your income producing investment assets.

The details of tax are extremely complex, but this is the basic principle. Now, as I said before, there are two ways to increase your wealth. First, you can receive income, as we have just discussed. Second, you can own an asset that increases in value. As the value of the asset rises each year, there is no tax to pay, and so the increase in your wealth belongs entirely to you. In order to combat this, some countries have a 'capital gains' tax.

This tax applies when you sell an asset. Again, this is extremely complex, but the basic idea is that you pay tax on the profit, which is the increase in the price of the asset from when you bought it to when you sold it.

Overall, though, you will find that this tax is far more gentle than income tax over a long period of time. Investments and wealth stored in the form of assets that increase in value are subject to far less tax than income.

Thus, income based investments such as fixed interest investments and deposits are subject to harsh tax treatment, as well as being subject to reduced value from inflation. There are many different taxes, Kate, and governments tax just about everything they can think of.

Some taxes are little more than fees for performing certain actions or buying certain products, whereas the two fundamental taxes, income tax and capital gains tax, apply to the true increase in a person's wealth.

There is also the issue of tax on companies and trusts, and this is an area that you should also develop a general knowledge of.

These rules change often, so you will need to keep up-to-date by reading magazines and newspapers.

Do not, however, bother becoming an expert on tax, or looking for obscure loopholes in the tax rules. It is important, however, to understand the basics, and I suggest that you look around for some small and simple guidebooks to tax.

A basic general knowledge, and a good accountant, is all you need to handle tax issues successfully."

Kate breathed a sign of relief. John's comments on tax had been pitched at a basic level, but she had even had trouble with these.

She decided to spend some time in the evening thinking over his words, and contemplating the concepts. It was heartening, though, that her grandfather had said that a basic general knowledge was all she needed.

To be honest with herself, the complexities of tax had scared the hell out of her, and had been a major factor in her reluctance to invest. She knew, though, that she had to put her fears aside and make the effort, and besides that there were many people who became wealthy with nothing more than enthusiasm and the willingness to learn and take action.

5.10 Evening

Kate and John rested in the cool of the evening. It was late winter now, and the days had become a little milder.

The earth was still cold, however, and John's breath condensed into a mist as he breathed.

Soft twilight illuminated the park and shadows danced around them. It had been a long day, and they have covered many topics. The talking had tired Kate's grandfather, but his strength returned as they sat quietly together. It was a peaceful, gentle evening.

Kate and John sat together on the park bench as the last of the light faded. They huddled together, sharing each other's warmth and strength.

6 Putting it into practice

6.1 Dealing with people

The worst of winter had passed now, and the days had become milder.

The ice had melted on the lake, and gradually the animals were returning to the park.

John sat on the park bench and stared thoughtfully into space.

"Kate," he said at length, "we have discussed many things over the past few months." He paused again, collecting his thoughts. "I began with the basics of money management and budgeting, spoke about the principles of business and investment, and then covered the specific investments in detail."

Kate could see that he was building up to something, but was unsure of how to broach the subject.

"As you say, grandfather," she said in a supportive tone, "we have covered a great deal. I have leant more than I ever dreamed I would when I first asked you about money. Please go on."

John was encouraged by his granddaughter's words, and he continued speaking.

"The time has come to talk about some practical aspects of your financial affairs, and address some problems that you may face when you put my suggestions into practice."

"Go on," Kate said with growing interest.

"Soon we will cover some specific advice for each stage in your life, but first we must speak about dealing with people."

"Oh?" Kate replied, surprised by the topic her

grandfather had chosen.

"Yes Kate, this is a very important subject. It is no use knowing the theory behind wise investment if you are confused, manipulated and ripped off when you deal with real people.

Although we live in a beautiful world, it is a dangerous one as well, and there are many sharks in the community who prey on the weak, innocent and naive.

Your business life is like living on a tropical reef; you will be surrounded by beautiful and exciting things, but some of the prettiest fish are the most deadly."

Colourful imagery, Kate thought to herself, but his point was a fair one.

"First I want to speak about business relationships. It is important that you build strong business relationships with the people you deal with.

This includes your accountant and your solicitor, and also any contacts with companies and institutions that you deal with regularly.

Always be prepared to pay money for good advice, as expert advice is invaluable in your business dealings.

Many people are not prepared to pay the fees that professionals charge, but end up loosing far more from making poor decisions. Good advice pays for itself in the long run.

Having said this, however, make sure that you get service and value for your money, and do not throw money away if you are not receiving benefits from it.

The next thing to realise is that a successful business relationship must be an equal, two-way partnership. Some people treat the people that they deal with as servants or slaves, believing that they have the right to do this because they are paying the bills.

I hardly need to tell you that this results in very little co-operation, even from a professional who is being paid by the hour. Other people take the opposite extreme, and take a very passive role. In the case of paid professionals, they simply leave everything up to the other person and make no contribution at all.

This may be due to apathy, or may be because they put the professional on a pedestal and believe that the person can handle everything perfectly without help.

Both these attitudes are dangerous. With their contacts, these people they don't make the effort to suggest compromises or alternative actions that can solve the problems for everyone.

To build a successful business relationship you must take the initiative.

Do your homework and learn the basics so that you can understand the language your accountant or solicitor speaks.

Remember that they are working for you, and make it clear as to what you are trying to achieve. Make suggestions, and discuss the suggestions that they put to you. Accountants, solicitors and other professionals need your input and contribution in order to do their job properly.

Never forget that there are many things that they don't know about you, and unless you have some idea of what to tell them they may never ask the right questions and learn the critical facts about your situation.

You must respect the opinion of a professional and take it seriously, but do not put the person on a pedestal and treat their words as fact either.

All people are fallible, and you will often get two quite different opinions from two different professionals.

Once you become involved in more complex investments, you will discover that there is often no exact answer to your questions.

It will often be a question of interpretation of a rule or law, and a professional's opinion is just that; an opinion.

Often you cannot be sure of the answer to a question until it is decided by a court, the tax department or whatever other body is involved.

Always remember that the final decision and responsibility is up to you.

Get the best advice that you can, but do not follow the recommendation of a professional blindly or you will suffer in the long run.

Be friendly and business-like when dealing with people.

Where possible, take an effort to make their job easier. Prepare the information they need before you meet, and be flexible with your requirements.

The appreciation you generate may be repaid with good service.

Finally, you need to choose people who are willing to take the same professional attitude as you, and give you good service and competent advice. If you are not happy with the attitude or the competency of one of your professionals or advisers, then change to someone else.

Remember, it is your whole future that is at stake."

These were reasonable suggestions, Kate thought.

She had taken a very passive role with her accountant herself, and simply went along at tax time each year and did what he told her to. John was right, she decided, and if she took a more active role then she could probably make a lot more progress with her finances.

"Next on the agenda we have negotiation. We could spend a whole year on this topic alone, but there are a few simple tips that I can give you. There are many situations during your life when you need to negotiate.

For example, the fence around your property may be in disrepair, and you need to agree with your neighbours as to the type of fence and the arrangements for paying for it.

Other common examples are negotiating for pay rises and negotiation changes in rent. The techniques can also be applied in everyday situations, such as a restaurant that has made a mistake with your booking and offers compensation in return.

First, it is essential to find out the background and facts to the situation before you enter into a negotiation.

Gathering information is the first step, and nothing can replace good preparation.

Next, you need to think through the approach that you are going to take before you begin the discussions.

Imagine the possible responses that the other party may give, and decide what your approach will be in each case.

Be careful, however, not so spend too much time on this. It is important to consider the possibilities briefly, but many people dwell on this for long periods of time and become very worried about problems that never arise.

Too much thought also distorts your perspective, and it becomes difficult to keep the original objective clearly in mind.

Think through the possibilities briefly, so that you are not confused and caught by surprise during a negotiation.

At these times it is easy to make poor decisions and be pressured into something that you don't want to do.

You should never negotiate or make important decisions when you are tired, hungry or uncomfortable.

Once you have considered the possible reactions, you must begin the discussions with an open mind and take each reaction as it comes.

Do not pre-judge how the other person will react, and keep a flexible attitude. When you are negotiating, it is important to look for a 'win-win' solution.

This means that you try and develop a solution to the dispute where everyone benefits, where both sides 'win'.

Negotiation is not about beating the other person into the ground, and this is seldom a winning approach in the long term.

Negotiation is not just compromise, although that is often part of a negotiation.

The most successful forms of negotiation are based on inventing new solutions, and suggestion new approaches to solve a problem so that everyone benefits.

To achieve this, you must understand the goals and desires of the other party.

Look at the situation from their point of view, and consider the issues that are important to them.

Look beyond the immediate disagreement to their basic goals, and look for solutions that avoid the dispute altogether and help promote the goals of both parties.

Often you may seem to be at odds with another party, but when you consider the other person's priorities, you can often give them something and get something for yourself as well.

When you are negotiating over price, the objective of both parties it generally to get the best deal for themselves.

Even here, however, it is not simply a case of meeting half-way on the price.

This leads me to an important point on negotiation.

There are things that you can offer in a negotiation that have no monetary value, and are cheap for you, but may be very useful to the other party.

Let me give you some examples Kate.

Imagine that you have been renting a home for a year, and the landlord decides to increase the rent. You may believe that you have little choice, but in actual fact you have several powerful bargaining chips.

Let us imagine that you have paid the rent on time every month and kept the house in good order.

This is a major benefit to the landlord, and he has no guarantee that new tenants will do the same thing.

There are costs and lost rent involved in changing tenants, and this is also a disadvantage to the landlord if you leave.

These two factors are strong bargaining points in your favour, and so you are actually entering the negotiation with a strong position, even though you may have no financial strength.

Consider another example.

A young couple has decided to purchase a particular house, and are negotiating the price with the owners. They are currently living with one of their parents, and can leave at any time.

The owners of the house, however, cannot move into

their new home for another four months.

It makes little difference to the couple when they move, but it would be a great inconvenience to the sellers of the house if they had to find temporary accommodation for a month or two while they were between houses.

In this situation, the couple has a powerful bargaining chip that costs them little.

The date they move in matters little to them, but it is vital to the other family.

By offering to pay the money immediately, so the owners can settle the bill for their new house, but letting them remain in the current one for the extra few months, the young couple will save them a great deal of money and effort. This may be used to negotiate a lower price for the house."

John paused, took a few deep breaths, and continued. "I will give you one final example, Kate, from the world of business.

A large corporation called for tenders for a major building project.

Several building firms submitted offers.

Surprisingly, however, the one that was chosen was not the cheapest.

In fact, the offer this builder made was significantly more expensive than the other builder's proposals.

At first, the builder's competitors could not understand how they had won the tender.

In order to win the building deal, however, the builder had included a very clever clause in his proposed contract. He offered a guarantee that the building would be finished on time and within budget.

If the construction was late, then the builder's fees would be reduced.

You must realise Kate that this guarantee was extremely useful to the corporation.

Their entire plans and cash flow were built around the completion date of the building, and if it was late then they would be in major trouble.

The building company, however, was very professionally operated, and they were confident that they could complete the construction within the set timeframe.

In fact, the agreements with their own workers included bonuses and penalties that ensured a quick completion.

In this case, Kate, the builder offered the corporation something that cost them nothing, but was very valuable to the other party. In this way, they won the contract and made a large profit for themselves."

Kate was listening carefully, and considering the examples that John had given her.

"The point I wish to make is this Kate.

When you are negotiating, look for things that you can give the other party or do for them that will be useful to them, but of little bother to yourself.

This may be something monetary, such as offering to pay for something in advance, or something intangible such as being a good tenant or offering to accept extra responsibilities.

The best settlement to a negotiation is where both parties get the things they need, and give up things they didn't really want.

Finally, remember to be calm, friendly but assertive.

Persistence has the power to level mountains, and if you are stubborn and persistent then you are likely to get what you asked for, even if people are just doing it to get rid of you.

Even if you are in a position of weakness, negotiating with a stronger opponent, this does not stop you putting forward win-win proposals, or nagging the other party until they give in.

It is essential to decide what you want, what you think is reasonable and morally right, and be assertive, sticking to your guns no matter how much criticism or rejection you suffer.

If you persist, then in the end you will reach an

acceptable settlement.

Winston Churchill once gave a speech before a crowd of schoolchildren in England, in which he said only nine words.

They were: 'Never give up! Never give up! Never give up!' For many people, Kate, these words are their only real power in a negotiation, but never underestimate how powerful they can be."

John paused for a break. In some ways, their discussions had come full circle. He had begun with simple, practical advice on budgeting, and then advanced to the principles of investment and business.

Now that they had laid the groundwork, the talks were becoming more practical again and Kate was almost ready to implement the strategies he had taught her.

"Having spoken a little about negotiation," he began, "I will say a few words about buying. There are many times during your life when you will buy things from another person, from small items like furniture to large items like a house.

The approach you take should always be the same, and can make a significant difference to the price that you pay. Before we discuss the details, however, there is one golden rule that you should always keep in mind.

When you are contemplating a purchase or an investment, you should always remember this: 'if you have a bad feeling about a deal, then just walk away'.

I must emphasise Kate just how important this is. There will be times when you are involved in an investment or a purchase, and things just don't feel right.

There will be nothing specific that you can identify, but you have an uneasy feeling about the whole situation.

When this happens, you should follow your instincts and pull out of the deal.

There will always be another time.

Often the unconscious mind notices things or makes connections that we are not consciously aware of, and this is reflected in a general feeling of unease.

These thoughts of the unconscious mind are often the most accurate of all.

You should not become paranoid, of course, otherwise you will never make any investments at all and you will die poor anyway.

You must always feel comfortable with the decisions that you make.

There will often be some nervousness, especially when a large amount of money is involved, but you should not have a strong feeling that something is wrong.

When you have this feeling, don't worry that you need any logical reason to cancel a deal.

Simply tell the other party that you have changed your mind. Don't bother justifying it to yourself, either, for the best reason in the world is the thought that 'it just didn't feel right'.

If you follow this advice, Kate, you will avoid many difficult situations before it is too late.

You may sometimes find that your fears were unfounded, and there was nothing wrong after all, but this does not mean that you made the wrong choice.

You must always feel comfortable with your investments and deals, and if you don't then that is a problem in itself."

Kate was paying great attention to John's words. He had always suggested a very calm and logical approach to investment, and Kate was a little surprised that he had raised such an emotional factor in decision making. She saw his point, though, and agreed that it was important to feel comfortable about a deal before taking the final step. From the way he spoke, Kate was sure that he had been caught out many times himself.

"Now," John said with renewed enthusiasm, "the approach to buying. The first thing that you must realise, Kate, is that the purchase of an item from another person involves the personalities of the two people.

The price may vary considerably depending on the

attitude and approach that the two parties adopt.

Remember that the other person will know almost nothing about you.

You may be desperate for the item, have plenty of money to spend and fall in love with it straight away, but there's no reason for them to know that. For all they know, you may be a wealthy businesswoman ready to out-bargain them, a brilliant judge of character who can see right through them or a homicidal maniac about to cut their throat.

It is this mystery that gives you all your power. The image you project will be crucial to the outcome of the negotiation.

First, you must act in a very businesslike manner.

Be friendly, but in a reserved and cautious way. Have a relaxed and confident attitude, but with a hint of formality. Apart from the introductions and a little small talk, do not speak very much. If you say little, conveys the impression that you are there strictly to do business and make a good purchase.

The less you speak, the less the other person learns about you and the more mystery and power you hold. There will be plenty of time for talking once the price is agreed and the money is paid.

After meeting the seller, you should carefully examine the item. You should look unimpressed, but say little and do not be overly critical. If you are overly critical, the person may be insulted and feel the need to defend the quality of their possession.

You do not want this.

While you are examining the item, you should decide how much you think it is worth.

If it is not what you want, or is not of good quality, then thank the seller for their time and leave.

Never buy something just because the price is good.

If it is what you want, then make a mental assessment of its value.

At this stage you need to decide the maximum amount that you will be willing to spend on the item.

Choose a figure so that it would still be a good deal it you paid the maximum. Never pay an amount that is verging on being overpriced.

You may offer a price of 10% to 20% below the asking price, however in some cases a price is a firm offer and is not negotiable.

The key point is whether the asking price is equal to or below the price that you consider to be a good deal.

If the price is a good deal, then accept the offer, otherwise walk away from the deal.

There will always be another item that is just as good but is priced more cheaply.

There is only one golden rule that you should not break. Do not pay more than the maximum price you decided on when you examined the article.

The seller may claim that a higher price is fair, and indeed it may be, but you are looking for a price that is good, not simply reasonable.

Be realistic of course and be prepared to offer an amount that is good for you but still reasonable for the seller.

Finally, if the seller is not willing to sell at your maximum price, then simply walk away. You must enter a negotiation with the knowledge that you will walk away if your price is exceeded.

Even if you love the item, and want it desperately, you must keep this attitude in the forefront of your mind. "

Kate was surprised, and a little shocked. John's words were very different to the other topics he had discussed.

These were personal, emotional issues and quite different to the things he had taught her about investment.

Still, Kate had to admit, it was useful advice and something she should remember.

"After discussing buying, Kate, we come to selling. The first step in selling something is to decide on the price.

You should do your homework here and find out the

prices that similar items are sold for.

Be realistic and objective when you compare your item to others.

You will only be hurting yourself if you over-estimate the true value of the asset you wish to sell.

Choose a price that will be good for you, but do not try and squeeze the last few dollars of value from the item. This will only lead to delays and drawn-out negotiations with buyers. Choose a price that is towards the high end of the range of reasonable prices, but not at the absolute top. Make sure you present the item in its best possible light.

I am constantly amazed Kate by the people who try and sell things without even bothering to clean them properly and fix minor faults.

Whether you are selling a chair or a house, always clean it to within an inch of its life.

People are emotional creatures and the appearance of an asset affects its price significantly.

Fix any minor problems with the item and present it in the best surroundings and in the best possible manner.

Next we come to dealing with the potential buyers. Like the situation where you dealt with a seller, the potential buyer knows little about you.

You must realise that their impression of the product will be largely based on their impression of you.

They can examine the item closely, but they have no proof of its past and they have to base their opinion of the product on what you tell them about it.

Be friendly and open when you greet the buyers. Do not be overbearing, however, and let them examine the item in their own good time. Relax, and give them all the time and space they need to examine the item fully.

Give them a brief history of the item, and mention its strengths. Also, mention one or two weaknesses and disadvantages. Your best approach is to be honest and open, and the buyer will sense this and have confidence in the product.

You should let the item speak for itself, and not spend too much time praising it.

This annoys people and makes them suspicious. Wait until the buyer is satisfied with his inspection and is prepared to discuss the purchase.

Let the buyer make the first move. Once the issue of money has been raised, tell the buyer the price, and state quite clearly that it is not negotiable. The buyer may try several tricks to change your mind, including criticising the item or claiming that he has other possibilities to explore.

Ignore everything he says, even valid criticisms.

You must maintain your confidence and determination not to alter the price. Eventually the buyer will realise that you mean what you say, and will either pay the price or leave.

If you have chosen the price well, then once the buyer has taken the trouble to come and see the item then he may go ahead with the purchase. If, however, three or four buyers all reject the price, then you should consider lowering it.

However, don't even consider this until a period of time has passed without interest at the current price. Never lower a price by a cent for the first or second potential buyer. If you hold fast to your chosen price, and the price is reasonable, then you will get all the money you ask for."

John stopped speaking, drained from the long monologue he had just delivered.

A cloud passed over the sun, and shadows danced on the lawns around the pair. John found it hard work talking about these things, organising his thoughts into logical groups and telling stories to illustrate the concepts.

A soft puff of cool air brushed past his face, and John breathed a sigh or relief. It was only the beautiful surroundings and the cool breezes that gave him the energy to continue.

Earlier in his life, John had sometimes wondered whether his knowledge was wasted, and whether he should attempt some form of teaching so that others could benefit from the lessons he had learnt. Now, though, the road he had travelled with Kate had been so draining and arduous that he was grateful he had never attempted something similar before.

He doubted that there would be energy left within him to ever attempt something of this scale again. "Kate, my dear," he said softly. "Walk with me. Walk with me a while, so I may rest my weary soul." Kate rose, helped her grandfather to his feet, and together they strolled thought the park. They walked a long time.

Refreshed at last, Kate and John sat once again on their favourite park bench. Kate sensed that John was ready to continue speaking, and she sat in silence, waiting expectantly.

"We have come, my dear, to my final words on dealing with people. There is one last situation we must explore, and unfortunately it is the most distasteful part of your business affairs."

John paused for a few moments. "

You will, during your life, deal with people who are dishonest or selfish, and there will be times when you must battle with people to get what is rightfully yours.

Imagine that you purchase a television from someone and pay in cash. The man you bought the television from has a physique like a truck and lives in a shady part of town.

On arriving home, you find that the television does not work properly. From time to time it simply stops operating for no apparent reason. Although you were very careful when you transported it, and you are sure that you didn't damage it, you have no proof of this. In this situation, what would you do?"

"What could I do?" Kate replied. "I paid cash, I have no proof, there is nothing I could do. Nothing at all."

"Wrong," John answered with determination. "Kate, lift your right arm into the air."

Kate was confused, but she trusted her grandfather and

so she fulfilled his request.

"Now, take it down. Kate, you have just illustrated the most powerful weapon in the world. Given time, you can achieve anything with this power. You could move mountains."

"What do you mean, John?" Kate asked. She was confused and didn't understand what he was trying to say.

"Kate," John said a little more calmly, "you have just controlled your body. You have exercised the power of the individual, the greatest power in the world.

You decide when to stand, when to sit, what to say and when to say it.

You are not powerless, in fact with determination and patience you can achieve almost anything.

There is one thing you can do that will ensure that you always get what you want in the end.

This is to hassle people, to nag them, to make a nuisance of yourself. Telephone them, visit them, interrupt them, make their life a misery.

Just as Samson gave in to Delilah and lost his tremendous power, everyone will eventually submit if you nag them enough.

This approach can also be used with institutions, although in this case you need to be careful to keep dealing with the same people, as they will try and transfer you to other parts of the organisation and you can end up going in endless circles.

Think back to the example of the faulty television, Kate, and I will suggest an approach to handling it.

As I mentioned previously, possession is nine-tenths of the law, and in these cases it is the other person who has possession of your money.

You are therefore starting with at a serious disadvantage. The other bad news is that the law will be of little use to you. The legal system is slow, expensive and full of loopholes.

If you find yourself in a situation like I have just

described, then forget about getting help from the legal system.

You can try, but keep this as a last resort.

The good news, however, is that you can get anything you want if you use the correct approach.

The first thing to realise is that the battle you are entering is a battle of wills, a battle of persistence.

It is not determined by physical strength, wealth, power or legal rights. It will be a test of who is more determined, and who uses the correct approach most effectively.

If you feel powerless sometimes, remember that there have been times when a single ordinary person brought down an entire government, simply through persistence, determination and refusing to give up.

Having realised this, you must now prepare for a confrontation. Follow the guidelines I give you, and you will be amazed at how effective they will be.

The first step is to determine your goal and the outcome you are trying to achieve. This must be reasonable, and try and include some minor benefit for the other person if possible.

For example, in the case of the television, you decide that you want to get your money back and forget the whole thing.

You believe this is fair and morally right.

However, you are prepared to do all the travelling, to deliver the television back to the seller, and you are also willing to forget about the inconvenience.

Do not press for too much, such as extra money as compensation, or you will make your task impossible.

Once you have decided on a solution that is fair, a solution that restores all your money to you and does not cause excessive inconvenience to the other party, then the next step is to make it happen."

"Go on, John," Kate said with muted interest. She was not entirely convinced that it would be that easy, but she was curious to hear what her grandfather had to say.

"When you contact the other person, the attitude you have will be critical. You must be calm and business-like, but also angry in a controlled way.

Make it plain to the other person that you are very unhappy about the situation.

You should remain polite, but also let the anger show clearly in your voice.

Never become agitated or excited, and never swear or be rude.

If you become agitated, then you loose power in the personal battle.

You cannot control the situation if you cannot control yourself, and the other person knows this.

You must remain very calm and controlled. If you do, then you will maintain control and power over the situation.

You should remain polite and not swear.

The more formal and controlled you are, the greater your power.

If you swear or become rude, the other person can focus the attention on your behaviour and accuse you of acting badly.

You must always keep the focus on the main issue, and do not give them any excuse to shift the attention to anything else.

Having chosen the correct attitude, the next step is to explain the actions that you are going to take, and tell the other person what you expect them to do. Make simple and direct statements such as 'I am coming over immediately with the television and I would like to have my money back'.

This is bold, but maintain your controlled approach and do not let the conversation venture into other issues.

Don't explain or justify your actions, simply state them as facts.

Answer each question and statement made by the other person, but keep returning back to the solution that you have decided.

While you are discussing the problem, be careful not to give away information about yourself or your private thoughts, feelings and beliefs.

The other person may try and steer the conversation away from the main issue, and any information they have about you gives them more power and control to do this.

Do not state your feelings and beliefs, simply state that you are extremely unhappy with the situation, and repeat what you are going to do and what you expect them to do.

Do not make threats.

Making threats weakens your power in a battle of personalities.

When you make a threat, you are stating that you believe that you cannot win the argument on your own and that you need something else to assist you.

The other person can ignore your threats, which weakens you and strengthens them, they can challenge your threat, which changes the focus from the main issue and delays the settlement, or they can make counter-threats, which leads to a deadlock.

You must keep the determination and pressure up, and do not let the conversation stray from your chosen settlement.

There are times, however, when you should consider making threats even though it damages your standing in the personal power struggle.

There are two main situations where a threat can be useful.

First, if the other person had something to fear from the law, then a statement that you intend contacting your solicitor immediately after the conversation can work wonders.

The second case is where the other person needs something from you. A prime example is a booking for a restaurant or leisure activity, where you are arguing about the details of the booking.

A threat to cancel the booking entirely can work

wonders in your favour.

Your prime goal at this stage is to keep repeating the actions that you expect to occur, and to make the person realise that you are angry and you are not going to give up under any circumstances.

The other party may then try various methods of emotional manipulation to change your mind. They may become aggressive, or attempt to physically intimidate you if the conversation is in person.

They make take the opposite tack, being friendly and apologetic in an attempt to win your sympathy.

They may use a ruthless and sarcastic approach in an attempt to break your spirit. Some people will even try several different methods in an attempt to find one that works.

The correct approach in all these circumstances in to completely ignore their behaviour.

Women sometimes feel that they are at a disadvantage in these battles, because a man can use physical intimidation to shift the power in his favour.

However, if she completely ignores this, then the damage to the man's ego will actually work to her benefit.

A man may feel at a disadvantage when fighting with a woman, as the sarcasm of a woman can be very cutting and effective. Should he ignore this completely, however, then her surprise at not getting the typical reaction will confuse and worry her.

At the end of the day, it becomes purely a battle of wills, and every person is equal.

Man or woman, large or small, rich or poor, in this battle it is one human being against another, and the most determined person will win in the end.

Regardless of the attempts made to intimidate you and make you drop your demands, ignore them all and the other person will eventually give up.

If the other person threatens you, then ignore their words and act as if they never said it.

Do not respond to the threat, discuss it, or mention it in any way.

Act as if you never heard it at all.

There is nothing more damaging to a person's pride, determination and power than to be ignored.

By ignoring their threats, you imply that you are not concerned in the slightest and you are not impressed by their abilities.

This is highly damaging to their ego and power. A threat by the other person is actually an advantage to you because it provides an opportunity to damage their pride and confidence by ignoring it.

The final technique, after distracting you from the issue and attempting emotional manipulation, is to suggest a delay.

This can be raised in many different ways, but the end effect is the same.

Once all else has failed, the person will try and postpone the argument.

They may have many excuses, but whatever they are, don't accept them.

Refuse to delay the issue.

Delays will drain your strength and determination.

It is essential that you maintain the pressure until they give in, and do not accept any delays.

Eventually, after all this, if you still maintain your original attitude and demands, then most people will give in.

By this point, they realise you are not going to change your mind, and the best thing they can do is give you want you want and get rid of you.

Alternately, they may try avoiding you altogether, and this is where the final step in the process comes in."

John took a deep breath, and Kate wondered nervously what he was about to say.

"When the conversation is over, Kate, carry out your part of the actions exactly as you described them.

Never fear, because in a situation like this you can

always get want you want.

The final step is to persist, and constantly harass the person.

Telephone them every day

Go around to their home or their work.

Contact them constantly, and don't be put off by secretaries of housemates who protect the person.

Demand to see them or speak to them, and wait at their office or home if they refuse to see you.

Keep the pressure on with frequent contact, and eventually they will give in and give you what you want, simply to make you go away.

By this time, you will have become the most persistent and annoying person they have ever met, and they will pray for the day when you simply leave them alone.

Believe me, Kate, it works. Most importantly of all, once you understand and believe that you can get what you want, then this shows in your voice and most people give in very quickly."

6.2 Some issues

John was weary. It had been a full year since they had begun discussing finance, and at times he had felt that their discussions would never be completed.

He pressed on from week to week, in the hope that they would finally reach an end.

John's voice was softer these days, and Kate worried that a permanent change had come over him.

As they sat in the cool air of the park, the sun slowly sank to the horizon and the shadows became longer.

"Katie my dear," he said finally. "Let us discuss finance once more. Soon, very soon, I will be finished, and it will be time for you to put it all into practice.

Never fear, for I will give you some practical suggestions to get you started.

Firstly though, I want to address a few of the common financial situations that you may meet during your life.

The first one we will examine is the investment of a lump sum of money.

Most people receive lump sums of money several times during their lives.

They may be from an inheritance, leaving a job or some other windfall.

These few large sums that you receive during your life are very important.

They can kick-start you to a brighter financial future, or they can be whittled away on minor expenses, until nothing remains.

Most people only get a few chances in their lives to manage a significant sum of money, so it is important to do the right things with it.

First, you should spend something on yourself. It is important to enjoy life to the full, and have a good time when you get the chance.

These chances may not come along very often, so make the most of them while you can.

If the amount is small, you may want to spend up to half of it on yourself.

If a larger amount is involved, then you may want to spend only 5 or 10 percent of the total on enjoying yourself, but ensure that you spend something as a sense of balance is essential to happiness.

Becoming obsessed with saving distorts your perspective, and many people with this attitude have poor financial success and suffer needlessly.

The money that remains after this should be split into two equal halves.

The first half should be used to repay your debts. Repay the debts with the highest interest rates first.

If these debts were for personal spending, then cancel the credit agreements otherwise you will just spend the money again and it will have been wasted.

Once the high interest loans have been repaid, the remaining money from the first half should be paid onto your home mortgage.

Having used half the money to repay debts, the other half should be invested.

If possible, try and maintain an equal split in the three sectors: property, shares and interest-bearing.

If you are already biased into one particular sector, such as owning your own home as a form of property investment, then invest the new money in the other sectors.

You should always have a portion of your money in all three sectors, and the closer you are to an equal three-way spilt, the more secure your long-term returns will be.

The next situation we will consider is a person with a large home mortgage.

Assuming that they are able to save some extra money, the question becomes whether they should pay off the mortgage early or invest the money elsewhere.

From a purely mathematical point of view, repaying the

mortgage is probably the best investment, as the rate is high and there is no tax to pay on the interest that is saved.

However, this leaves the person with little free cash, and they are vulnerable to changes in property prices and will miss out on profits from shares.

Wherever possible, Kate, you should try and keep your wealth in an equal three-way split between the sectors.

On balance, I suggest the following approach. Any spare money you save should be split into two equal parts.

Use the first part to make an extra payment on the mortgage, and invest the other part in fixed interest deposits, shares, and perhaps a little in property trusts.

This approach will give you the best balance between flexibility and returns.

If you purchase a home, then you will have a major exposure to the property sector, regardless of your mortgage.

This should be balanced by keeping some of your wealth in the other two sectors.

Next we have a situation that many people encounter during their lives. I want to say a few words about financial problems, and give you some practical advice on what to do if you run into serious financial difficulties.

Many good people, both rich and poor, have found themselves in this situation. Listen carefully to what I say and remember it, for one never knows what is around the corner."

Kate listened carefully. Somehow, this topic seemed particularly relevant to her.

"If you find yourself in serious financial difficulties, then there are two things you must realise. First, you will need to take firm and decisive action to change the situation.

Some decisions may be difficult, but if action is not taken then things may become even worse.

The long term solution to financial problems is improved money management, but in the short term more drastic action may be required.

The second thing that you must realise is that financial problems are almost always associated with debt. I have never seen someone who has major financial problems and who doesn't have debts. When you encounter problems, and decide to take action to improve the situation, then your first goal is to manage and reduce your debts.

Investigate ways of reducing your interest rates, perhaps by combining several high interest forms of credit into a single low interest loan.

Re-arrange your loans and credit so that you are paying the lowest possible interest on your debts.

Simply doing this will give you some breathing space, and free up some cash to begin solving the problem.

After rearranging your debt to get the lowest possible rate, the next step is to look at your expenses.

Keep a record for a month of every single cent you spend.

You may be surprised as to where all your money is going.

Examine every single item on the list of expenses, and consider ways to reduce or eliminate the expense.

If you have reached the point of significant problems, then should consider spending less on personal needs and entertainment.

The quicker you get back on your feet, the sooner you will be able to enjoy yourself once again without creating new problems.

It is essential to spend less than you earn.

This is the fundamental ingredient in financial success.

The extra cash should be used to pay off your debts as quickly as possible.

A person in this position is highly vulnerable if something goes wrong, and it is essential to reduce the debts as quickly as possible.

Owning assets leads to security and freedom, and having debts leads to vulnerability and enslavement.

Having reduced your expenses, and used the extra cash

to begin reducing your debts, the next step is to examine ways to increase your income.

If you are in serious trouble, then extra work may have to be considered in the short term.

However, if you do this, then make sure that you use the extra money to repay debts and build assets. Do not spend it. Some people work longer and longer hours, then spend more and more, and lock themselves into an expensive lifestyle which they can't escape.

This is a recipe for financial disaster and misery.

When you are in financial trouble, Kate, every extra cent you can earn must be used to improve your financial position.

Finally, you should make a list of everything you own of value.

You should consider selling some of your assets and using the money to reduce your debts.

Selling assets to reduce debts is the primary way that companies restore their financial health when they strike trouble, and individuals need to consider the same strategy.

Sentimental feelings may make it difficult to sell some assets, but the extent of the problems must be faced, and if they are severe then drastic action must be taken.

Once you take these steps, your financial position should improve quite quickly.

It may take a long period of time to eliminate your debts and build a reserve of assets, but your position should be improving as time goes by, rather than getting worse.

Once you have taken these actions, made a plan and seen some improvement, your morale will improve drastically.

As long as you can see some improvement each week, even if there is a long way to go, then you will feel as if a burden has been lifted from your shoulders.

Finally, these suggestions relate to the short-term actions needed when serious financial difficulties arise.

They are not a long term solution to your problems. If your habits and money management do not change, then you will fall into debt again, and this time it will be even worse.

It will be worse because you will have fewer assets to sell, and less expenses that can be trimmed. Once the short term problem is reduced, then you must start to save and invest, and build your wealth for the future as I have already described."

6.3 Putting it into practice

John and Kate sat together, relaxing in the park, and John prepared to speak once more about finance.

"Kate, we have almost come to the end of our discussions on money.

It has been a long road, but I have covered all the issues that I feel are important.

We could speak for years on this subject, and still not exhaust the things I could teach you, but I believe that I have told you everything you really need to know.

This knowledge is enough for you to manage your money successfully and become an independent and wealthy woman.

Before we finish, though, I want to suggest some specific actions that you should take to put my words into practice.

First, you must become more organised with your finances.

You must gain a clear understanding of your expenses, your income, your debts and your assets.

Becoming organised is the first essential step on the path to financial success.

Make a list of all your insurance policies. Summarise them on a single page, with a list of their premiums, purpose, and the amount of cover involved.

Ensure that you have adequate cover, as I have already described, but don't pay for anything that is not absolutely necessary.

Insurance is a significant expense for many people and you should be careful not to have too much cover, or too little.

Next, record all your expenses.

This should include everything you spend money on, from bank charges to savings for Christmas presents.

Examine each expense carefully, and consider ways to reduce or eliminate the expense.

We have already discussed several suggestions in detail.

Having done this, you should make a budget and plan the way in which you are going to divide your income.

You must save a certain part of your income, and use this money to improve your financial position for the future.

Ten percent of your income is a good guideline to begin with.

The more you save, however, the faster your financial position will improve.

Make a list of all your loans and debts.

Include everything that you owe, from personal loans to credit through stores.

Anything where you must make payments for something that you have purchased comes into this category.

You should aim to repay these loans as quickly as possible.

Use any assets you have, such as money in the bank, to repay these loans.

Although loans can be useful for investment purposes, you should avoid loans for personal purposes wherever possible.

Home mortgages take many years to repay, but other loans should be repaid in the shortest term possible.

If you do not have sufficient assets to repay your debts, then use the assets that you do have, and use your regular saving to repay the rest as soon as possible.

Next, make a list of all your assets.

All investments, significant assets and money should be listed.

Critically examine the assets you own and the places that you keep your money.

You may find, for example, that money in a bank account or insurance policy is earning a low rate of interest.

Financial success depends on making the absolute most of all your assets.

Do not let any of your wealth linger in places where it earns a poor return.

Sell assets that are not providing good profits and cancel any investments that are showing poor returns.

It is essential to place all your wealth in forms that increase in value and provide healthy profits.

Never leave money in places where it receives a poor return. Having looked at these issues, we now look to the future.

Read the newspapers and develop a general knowledge of finance and investment.

The aim is not to become an expert, or understand the complex details, but to understand the principles.

It is also important to have a good feel for the current environment, and which investments are likely to perform well and which aren't. You may also want to look for some simple books on property and shares.

I suggest that you read the smallest and simplest books, as these have everything that you really need to know.

The larger ones may contain complicated and obscure strategies, detailed mathematics or large amounts of meaningless waffle.

All three are of little use to the average investor, and in fact they are little use to anyone at all.

As your knowledge and experience of investment grows, you will be able to build your wealth and ensure a secure financial future.

6.4 A month later

Kate and John sat on their favorite park bench, as usual.

Several weeks had passed since they had finished discussing finance.

Spring was in full flight now, and the park was full of animals. Tender green shoots spread out from the bushes

340

and rose from the ground.

John had weakened steadily over the past year, and Kate had worried that he had suffered a permanent blow to his energy.

As the weeks passed, however, the brightness in his eyes seemed to gradually return.

It was as if a great weight had been lifted from his shoulders.

His strength was returning slowly, and he was healing from the long struggle.

"John", Kate said at last, "Thank you. Thank you for everything that you have done over this past year."

"You are most welcome, Kate," John answered softly.

"I feel like we have reached the end of a long journey," Kate replied.

They rose from the bench and began to walk slowly through the park,

"Oh no, my dear," John said.

"The journey had only just begun.

Its only just begun."